Motorbooks International
**WARBIRD HISTORY**

# B-29
## SUPERFORTRESS

469988

Chester Marshall

First published in 1993 by Motorbooks International Publishers & Wholesalers, PO Box 2, 729 Prospect Avenue, Osceola, WI 54020 USA

Motorbooks International books are also available at discounts in bulk quantity for industrial or sales-promotional use. For details write to Special Sales Manager at the Publisher's address

Library of Congress Cataloging-in-Publication Data
    Marshall, Chester.
        B–29 Superfortress/Chester Marshall.
            p. cm. — (Motorbooks International warbird history)
        Includes index.
        ISBN 0-87938-785-8
        1. B–29 bomber—History. 2. World War, 1939–1945—Aerial operations, American. I. Title. II. Series.
        UG1242.B6M29          1993
        358.4'283—dc20          93–24759

**On the front cover:** The *Enola Gay* rests quietly in its hardstand after dropping the first atomic bomb, which destroyed much of Hiroshima, Japan. *Warren Thompson*

**On the back cover:** Top, the author's B-29, *Mary Ann,* of the 878th BS, 499th BG, 73rd BW. *Chester Marshall.* Center, *Flak Maid* flew with the 444th BG, 58th BW, from Tinian Island. *Ken Rust.* The B-29 *20th Century Fox* flew with the 501st BG, 315th BW, from Guam. *Josh Curtiss*

**On the frontispiece:** This picture shows some of the women who made up a large part of Boeing's work force, inserting wiring in the bomb bays and in the pressurized tunnel passageway from one compartment to another, above the bomb bays. *Boeing Archives*

**On the title page:** This Superfortress portrays an unusual appearance, as if it was a pregnant airplane with its large boat attached to its belly. The fortress was designated an SB-29, and its primary duty was air rescue. The SB-29s operated out of Kadena in the early 1950s. *R. Mann*

Printed in Hong Kong

# Contents

# Foreword

In the pages that follow, Chester Marshall takes you on a fascinating journey chronicling the great World War II B-29 bomber program. With anecdotes, accurate historical coverage, pictures, and personal recollections, he guides you through the evolution of the B-29 from a troubled beginning to a very successful combat airplane.

Chester and I were in two different arenas during the war. He was in the military, and I was in a civilian industry, heavily involved in experimental flight tests of the no. 1 XB-29, which continued through the end of World War II. Chester has integrated these two perspectives and many other facets of the B-29 program, and the result is an outstanding story.

The B-29 was radical for its time and its development was unique for many reasons. It was conceived of in an atmosphere of great urgency to do a job that no other airplane could do: to effectively bomb an enemy from very distant bases. Its gestation period was plagued by changing requirements, and it was severely criticized and subjected to pressure to move faster.

*Robert M. Robbins, a Boeing experimental test pilot, poses by* The Flying Guinea Pig, *the first prototype B-29 built, known as no. 1 XB-29. As aircraft commander, Robbins accumulated more than 400hr on no. 1 XB-29. Boeing Archives*

By the time of its birth—the first flight of the no. 1 XB-29 was on September 21, 1942—this urgency had greatly intensified to meet the threat of Japanese forces ravaging the Pacific. The need was so great that firm orders had already been placed and production initiated for 764 B-29s. It was recognized as a necessary fly-before-buy program so that assembly lines could begin production as soon as possible.

The urgency had grown "white hot" by the time the troubled flight test program was only five months old. Orders had increased to 1,600 airplanes and the massive production effort was now rapidly accelerating and beginning to swell assembly lines. However, only two XB-29s had flown and, due to many problems, fewer than 35hr and only thirty-two flights had been possible in those five hectic months. There were lots of problems and questions but as yet few solutions or answers. When the no. 2 XB-29 crashed and its entire crew was lost on February 18, 1943, the already-troubled program was in even more desperate straits. The no. 1 XB-29 was grounded indefinitely until reasons could be found for the accident and safety measures taken in it and the other B-29s in production.

Many changes resulted from the accident investigation. It took more than three months of intensive effort

before the next B-29 in the "infant" program was ready to fly, on May 29—and it, too, nearly crashed because the aileron control cables were crossed! After that, almost all of the truly serious flight test crises were behind us. High-priority engineering and developmental flight testing continued throughout the war to further improve the airplane and increase its capability. Much of this flight-testing involved the engines, which, although greatly improved, were always troublesome.

Early-production airplanes of late-1943 and early-1944 were built by dedicated but mostly inexperienced people from all walks of life who had been quickly trained. In addition, numerous changes had to be retrofitted in "finished" airplanes, a job normally assigned to experienced mechanics, who now were spread very thin. The resulting problems led to the "Battle of Kansas" to correct discrepancies in already-delivered airplanes.

In the China-Burma-India (CBI) theater, the B-29 was troubled but its effectiveness was improving. The program matured fully in the Mariana Islands, reaching its awesome combat potential as it destroyed the war-making capability of industrial Japan and decimated the will of that nation's people to continue fighting. It brought World War II to an end just two-and-one-half months before the planned invasion of the Japanese homeland, an invasion that was expected to cost five million US casualties.

The B-29 program started "behind the eight-ball" with extreme requirements and too little time. Problems were solved and capability was increased, and despite persisting engine troubles, the resilience, toughness, and survivability of the B-29 endeared her to most of her crews. It was the second-largest World War II industrial program in scope and dollars. Only the Manhattan Project was bigger—and that program's product, the atomic bomb, still had to be delivered by B-29s to abruptly terminate the war.

The Boeing B-29 Superfortresses were the Air Force's mainstay immediately after World War II. They were the first to go into battle at the onset of the Korean War as the youthful, vigorous jet age was beginning to evolve and propeller-driven combat airplanes were becoming obsolete. Many of the Superfortresses that escaped being melted down into aluminum pots and pans were converted to tankers for refueling the new short-range jets. Others were used in the experimental atomic drops at the Bikini Atols in the Pacific and in the lifting of the X-1 experimental airplane to altitude on its way to breaking the sound barrier for the first time in the history of aviation.

This unique story of the B-29 program is graphically told by Chester Marshall. I'm sure you'll find it fascinating.

—*Robert M. Robbins*
*Boeing Experimental Test Pilot on the no.1 XB-29*

*End of the road for* The Flying Guinea Pig.
*At Boeing scrap yard, about May 1948.*
Bob Robbins

# Acknowledgments

Professional writers, historians, and aviation buffs came to my assistance when they learned I was writing this book. I'm grateful to them all, especially Wilbur Morrison, Tom Britton, Bill Hess, and Warren Thompson, for helping me accumulate photographs, color slides, and historical facts about the B-29. I also thank Josh Curtis, a young aviation enthusiast who is dedicated to helping preserve the history and to keeping the memory of the famed World War II airplane alive for his and future generations.

I thank the people at Boeing Aircraft Co. for their help, valuable information, and pictures—especially the gracious assistance of both Marilyn A. Phipps, the archivist specialist at the Boeing Historic Services, and Bob Robbins, a former experimental test pilot at Boeing and command pilot of the no. 1 XB-29, the first Superfortress built.

I am also indebted to the wing and group historians in the old 20th Air Force who sent information and pictures, among them Bill Rooney, Denny Pidhayny, Larry Smith, and Fiske Hanley. I deeply appreciate the invaluable information given me by Lt. Gen. (Retired) James V. Edmundson, Maj. Gen. (Retired) Earl Johnson, Maj. Gen. Winton Close, and Maj. Gen. Henry Huglin.

I am grateful to Robert C. Tharratt, Albert E. Conder, and Ray Brashear for information, photographs, and slides pertaining to the B-29 Superfortress between wars and during the Korean War. Ray Ebert, 73rd Wing historian, opened up his collection of pictures for use in this book, as did Carl Dorr and Harry Mitchell. And many thanks to John V. Patterson, Jr., a former Boeing employee who furnished me with many contacts.

And, finally, I want to say thanks to my wife, Lois, who encouraged me while I toiled to finish this manuscript.

The following individuals contributed first-person anecdotes or described episodes from their combat experiences; the number-letter combination to the right of each name represents the unit in which the person served:

Cleve R. Anno, 29th BG
Stephen M. Bandorsky, 504th BG
Jake Beser, 509th Composite Group
Ray Brashear, 499th BG
Charles G. Chauncey, 9th BG
Arthur Clay, 6th BG
John Cox, 499th BG
Russell Crawford, 444th BG
Harry Crim, 7th Fighter Command
Harold Dreeze, 73rd BW
Clyde Emswiler, 498th BG
Richard Field, 73rd BW
Jack Grantham, weather observation
Ray "Hap" Halloran, 499th BG
Jim Handwerker, 19th BG
Fiske Hanley, 505th BG
George Harington, 315th BW
Allen Hassell, 499th BG
Ed Hiatt, 499th BG
Carl Holder, 9th BG
Edwin L. Hotchkiss, air-sea rescue
Elmer Huhta, 500th BG
Murry Juveluer, 498th BG
Victor King, AS GP
William Leiby, 19th BG
Norman Lent, 3rd PRS
Roger Marr, 16th BG
Glenn McClure, 500th BG
Hal McCuistion, 315th BW
Jack McGregor, 497th BG
Robert W. Moore, 15th FG
Warren G. Moss, 498th BG
Jim O'Donnel, 499th BG
James O'Keefe, 40th BG
Fred Olivi, 509th Composite Group
Van Parker, 19th BG
Edward Perry, 462nd BG
Sture Pierson, 498th BG
Stubb Roberts, 468th BG
Gerald Robinson, 498th BG
William Roos, engineering
Mary Thomas Sargent, Red Cross
Daniel J. Serritello, 444th BG
George A. Simeral, 29th BG
Lawrence S. Smith, 9th BG
Chuck Speith, 498th BG
Wilbur N. Stevens, 509th Composite Group
Jim Teague, training
Kelcie Teague, 314th BW
Rudy L. Thompson, 462nd BG
Robert D. Thum, 549th Night Fighter Group

# Introduction

As war clouds gathered in Europe during the late-1930s, there was great concern among US military leaders because of the strong isolationist mood prevalent throughout the country. People in high places were extolling a hands-off policy, lest we make Hitler angry at us. A war was the last thing we needed, they said.

America had struggled for most of the decade to throw off the shackles of the Great Depression, and it was hard to find funds to keep the military services supplied with even enough necessary equipment to maintain a ghost of an army or navy. Lack of funding plus myriad restrictions imposed by Congress delegated our armed services to a defensive role only. As late as 1938, when Maj. Gen. Henry H. ("Hap") Arnold became its chief, airplanes in the Army Air Corps were not allowed to venture beyond 100mi from our shores.

Arnold was a long-time believer in strategic bombing, and thought the Air Corps should be in a position to carry out such an offensive undertaking if faced with a shooting war. He had many friends in the Air Corps—including Gen. Frank Andrews, Col. Oliver Echols, Col. Carl Spaatz, and Maj. Bill Irvine—who were also strong advocates and agreed that the country needed a fleet of long-range bombers.

By early-1939, General Arnold was able to convince the soon-to-retire Army Chief of Staff, Gen. Malin Craig, that there was an urgent need to set up a board to study types of long-range bombers which were needed, he suggested, for the defense of our hemisphere. Under these pretenses, a board was formed in May 1939, headed by Gen. Walter Kilner. Other members of the board included Col. Carl Spaatz, Arnold's top assistant; Charles Lindberg, America's favorite aviation hero; and two other officers. It took only one month for the board to draft its first report, recommending, among other things, the development of long-range bombers.

The Kilner report was delivered September 1, 1939—coincidentally, the last day of General Craig's tenure as Army Chief of Staff and ironically, on the same date that Hitler's goose-stepping Army and dive-bombing Air Force attacked Poland. World War II was underway in Europe. Things would never again be the same.

The Air Corps luckily found a friend in the new Army Chief of Staff, Gen. George C. Marshall. His firm decisions, especially those pertaining to long-range bombers, were instrumental in moving the Air Corps to a higher level of responsibility and toward a self-sustaining operational Air Force.

In November 1939, General Arnold stepped up his efforts to get approval from the War Department to let contracts for a very long-range, very heavy, four-engine bomber. On December 2, 1939, he got the green light to proceed. Capt. Donald Putt, an Air Corps test pilot and engineer at Wright Field, Ohio, was given the task of writing a "statement" of requirements for a super-bomber. Putt was well qualified for the job and knew first-hand what was needed: He had been in the flight testing program at Wright Field for several years and in the mid-thirties had participated in the flight-testing of the Boeing B-17, the first of which crashed while he was testing it.

On January 29, 1940, the Air Corps requirements document requesting a heavy, four-engine airplane that could fly at a speed of 400mph, with a range of at least 5,333mi carrying a maximum bomb load of 1 ton, was sent to four airplane manufacturers, resulting in four Air Corps mission-design-series designations: B-29, Boeing Model 345; B-30, Lockheed Model 51-81-01; B-31, Douglas Model 332F; and B-32, Consolidated Model 33. For various reasons, Lockheed and Douglas dropped out of the running, and Boeing and Consolidated-Vultee were declared winners of the competition.

Boeing was considered way ahead of Consolidated. Its design teams were familiar with four-engine airplanes, having experimented with various concepts of long-range, heavy bombers since 1939. Their experiences with both the unsuccessful huge, underpowered XB-15 and the very successful B-17 led to the development of the Model 322, the design they hoped would win the competition. They had experimented with several versions, one of which was a pressurized B-17 with tricycle landing gear. After selecting Wright Aeronautical's 2,200hp R-3350 twin-row radial engines to power their design, they came up with specifications that they designated Model 341. This was the model Boeing submitted to Wright Field, but to make it more combat-ready, the model was modified later and designated the Model 345.

This is the story of that airplane, World War II's premier bomber—about the people who designed and built it, and those who suffered through its development. The Boeing B-29 Superfortress was indeed the forerunner of today's modern Air Force bomber fleet. Many of the innovative ideas incorporated in the B-29 more than fifty years ago are still in use.

*Fifi is the last of the flying B-29s. This grand warbird is operated by the Confederate Air Force.* Glenn Chaney

*Chapter 1*

# Birth of the Boeing B-29 Superfortress

The Air Corps requirements document found its way to Boeing Aircraft Co. president Philip Johnson on February 5, 1940. Within three weeks, Boeing's Model 341 was submitted to Wright Field's Col. Oliver Echols.

Because of Boeing's interest and experience in building four-engine airplanes, company officials for years had maintained a close, cordial relationship with Air Corps leaders. They were so convinced that, sooner or later, very long-range bombers would be built that Boeing used company funds to conduct experiments and construct mock-ups before Congress ever approved any appropriations for such a project. Such men as Edward Wells, Claire Egtvedt, and Wellwood Beall had advance knowledge of the Air Corps' super-bomber hopes and plans. The gamble was about to pay off for Boeing.

Fortunately, at the same time that the Air Corps was requesting bids for its new bomber, the British were giving the War Department the inside scoop on the German Luftwaffe—warning that Allied airplanes needed better crew protection, self-sealing fuel

*The forward pressurized section, which was occupied by two pilots, the bombardier, the flight engineer, the navigator, and the radio operator, are shown ready for the assembly line.* Boeing Archives

tanks, and more defensive armament. Though Boeing had a contract to build three prototype XB-29s, these revelations caused Boeing to change some of the specifications in its Model 341. Among the changes were the addition of armor plating and heavier guns which increased the weight of the airplane from 97,700lb to about 105,000lb. This new Model 345 was the prototype from which the B-29s were built.

## Boeing Receives First Appropriation

Boeing's Model 345 was judged to be superior to the others submitted, and the company was appropriated $85,000 for further study and wind tunnel tests. On August 24, 1940, Boeing received $3,615,095 to build two prototypes. The contract for this appropriation was not signed until September 6, and was amended on December 2 to include a third prototype.

About the time Boeing received the original contract, both Lockheed and Douglas pulled out of the competition and Consolidated received a similar contract to proceed with development of its XB-32. This decision meant that two super-bombers would begin development simultaneously with hopes that at least one of the two would live up to expectations.

By mid-1941, the Germans had violated the Neutrality Act by sinking

two American ships. President Franklin D. Roosevelt acted immediately, calling upon the War Department to step up production requirements and to "shoot if necessary" if the Axis nations continued violations against the United States.

A committee of Air Corps officers, headed by Col. Harold L. George, prepared an "air plan" in August 1941 in response to the president's urgent call for action. The plan was called "Air War Plan Division—1" (AWPD-1). Serving with George were Lt. Col. Kenneth Walker, Maj. Haywood S. Hansell, Jr., and Maj. Lawrence Kuter. Among other radical changes in the future role of the Air Force, the plan stressed the urgent need for very long-range heavy bombers should strategic bombing be necessary.

General Marshall sided with General Arnold and the plans committee. He approved the plan with the remark, "This plan has merit," but the approval did not come easy. Some of Marshall's staff thought the plan would counteract the traditional role of the Air Corps, that of a secondary mission of aiding the Army in a combat situation.

Many in the Air Force considered the Marshall decision in August 1941 as the turning point in the Air Force's future. It was, they say, the real "birth of the United States Army Air Forces (USAAF)" The name change from Air

*Boeing's Model 345 from which the B-29 Superfortress was built.* Boeing Archives

*The no. 1 XB-29 at Boeing Field, Seattle, in September 1942 before the first test flight by chief test pilot Eddie Allen.* Bob Robbins

Corps to USAAF took place June 20, 1941.

To give the USAAF and General Arnold a more authoritative position in the War Department's chain of command, the Chief of Staff made Arnold his Deputy Chief of Staff for Air of the United States Army. This was a tremendous improvement in the struggling Air Corps' hopes for a strong Air Force. The decision also gave assurance that more appropriations would come quicker for the development of the B-29 Superfortress.

## Building of the Superfortress Begins

As 1940 came to a close, a mockup of Model 345 was inspected and given final approval, along with an order from the Air Force to build a third prototype and a fourth airframe for static tests. The design engineers sent the first engineering drawings to the Boeing shop in Seattle on May 4, 1941, calling for the completion of the first B-29 to be no later than August 1942.

On May 17, 1941, Boeing received a conditional contract from the Air Force to build 250 B-29s. The "condition" asked that the company expand its Wichita, Kansas, facilities, where the much-needed Stearman trainer was produced, to meet demands for the production of the B-17 Flying Fortress, along with a quota of B-29s.

As the plant expansion at Wichita proceeded and production at Boeing's home plant in Seattle geared up to a giant undertaking, the Japanese pulled their sneak attack on Pearl Harbor. With the country now at war, the Air Force wasted no time in upping the order for more B-29s, even though not a single B-29 had been built at that time. More than nine months would come and go before one would leave the ground for the first time. On January 31, 1942, Boeing's "conditional" contract for the original 250 airplanes was not only signed but was amended to increase the number to 500 airplanes, plus $53 million for spare parts for the B-29s.

## The Wing

The new bomber was revolutionary in so many ways that designers were faced with extreme challenges as specifications changed. The huge wing

presented one of the greatest challenges. A search for a suitable wing by Boeing's chief aerodynamicist, George Schairer and flight-test pilot Eddie Allen was unsuccessful. The wing had to have low drag at cruising speed and good high-speed and stall characteristics. Finally, Wellwood Beall, Boeing's chief engineer, decided that Boeing should develop its own wing. After eight different designs and thousands of hours of work, the excellent Boeing "117" wing was developed.

What made the new wing so successful was the size of its flaps. They were the equivalent of one-fifth the area of the entire wing, which allowed the aircraft to take off and land at a lower speed than it would have if it had conventional wings and flaps. George Schairer was credited with being the father of the huge wing.

Self-sealing fuel tanks were installed in the inboard wing structure. At the time, the two wing spars were the longest and heaviest Duralumin extrusions ever used in a production aircraft. Development of the Boeing "117" wing was a major contribution to the success of the B-29.

## Pressurization

Pressurization of large areas in the new bomber presented the design-

ers with more challenges. Faced with the problem of maintaining pressurization while opening bomb bay doors in order to drop bombs, designers came up with a unique solution by connecting two pressurized sections with a 40ft tunnel large enough for men to crawl through. The tunnel had a diameter of 34in and was located at the top of the fuselage above the two bomb bays.

The two pilots, the bombardier, the navigator, the flight engineer, and the radio operator were located in the forward section, and the central fire control gunner, two side gunners, and the radar operator were located in the mid-ship section. The tail gunner position was pressurized by two 6in pipes connected between the central section and the tail gunner. Between these two sections was an unpressurized part of the aircraft where the oxygen bottles were stored. Also in this section was a gasoline-operated auxiliary generator, called the "putt-putt." This auxiliary unit had to be started and its power placed on-line with the main electrical system before the engines could be started or the bomb bay doors raised. It also had to be started before landing.

The Americans were not the first to incorporate pressurization in their

*The various sections of the Superfortress, produced separately, are shown here at the Boeing-Wichita, Kansas, plant. Boeing Archives*

combat bombers. The German and English air forces had experimented with pressurizing cockpits of combat aircraft, but none were as sophisticated or could accommodate large areas as the B-29 Superfortress could.

A pump located under the floorboard in the radar room which dispensed supercharged air to the pressurized areas in the B-29 maintained the equivalent of an 8,000ft altitude when flying at 30,000ft. With the development of the B-29, for the first time in American aviation history, a combat crew could be comfortable at high altitude.

## Remote-Controlled Gunnery System

The development of a remote-controlled defensive gunnery system for the B-29 put the aircraft in a class of its own. Four companies competed for the contract to develop this innovative system, including Bendix, General Electric, Sperry, and Westinghouse. With its retractable turrets and periscope sights, the Sperry system

The B-29B is shown at the Renton, Washington, plant, in its final assembly. The B-29B was a modification of the A-model in which all gun turrets and the remote controlled firing system were removed. Only the tail gun position remained. The deletion of the turrets added about 10mph to the B-29B's speed. As the air war against the Japanese cities progressed, fighter opposition became almost nil, so the defensive weaponry was no longer needed. This plane was used in the 315th BW and the 509th CG. The 315th BW flew most of their missions at night against Japanese fuel dumps and oil refineries, with great success. The 509th CG was the atomic bombing group. Boeing Archives

won the original contract. After experimenting with the system on the first three XB-29 prototypes, however, the contract was given to General Electric because General Electric's system fea-

tured stationary turrets and computerized sights.

There were five gun positions: upper-forward, upper-aft, lower-forward, lower-aft, and tail. The bombardier and each gunner except the tail gunner could aim and fire two turrets simultaneously. Each of the turrets except for the upper-forward turret and the tail gun position mounted two .50cal machine guns. A 20mm cannon was mounted in the tail position. The cannon was later removed because most of the Japanese fighter attacks came from the front, and two extra .50cal machine guns were incorporated in the upper-forward turret.

The system developed by General Electric was a computerized and flexible system that gave control of turrets to more than one gunner. Each of the gunners had primary guns, but could operate two turrets at the same time if

necessary. The central fire control gunner, located in the central gunner's section, sat in an elevated seat between the two side gunners. Since he had a better overall view by looking through a plexiglass blister, he controlled the master gunnery panel. He could also flip a switch and assign turrets to gunners who had a better view of an attacking plane, thus increasing firepower where needed.

Mounted gun sights were at each of the gunner's position, about 1ft high with the reticule sight near the top. The gunner gripped it by two round knobs about the size and shape of oversized iced tea coasters. The sight swiveled horizontally at the base, and the upper section rotated in elevation by forward and backward twisting of the wrists. The sighting mechanism included an incandescent light source that sent a pattern of dots upward through a lens from inside the sight. This pattern struck a piece of clear glass set at a 45deg angle in the center of the part of the sight the gunner looked through. The image appeared as a circle of bright red-orange dots with one dot in the center. The right-hand sight knob rotated independently of the left-hand one. By twisting this knob back and forth through a few degrees, the gunner could make the circle of dots shrink in on the center dot or expand to fill the sight. There was a dial on the back of the sight with which to set the wingspan of the attacking aircraft. The right-hand knob also had a metal flap on it which was spring loaded to hold it out at a 30deg angle. This was the action switch. Unless it was held down by the palm of the hand, the turret would not activate.

With the computer switched on, a target could be tracked smoothly. Gyroscopes scanned the enemy plane's wing tips, and those electrical signals were sent to the turret, allowing it to lead the target and to elevate the guns to compensate for range from the target. When correct data, such as air speed, altitude, and so on, were fed into the computer system, the gunners' bursts of fire were significantly more accurate than those fired from conventional turrets.

Central fire control gunner Kendal Chance, member of the author's crew, explains how he directed fire at multiple attacking planes: "Since I had an overall better view of attacking planes, I used the in-plane intercom to direct the fire. If I had a better shot advantage, I would take control of two guns and fire them simultaneously. Each of the other gunners could fire two guns also, except for the tail gunner."

The gun sights included a deadman's switch; if a gunner were knocked out of action, his turret automatically was assigned to the gunner with secondary control. To prevent a gunner from shooting parts of his aircraft when tracking a target, a switch would cause firing to stop momentarily while passing scanned parts of his own aircraft.

There were a few instances of gunners' blisters blowing out after being hit by shrapnel or bullets. Crew members were instructed to wear oxygen

masks while over the target area because of the danger of losing pressurization while under attack.

Though this turret system was complex, it was maintainable under combat conditions.

## B-29 Radar Units

Another first for the Superfortress was that each of the B-29s that went to combat had a radar unit installed, and each crew of eleven members included a radar operator trained to aid the navigator in navigating and locating the target. If the target were covered with overcast or the weather were extremely bad, the targets were located by radar. During the incendiary raids on Japanese cities, the radar units were helpful in preventing collisions by B-29s merging on the same target area during extremely bad weather. Most of the B-29s were equipped with the AN/APQ-13 radar equipment developed by Bell Telephone Laboratory and the Massachusetts Institute of Technology (MIT) Radiation Laboratory. The radar antenna for this unit was a 30in hemispherical radome located between the bomb bays and protruding below the fuselage a couple of feet.

*A graphic picture of side blister of Superfort, showing how gunner sights and fires by remote control at target.* Albert Conder

Later in the war, a new and more efficient radar unit was developed. It was also developed by MIT's Radiation Laboratories and Bell Telephone and was called the AN/APQ-7 Eagle radar unit. Western Electric Co. actually built both radar units.

The Eagle unit was used primarily by the 315th Bombardment Wing (BW) at North Field at Guam, in its campaign of precision attacks on oil fields and fuel targets. Most of these highly successful missions were carried out at night. The Eagle antenna was wing-shaped in a housing installed underneath the forward section of the fuselage. It spanned 17ft, had a 31in chord, and was about 8in thick.

As war in the Pacific progressed, the AN/APN-4 Loran system was also used by the B-29s. This was a long-range navigation aid that helped navigators determine their plane's position by means of Loran signals broadcast from known positions. When Iwo Jima was captured, a Loran signaling station was installed on Mount Suribachi,

50th Anniversary
BOEING 1942 1992
B-29 Superfortress

further assisting navigators regardless of the weather. Philco built the AN/APN-4.

Late-model B-29s carried the AN/APN-9 Loran system, which was an improved version of Loran equipment, built by RCA.

Boeing's refined Model 345 was submitted to Wright Field on May 11, 1940. Model 345 would be powered by four Wright 2,200hp R-3350 twin-row radial engines (also refined). Four retractable (later stationary) turrets mounted twin 50cal machine guns and a tail turret held twin 50cal machine guns and a 20mm cannon (which was later removed). Three pressurized compartments—a forward section, a mid-section, and a tail gun section—were connected by a tunnel over the two bomb bays. Its landing gear was tricycle, with double wheels all around. The specs for this model called for a 5,333mi capability carrying 1 ton of bombs and a maximum bomb load of 16,000lb. It would carry a twelve-man crew.

A final production program for the B-29s was decided on at a meeting of military and industrial representatives in February. Boeing-Wichita would have the responsibility of production and assembly of the B-29s. In a plant yet to be erected, Bell Aircraft Co. would build B-29s at Marietta, Georgia. Two other plants would build the super-bomber, but the companies and locations were shuffled around before production actually began: Boeing at Renton, Washington (just north of the Seattle headquarters), took the place of North American Aviation in Kansas City, in a swap with the Navy, and Glenn L. Martin Co. at Omaha got the job of producing B-29s when Fisher Body was asked to concentrate on the P-75 fighter plane.

Wright Aeronautical Corp. received an order to triple its production of engines on the original order in April. The giant R-3350 engine would become one of the major headaches from day one because of excessive overheating. Many modifications were made to correct the problem—the en-

*This cut-away shows the three pressurized compartments for crew members. Boeing Archives*

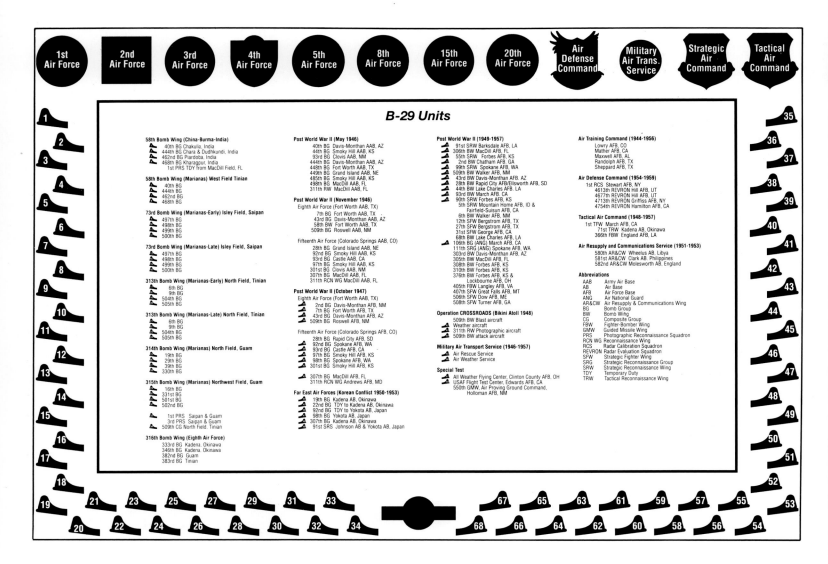

**B-29 Units**

**58th Bomb Wing (China-Burma-India)**
- 40th BG Chakulia, India
- 444th BG Chara & Dudhkundi, India
- 462nd BG Piardoba, India
- 468th BG Kharagpur, India
- 1st PRS TDY from MacDill Field, FL

**58th Bomb Wing (Marianas) West Field Tinian**
- 40th BG
- 444th BG
- 462nd BG
- 468th BG

**73rd Bomb Wing (Marianas-Early) Isley Field, Saipan**
- 497th BG
- 498th BG
- 499th BG
- 500th BG

**73rd Bomb Wing (Marianas-Late) Isley Field, Saipan**
- 497th BG
- 498th BG
- 499th BG
- 500th BG

**313th Bomb Wing (Marianas-Early) North Field, Tinian**
- 6th BG
- 9th BG
- 504th BG
- 505th BG

**313th Bomb Wing (Marianas-Late) North Field, Tinian**
- 6th BG
- 9th BG
- 504th BG
- 505th BG

**314th Bomb Wing (Marianas) North Field, Guam**
- 19th BG
- 29th BG
- 39th BG
- 330th BG

**315th Bomb Wing (Marianas) Northwest Field, Guam**
- 16th BG
- 331st BG
- 501st BG
- 502nd BG
- 1st PRS Saipan & Guam
- 3rd PRS Saipan & Guam
- 509th CG North Field, Tinian

**316th Bomb Wing (Eighth Air Force)**
- 333rd BG Kadena, Okinawa
- 346th BG Kadena, Okinawa
- 382nd BG Guam
- 383rd BG Tinian

**Post World War II (May 1946)**
- 40th BG Davis-Monthan AAB, AZ
- 44th BG Smoky Hill AAB, KS
- 93rd BG Clovis AAB, NM
- 444th BG Davis-Monthan AAB, AZ
- 448th BG Fort Worth AAB, TX
- 449th BG Grand Island AAB, NE
- 485th BG Smoky Hill AAB, KS
- 498th BG MacDill AAB, FL
- 311th RW MacDill AAB, FL

**Post World War II (November 1946)**
Eighth Air Force (Fort Worth AAB, TX)
- 7th BG Fort Worth AAB, TX
- 43rd BG Davis-Monthan AAB, AZ
- 58th BW Fort Worth AAB, TX
- 509th BG Roswell AAB, NM

Fifteenth Air Force (Colorado Springs AAB, CO)
- 28th BG Grand Island AAB, NE
- 92nd BG Smoky Hill AAB, KS
- 93rd BG Castle AAB, CA
- 97th BG Smoky Hill AAB, KS
- 301st BG Clovis AAB, NM
- 307th BG MacDill AAB, FL
- 311th RCN WG MacDill AAB, FL

**Post World War II (October 1947)**
Eighth Air Force (Fort Worth AAB, TX)
- 2nd BG Davis-Monthan AFB, NM
- 7th BG Fort Worth AFB, TX
- 43rd BG Davis-Monthan AAB, AZ
- 509th BG Roswell AAB, NM

Fifteenth Air Force (Colorado Springs AFB, CO)
- 28th BG Rapid City AFB, SD
- 92nd BG Spokane AFB, WA
- 93rd BG Castle AFB, CA
- 97th BG Smoky Hill AFB, KS
- 98th BG Spokane AFB, WA
- 301st BG Smoky Hill AFB, KS
- 307th BG MacDill AFB, FL
- 311th RCN WG Andrews AFB, MD

**Far East Air Forces (Korean Conflict 1950-1953)**
- 19th BG Kadena AB, Okinawa
- 22nd BG TDY to Kadena AB, Okinawa
- 92nd BG TDY to Yokota AB, Japan
- 98th BG Yokota AB, Japan
- 307th BG Kadena AB, Okinawa
- 91st SRS Johnson AB & Yokota AB, Japan

**Post World War II (1949-1957)**
- 91st SRW Barksdale, LA
- 306th BW MacDill AFB, FL
- 55th SRW Forbes AFB, KS
- 2nd BW Chatham AFB, GA
- 99th SRW Spokane AFB, WA
- 509th BW Walker AFB, NM
- 43rd BW Davis-Monthan AFB, AZ
- 28th BW Rapid City AFB/Ellsworth AFB, SD
- 44th BW Lake Charles AFB, LA
- 93rd BW March AFB, CA
- 90th SRW Forbes AFB, KS
- 5th SRW Mountain Home AFB, ID & Fairfield-Suisun AFB, CA
- 6th BW Walker AFB, NM
- 12th SFW Bergstrom AFB, TX
- 27th SFW Bergstrom AFB, TX
- 31st SFW George AFB, CA
- 68th BW Lake Charles AFB, LA
- 106th BG (ANG) March AFB, CA
- 111th SRG (ANG) Spokane AFB, WA
- 303rd BW Davis-Monthan AFB, AZ
- 305th BW MacDill AFB, FL
- 308th BW Forbes AFB, KS
- 310th BW Forbes AFB, KS
- 376th BW Forbes AFB, KS & Lockbourne AFB, OH
- 405th FBW Langley AFB, VA
- 407th SFW Great Falls AFB, MT
- 506th SFW Dow AFB, ME
- 508th SFW Turner AFB, GA

**Operation CROSSROADS (Bikini Atoll 1948)**
- 509th BW Blast aircraft
- Weather aircraft
- 311th RW Photographic aircraft
- 509th BW attack aircraft

**Military Air Transport Service (1946-1957)**
- Air Rescue Service
- Air Weather Service

**Special Test**
- All Weather Flying Center, Clinton County AFB, OH
- USAF Flight Test Center, Edwards AFB, CA
- 550th GMW, Air Proving Ground Command, Holloman AFB, NM

**Air Training Command (1944-1956)**
- Lowry AFB, CO
- Mather AFB, CA
- Maxwell AFB, AL
- Randolph AFB, TX
- Sheppard AFB, TX

**Air Defense Command (1954-1959)**
- 1st RCS Stewart AFB, NY
- 4613th REVRON Hill AFB, UT
- 4677th REVRON Hill AFB, UT
- 4713th REVRON Griffiss AFB, NY
- 4754th REVRON Hamilton AFB, CA

**Tactical Air Command (1948-1957)**
- 1st TFW March AFB, CA
- 71st TRW Kadena AB, Okinawa
- 366th FBW England AFB, LA

**Air Resupply and Communications Service (1951-1953)**
- 580th AR&CW Wheelus AB, Libya
- 581st AR&CW Clark AB, Philippines
- 582nd AR&CW Molesworth AB, England

**Abbreviations**

| | |
|---|---|
| AAB | Army Air Base |
| AB | Air Base |
| AFB | Air Force Base |
| ANG | Air National Guard |
| AR&CW | Air Resupply & Communications Wing |
| BG | Bomb Group |
| BW | Bomb Wing |
| CG | Composite Group |
| FBW | Fighter-Bomber Wing |
| GMW | Guided Missile Wing |
| PRS | Photographic Reconnaissance Squadron |
| RCN WG | Reconnaissance Wing |
| RCS | Radar Calibration Squadron |
| REVRON | Radar Evaluation Squadron |
| SFW | Strategic Fighter Wing |
| SRG | Strategic Reconnaissance Group |
| SRW | Strategic Reconnaissance Wing |
| TDY | Temporary Duty |
| TRW | Tactical Reconnaissance Wing |

gine nacelle was redesigned and the baffling shortened to reduce drag when opened to allow more air to the engines—but the problem remained.

One of the reasons for this overheating was the material used to build the engine crankcases. Engineers first used magnesium because it was lighter than aluminum and could yield a ratio of 1lb weight in an engine to produce 1hp, a ratio that was considered ideal in helping to reduce overall weight of the huge aircraft. The magnesium proved to be problematic, however, getting much hotter than aluminum under sustained use and causing the engine to crack. Another engine problem was the oil pumping system, which did not feed oil to the top cylinders; this was the reason for so many "swallowed" valves. A swallowed valve meant having to shut down the engine and feather the propeller.

To those first assigned to the B-29 program, these problems were very frustrating, and some tried in vain to be transferred to B-17 units. An early assignee to the B-29s was M/Sgt. Russell Crawford, who served as crew chief on one of the first seven Superfortresses, designated the YB-29 and built at the new Wichita plant. Assigned to the 468th Maintenance Squadron, 444th Bombardment Group (BG), 58th BW, Crawford had this to say about the early B-29s: "I learned about the mysterious bugs and gremlins that filtered into and around the early B-29s before the USAAF even ran the acceptance check on them. Rumors floated around that the rise and fall of the tide in the nearby Pacific Ocean affected the construction of the aircraft during the building of the first three prototypes at the Boeing no. 1 plant in Seattle. I was crew chief of

one of the first seven YB-29s to come off the assembly line at the new Boeing-Wichita plant. Like most people associated with the Superforts at first, I lived through the frustrations and disappointments as we tried to iron out the kinks."

**Flight Tests Begin**

In early September 1942, the first XB-29 was rolled out of the assembly shed for its first taxi tests. A few days later, Eddie Allen and crew boarded no. 1 XB-29 for a series of more serious taxi tests. He almost got the airplane airborne three times during the faster taxiing, bouncing it into the air about 15ft each time, then settled her down on the runway, as his confidence surged.

Edmund T. Allen, affectionately known as "Eddie," had the reputation of being the most experienced and possibly the best test pilot in the United States. He learned to fly after joining the Air Service in 1917, and became a flight instructor and taught advanced acrobatics. During World War I, he was sent to England to learn about British aircraft flight-testing techniques. After the war, he became a test pilot for the National Advisory Committee for Aeronautics, and then for two years flew World War I De-Havillands as an air mail pilot for the Post Office Department until the department got out of the flying business in 1927. He then worked for various airlines and manufacturers as a pilot and a free-lance test pilot.

On April 26, 1939, Eddie Allen became Boeing's first and only director of aerodynamics and flight research, a position that gave him the opportunity to influence the research, testing, and development of several aircraft, especially the B-29. Allen surrounded himself with some of the best brains in the business, including Al Reed, chief of flight testing and chief test pilot, who was in charge of the Flight Research Department; and MIT-educated and renowned aerodynamicist George Schairer, who was responsible for developing the Boeing "117" wing. (The large high-lift wing flaps on the "117" allowed takeoffs and landings to be made in reasonable distances with the smallest wing surfaces, greatly reducing drag and, thus, maintaining the speed of the aircraft. The fuselage, nacelles, fairings, and other equipment were also designed to produce a minimum of drag.)

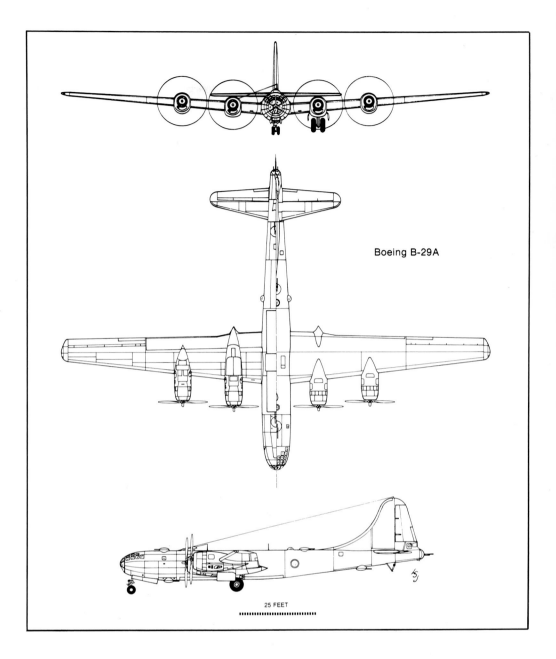

Boeing B-29A

25 FEET

## "She Flies!"

With satisfactory taxi testing completed and after 1,400,000 man hours spent on Model 345, the wind tunnel tests, the research, and the development work done by Eddie Allen and George Schairer and their people finally paid off. On September 21, 1942, no. 1 XB-29 taxied out onto the runway at Boeing Field in Seattle. Eddie Allen was in the pilot's seat and Al Reed occupied the co-pilot's seat. At various stations in the aircraft were eight more members of the flight test crew, each ready to monitor and record specific readings and observations during the flight.

The takeoff was uneventful. Allen climbed to 6,000ft and made the lateral, directional, and longitudinal stability and control checks. Everything that should be checked on a first flight was satisfactorily accomplished in 1hr, 15min.

As the engines were shut off, Allen told the waiting crowd of co-workers, "She flies!"

The day after Allen's first flight, Capt. Donald Putt, now an Army project officer, took the no. 1 XB-29 up for a short flight. Upon landing, Putt declared, "She's easier to fly than the B-17." He could claim the distinction of being the second man to test-hop the

XB-29 and the first USAAF man to fly it.

Soon after the first two flights, though, troubles began to plague almost every flight. It seemed that Murphy's Law was originated to apply to the B-29 program: If something bad could happen it usually did! Allen was able to get only 27hr in the air out of twenty-three flights by December 1942. During the first three months since the first flight, sixteen engines had to be changed, nineteen exhaust systems had to be revised, and twenty-two carburetors had to be replaced. There were many other problems, including governor and feathering diffi-

*Test pilot Bob Robbins takes no. 1 XB-29 off from Bolling Field in December 1943.*
Bob Robbins

culties with the four-blade Hamilton Standard propellers, which caused runaway engines.

Allen and his crew had trouble accumulating enough data with such short flights, which averaged just a little over 1hr. Half of the flight was usually spent fighting mounting odds trying to get back to the field.

One bright spot was the fact that the B-29's performance and handling qualities were excellent. Other than the rudder boost being removed, no significant aerodynamic changes were ever made.

On December 30, 1942, no. 2 XB-29 was ready for its initial flight. Allen was at the controls for this flight also. Engineers had cleared three of the engines for a maximum of 35hr flying time. Trouble erupted early, and Allen elected to discontinue the flight and return to the field. Six minutes from the field, fire broke out in the fourth engine and soon the smoke in the cockpit was so thick that Allen could hardly see the ground. Luckily, the crew made it in and the fire was put out on the ground.

Fires continued to haunt the B-29s. Boeing engineers reported that at least part of the cause was a faulty engine fuel induction system—a charge denied by Wright. It was fifteen months before there was positive proof that the R-3350 was susceptible to induction system fires, and that these fires would escalate rapidly and become uncontrollable magnesium fires, which then destroyed the evidence of the original fire's origin. The proof

came during a routine test flight of no. 1 XB-29 on March 24, 1944, while Boeing test pilot Robert ("Bob") Robbins was feathering the engines: a fire started in the fourth engine. Fortunately, he was able to get the engine feathered and the fire extinguished before the fire spread beyond the induction system and became an external fire.

More tests were needed on no. 2 XB-29 and no. 1 was out of commission until modifications were finished—so the engines from no. 1 were removed and put in no. 2. Everyone at Boeing, especially Eddie Allen, was anxious to get the problems solved and testing behind them.

## Disaster in Seattle

At 12:09pm, February 18, 1943, with Bob Dansfield flying as co-pilot and nine crew members aboard, Eddie Allen took off in no. 2 XB-29 on a flight that resulted in the most shocking air accident anyone could remember. The entire B-29 program, on which so much hope was riding, was placed in jeopardy, instantly.

Eight minutes into the flight, the first engine caught fire. The engine was routinely shut down and the props feathered. All aboard thought the fire was out, but Allen decided to abort the flight and return to the field. At 12:24pm, the radio operator reported the plane's altitude as 1,500ft about 4mi from the field. At this time, no one suspected that the fire was still alive, but it had spread into the wing section front spar. Allen was making a routine landing pattern when the raging fire was discovered.

At 12:25pm they had just completed turning onto the base leg and had just crossed the heavily populated west

shore of Lake Washington. At that time, ground witnesses heard an explosion that sounded like a loud backfire and saw a piece of metal fall from the airplane. About this time, the radio operator, who could see into the forward bomb bay and the wing center-section spar, yelled to Allen, "You'd better get this thing down in a hurry. The wing spar is burning badly."

In a desperate effort to get the airplane on the ground, Allen turned on final approach at an altitude of 250ft. Three crew members jumped from the burning plane, but they were too low to the ground for their parachutes to open and they died when they hit the ground. At 12:26pm, just 3mi from Boeing Field, no. 2 XB-29 crashed into the Frye Meat Packing Plant, killing all aboard and about twenty in the building. Allen and the others aboard were killed instantly.

Bob Robbins summed up the tragic accident and aftermath: "The flight test team that Eddie assembled and trained was decimated, devastated, and demoralized. Some of its members would probably never completely get over his loss—but they did put the pieces back together and continued to fight the battles and get the answers as Eddie would expect them to."

The third prototype XB-29 made its initial test flight on June 16, 1943. The next month, Boeing made its first delivery to the USAAF, which included seven of the YB-29 service test series from the Wichita plant.

## Gen. K. B. Wolfe's Special B-29 Project

The tragic crash of no. 2 XB-29 caused ripples up the chain of command all the way to President Roosevelt, who was already unhappy with the lack of progress being made in the airplane's development. He had promised Generalissimo Chiang Kai-shek an early deployment of the giant aircraft in the hopes of bolstering US-Chinese relations. He wanted B-29s on the way to India by the end of 1943.

After the tragedy, there were more investigations. General Arnold was eager to find the causes of these fires and steer the super-bomber away from ensuing political upheaval. Somebody had to come up with something real soon to quick-start the project, find some solutions, and get the B-29s rolling off the assembly line and headed for combat—or else.

Senator Harry S. Truman, who had made a name for himself as the head of a Congressional Investigating Committee that had exposed fraudulent overcharging and other violations in defense acquisitions, even looked into the troubles associated with the B-29 program. His committee's report stated that, "Quality had run second to quantity in building engines for the Superfortresses," and placed blame for substandard or defective engines equally on Wright Aeronautical Co. and the USAAF for applying too much pressure on the engine-building company to speed up production.

General Arnold had called on some of the most experienced pilots in the USAAF, including Brig. Gen. Kenneth B. Wolfe, Col. Leonard ("Jake") Harman, Col. Haywood ("Possum") Hansell, and Col. LaVern ("Blondie") Saunders. As trouble continued to mount and with time running out, something had to be done—and done quickly—to move the B-29 program forward.

And something did happen! A bombardment project officer at Wright Field came up with what turned out to be the solution to getting the B-29 project rolling. Colonel Harman, who worked with the B-29 project and had even flown in a B-29 with Eddie Allen, was the man who came up with the bright idea. Harman wasted no time in going over his plan with his boss, General Wolfe.

Harman's idea was that the B-29 program needed a "special project" tag with teeth in it. This special project would exercise full control over every-

thing pertaining to the B-29 program. In other words, a single command would have full control for flight tests, production, modifications, and the selecting and training of combat crews. The idea was so unique that General Wolfe thought it would not only work, but could be sold to the top people in Washington. "Write what you just told me down on a piece of paper," he told Harman, "and we'll take a trip up to Washington and see what General Echols thinks of the idea, before going to General Arnold."

Echols read the proposal, studied it for a while, and handed it back to Harman. "Take it down the hall and show it to General Arnold," he said. "I like the idea and I think he will!"

Colonel Harman had the proposal neatly typed with a place for General Arnold to sign above his name if he approved it. After the general read the proposal, he also studied it for a minute or so, and then said, "Why can't somebody else do something for

*Left to right: Bob Robbins, co-pilot; Jim Werner, flight-test project pilot; and Jim Fraser, flight-test project pilot. Bob Robbins*

me like this? Yes," he said, "I think it will work." He signed the paper.

The short proposal developed into what was called "The K. B. Wolfe Special B-29 Project." As the project got underway under the leadership of General Wolfe and Colonel Harman, things began to improve noticeably. Although the gremlins and bugs would continue to hamper the engine performances and other setbacks would occur, the B-29 Special Project could claim considerable responsibility for getting the giant bombers through the assembly lines, to the modifications centers, and ready for combat. Also, crew members from across the country, if they were thought to be B-29 combat crew material, were brought into the program.

23

## Chapter 2

# Three-Pronged B-29 Battle Erupts

The beginning of 1943 brought with it three distinct "battles" not pertaining to the "hot" war, but all associated with the B-29 Superfortress program: battle of the political decisions, battle to eliminate setbacks in production of the B-29, and the "Battle of Kansas," in which all hands pitched in to make the Superfortress ready for combat and to train combat crews and ground crews to maintain the planes in combat.

After the January 1943 Casablanca Conference, President Roosevelt made a decision to inform Generalissimo Chiang Kai-shek that all possible aid would be sent to prevent the Japanese from taking over China. Japan's army had cut off all land-deployed help to the USAAF by capturing Burma. Normally, supplies to China came over the Burma and Lido Roads, but now they would have to be flown in. Both Army Gen. Joseph Stilwell and USAAF Maj. Gen. Claire L. Chennault, newly appointed head of the 14th Air Force in China, were trying to exert pressure on the president to initiate this plan. They and Chiang

*Jacob Beser, standing before the atomic bomb-carrying Superfortress at Tinian Island, was the only man to fly in the strike plane on both atomic missions: in the* Enola Gay *to Hiroshima and* Bock's Car *to Nagasaki.* Jake Beser

Kai-shek wanted the B-29s sent to China so that they could begin and maintain an air offensive against Japan.

General Marshall was cautious because he realized the enormous problems that would develop from trying to supply bombers in China from bases in India before each bombing raid could take place. He thought the war in Europe, at this stage, would suffer if transport planes were taken from that theater and moved to the CBI theater. Major decisions had already been made with Allied forces to win the war in Europe before turning full force on Japan.

President Roosevelt still insisted on getting help to Chiang Kai-shek. He suggested sending up to 300 US bombers, not necessarily B-29s, to China.

**Service Tests Begin**

In the meantime, General Arnold had more or less staked the future of the USAAF on the early deployment of the B-29s against Japan. He depended heavily on the K. B. Wolfe Special B-29 Project to get this done.

The Wolfe Special B-29 Project had been given top priority in men and material, second only to the secret "Manhattan Engineer District Project." General Wolfe used this priority treatment to request the transfer of the Accelerated Service Test Branch

(ASTB), headed by Col. Abraham Olsen from Wright Field to Smokey Hill Army Air Field in Salina, Kansas. The new Boeing-Wichita plant, with orders to produce fourteen YB-29s that were to be tested and used for USAAF acceptance checks, began rolling planes off the assembly line in June 1943. On June 27, Colonel Harman flew the first service-test YB-29 at the Wichita field. Because Smokey Hill had extra-long, 10,000ft runways, built especially for one of the first B-29 groups for combat training, Harman decided that the service testing be done there, rather than at the shorter field at the Wichita plant.

The high priority of the Special B-29 Project allowed General Wolfe to choose the top aides who worked for him at Wright Field when the 58th BW was organized on June 1, 1943. He chose Colonel Harman as his deputy and General Saunders, who had commanded a B-17 group and served as group commander of the 11th BG in the South Pacific early in the war, to direct the B-29 crew-training program.

On August 14, 1992, many B-29 veterans gathered at Boeing Field to commemorate the fiftieth anniversary of the first flight of the B-29. Lt. Gen. James V. Edmundson, US Air Force (Retired), related an interesting account of his first encounter with the B-29: "I first met the B-29 in the sum-

A Superfortress from the 331st BG, 315th BW, proudly flies overhead. Many of those who fought to take the Mariana Islands, to make the B-29 operation possible, rest below at Guam. Josh Curtis

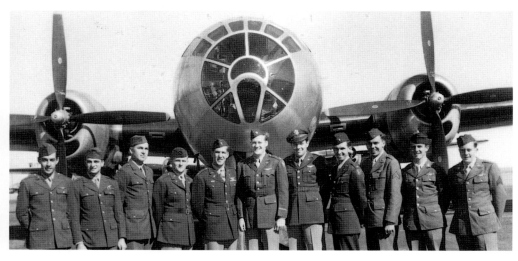

The Maj. Robert Goldsworthy crew pose in front of their new B-29 at Herrington, Kansas, before flying it to Saipan in October 1944. Goldsworthy, center, was shot down over Tokyo in December 1944, and remained a POW until the war ended. He remained in service after the war and retired as a major general. Hurth Thompkins

mer of 1943. After returning from the South Pacific in the spring of that year, I was assigned to Washington. Blondie Saunders had been promoted to brigadier general and was also assigned to the Pentagon. One day, he called me into his office and told me that he was involved in the B-29 program. He told me to grab an airplane and make a quick trip around the States to see how many of the old 11th Group troops I could find and how many of them would like to go back to war.

"I went out to Bolling Field and was assigned an airplane that, I guess, in this company should remain nameless. If I told you that it was shaped like one of General LeMay's cigars, had almost no wings at all, and was built in Baltimore, you'd be able to guess what kind of an airplane had been issued to me.

"Anyway, I toured the country in my flying cigar and ran into a bunch of the old 11th Group troops. I couldn't tell them where we would be going or what we would be flying. I could tell them that General Saunders would be going with us, and virtually to a man, they volunteered. I told them to sit tight and within a couple of weeks they would be getting orders assigning them to the 58th BW in Marietta, Georgia, and I'd see them there.

"The 58th BW, under the command of General K. B. Wolfe, with General Blondie Saunders as director of operations, had its headquarters in an old farmhouse in the back acres of the base at Marietta. There was a big hangar on the flight line where a YB-29 was safely hidden when it wasn't flying. The ramp was full of those little, twin-engined, cigar-shaped birds— B-26s! There, I said it!

"During those early days in Marietta, as my old 11th Group buddies came driving in to report for duty, they would have to phone me from the gate in order to get on the base. I'd take them for a tour around the ramp loaded with B-26s and they were not bashful about asking me just what in the hell I'd gotten them into. I'd say something about not letting anybody talk you into volunteering for any-

thing. It went over like a lead balloon. When we'd just about reached the point where they were ready to tear me limb from limb, I'd take them inside the hangar where they got their first look at that great big, beautiful YB-29. It was fun to watch their eyes light up. Since Jake Harmon had just checked me out in that YB in July, I was real proud of her.

"It isn't often realized what a big contribution the troops from Blondie Saunders' old 11th BG made to the early B-29 program. Of the sixteen squadrons in the 58th BW, eight were commanded by guys from the 11th BG. And others were scattered through the four groups in key staff positions."

Boeing and the USAAF were very congenial during the stepped-up testing program. The plan was for the USAAF to evaluate the airplane's speed, range, and engine cooling. Boeing ground crews would maintain the airplanes, and military pilots would teach Boeing flight personnel so that the company could build a staff to fly the B-29s as they rolled off the production lines.

General Wolfe was named commander of the newly formed 58th BW, VH (the VH designating "very heavy" aircraft), with headquarters in Marietta, Georgia. Along with the ASTB, Wolfe and his skeleton staff moved the 58th headquarters to Smokey Hill. One of Wright Field's brightest project officers was Maj. Vic Agather, who went to India with the 58th BW to help with maintenance as combat against Japan got underway.

Brig. Gen. "Rosey" O'Donnell (left), 73rd BW commander at Saipan, chats with Maj. Gen. Curtis LeMay (right), commander of the 21st BC after January 1945. Hurth Thompkins

Of the engine-fire problems, Major Agather said, "We had long since determined the troubles went back to the original design by Wright Aeronautical. Because a lighter-weight material was used to build the engine crankcases, the magnesium which was used rather than a heavier material such as aluminum, resulted in getting hotter, and when used on a sustained basis, it eventually exploded, or would swallow a valve, causing engine failure and, in most cases, fires.

"To correct this problem would require a redesign, and time had run out for any such delay. Consequently, we did patchwork, such as shortening the length of baffles and installing cuffs on the base of each propeller blade to increase airflow to exhaust valves."

## Trained Mechanics Brought In

At Smokey Hill Army Air Base, USAAF-trained mechanics were brought into the B-29 program to assist in the ASTB testing of the YB-29s. John Mitchell was one of the USAAF mechanics. He recalls some of the things that took place during those days: "A Captain Morris was the engineering officer from Wright Field in charge of mechanics and support personnel. These people were drawn from all over the USAAF. For the most part, they were as new to the B-29 as the plane was new to the USAAF. The manufacturers of the airframe, engines, and other components sent technical representatives to lend assistance, but these men also had to learn the details of the equipment as testing proceeded.

"Slowly, the problems were mastered and by the end of the service test program, the ASTB produced the most highly trained and skilled B-29 mechanics and technicians then in the USAAF."

General Arnold personally selected the commanders of the four groups that made up the 58th BW, VH, which was activated on June 1, 1943. Four huge airfields with wide runways about 10,000ft long were built in Kansas to accommodate the new airplanes. Col. Lewis Parker was Arnold's choice to command the veteran 40th BG, to be located in Pratt, Kansas. To head the 462nd BG at Walker Field in Victoria, Kansas, was Col. Richard H. Carmichael. At Great Bend, Col. Alva L. Harvey would head the 444th BG, and Col. Howard F. Engler was named to head the 468th BG at Smokey Hill.

During the ASTB testing, Colonel Olson checked out Colonel Parker, who took a YB-29 to Pratt Army Air Field, and began setting up the 40th BG. Within three weeks, he had received two more B-29s. Colonel Harvey took the next three production planes to Great Bend to begin training the 444th BG. Harvey had served as B-29 project officer at Boeing Aircraft Co. and was moved to Wichita early in 1943, before assuming command of the 444th BG. Engler's 468th BG received the next three production B-29s from Wichita, and Carmichael took the next three for his 462nd BG at Walker Field.

Colonels Harvey and Parker were sent to England to observe the 8th Air Force combat operations and as observers to participate in a few combat missions. Parker's plane was shot down on his fifth mission and he sur-

A 9th BG Superfortress showing the group's insignia. Al Browne/Josh Curtis

vived the war as a German prisoner of war. Colonel Harvey returned to the States after five missions over Europe. He was the senior group commander of the 58th BW.

As future crew members were selected to fly and maintain the B-29s in combat, various schools were set up around the country. At Harvard, MIT, and Boca Raton, Florida, men were trained to operate the new AN/APQ-13 radar set that would be aboard each B-29. Wright Field set up a school to familiarize ground crew with the R-3350 engine. Gunners had to be taught how to operate the innovative new remote-controlled gunnery system, and the maintenance crew had to be taught how to maintain the pressurization system.

The author's first encounter with the B-29 Superfortress went something like this: The date was June 26, 1943. It was graduation day for about 200 aviation cadets of Pilot Class 43-F at Blackland Advanced Twin-Engine School in Waco, Texas. I was still more or less floating on Cloud Nine, having just received my new second lieutenant bars and, best of all, a pair of silver pilot's wings, when my flight instructor, Pilot Officer Donald Laver of the Royal Air Force (RAF), stopped by our table while we ate lunch in the officers' club. After lunch, we would get our assignments, preceded by a much-awaited two-week leave, before reporting to our new flying assignments; then after a much-awaited two-week leave, we would report to our new flying assignments.

Pilot Officer Laver was a product

*Another B-29 crew poses in front of their new plane before heading to Guam. Pictured is crew no. P10 of the 60th BS, 39th BG, 314th BW. Elmer Jones, shown left, standing.* Elmer Jones

of America's Lend-Lease agreement with England in reverse. He was one of the many RAF pilots loaned to the USAAF to assist in training much-needed pilots to man the many bombers, fighters, and other aircraft rolling off the assembly lines of factories across the country. I considered it a special honor to have been one of his students. Laver wasted no time in giving me a hint of what was to come at the upcoming meeting.

"Mister 1, eh, I mean Lieutenant Marshall," my former instructor began. As he stood there beside our table, my mind pictured him as the perfect RAF pilot, in his royal blue uniform and well-trimmed mustache, reminding me of the newsreels or a movie portraying one of the few who Prime Minister Winston Churchill proudly told his nation about: "Never in the history of civilisation have so many owed so much to so few." He was, of course, talking about the heroics performed by the outmanned RAF pilots during the Battle of Britain when they defeated Marshal Goering's highly touted German Luftwaffe. "Have you had any mechanical engineering training in civil or military life?" Laver continued.

I was somewhat baffled at the question. "No sir," I replied immediately. The fact that I had completed an aircraft mechanics course at Chanute Field in 1941 before entering the aviation cadet program never crossed my mind. I asked him why the question at this time.

"Well," he said, "I heard a rumor that a few of you fellows will be assigned to some kind of special project, and I think your name is on that list."

"What kind of project?" I quizzed, as my pulse picked up.

"Nobody knows," he said. "Sounds like some sort of interesting experimental project, though. I wish I could tell you more, but I'm sure you will find out shortly!"

At the assignment meeting, the officer went through the list alphabetically, announcing assignments. As each name was called out, the recipient left the room after collecting his orders, which included a two-week leave. Most names called out were going to B-17 or B-24 transition school and a very few to fighters or instructor school. Bomber pilots were needed most at this time to carry the stepped-up air war to Germany.

Eleven of us were left seated in the near-empty room when the names and assignments were all called.

"O.K. fellows," the captain said, "You have been pegged for a special project and our orders are to hold you here at Blackland until we receive word about your new assignment."

*Ground crewmen repair T-Square-44 Patches, s/n 42-24624, of the 498th BG, after a Japanese Zeke fighter strafed it on a retaliation raid on Saipan, November 24, 1944. This Superfortress still has the 20mm cannon in the tail.* Josh Curtis

That was it. Nobody knew anything! No leave, no word, no nothing—that's how it was for the next four days. The order finally came on July 1: We would clear the field, catch the 6:00pm train for Salina, Kansas, to become part of the K. B. Wolfe Special B-29 Project. The assignment was the most disheartening news we'd received since entering the cadet program. We would be enrolled in the first class of B-29 flight engineer school at Smokey Hill Army Air Field!

Beginning July 1, 1943, newly commissioned pilots gathered at Smokey Hill. We soon learned that all were former GIs who had completed airplane mechanics or specialty school before entering pilot training. It seemed that General Saunders, General Wolfe, or somebody had come up with the big idea that "These bright young men who had survived airplane mechanics school and also pilot training would be ideal people to become the third pilot aboard the new Super-

Joltin' Josie, *the first B-29 to land in the Mariana Islands on October, 12, 1944. Aboard were Brig. Gen. Haywood Hansell, commander of the 21st BC, and Maj. Jack Catton and crew.* Josh Curtis

Dauntless Dotty, *piloted by Bob Morgan of Memphis Belle fame, led the first B-29 raid on Tokyo, on November 24, 1944. Later, Dotty crashed into the sea on takeoff at Kwajalein Island en route to the United States just prior to the end of the war.* Warren Thompson

fortress, with primary duty of flight engineer." Having not yet even seen a B-29, we learned that the flight engineer would ride facing aft behind the pilots, monitoring a huge panel of instruments.

We crashed through the flight engineer course, saw our first B-29 later that month, but that's about all. No hands-on instruction was available,

but we did graduate. There would be no "washing out" and we were scattered among the four Groups that were forming in the new bases in Kansas. I went to Colonel Carmichael's 462nd BG at Walker Field. So far, to most of us flight engineer-pilots, the K. B. Wolfe Special B-29 Project was like cold water splashed in our faces. Had it not been for the pretty little "Rosie the Riveters" who were building the B-29s down at Wichita, our morale would have been much lower.

Fall weather in Kansas that year came on like a lion. B-29s began to trickle to the four bases. Before the airplanes could be delivered to the bases, however, they had to go to a modification center. In addition to Wright Field and others, a huge center for modifying the B-29s was opened in Birmingham, Alabama, where more than 9,000 people were employed to accelerate the changes to be made.

Before the real "Battle of Kansas" got underway, policy makers changed courses again to get better-qualified people to man the flight engineer seats. All of the pilot-flight engineer (FE) officers were shipped out to Roswell, New Mexico, to go through B-17 transition and rather than releasing us for a combat unit in Europe, we were held over to join the 73rd BW

Lucky 'Leven *carried some of the best nose art over Japan, but then orders came down in April 1945 banning "girlie" art. Lucky flew with the 498th BG, 73rd BW, Tinian Island.* Warren Thompson

that would follow the 58th BW as they vacated the bases in Kansas. Ground crew chiefs or experienced mechanics were given the jobs of flight engineers.

Also changed was the original plan for the newly formed 20th Bomber Command (BC). Originally, the 20th BC would include both the 58th BW and 73rd BW, which was also formed in June, and would go to the CBI theater. General Wolfe was made commander of the new bomber command and Colonel Harmon took over the job of commanding the 58th BW. The 73rd BW became the initial wing of the 21st BC, and the 58th would join the CBI theater and go into combat under the Matterhorn plan. Under this plan, the B-29s would be based in India, with forward bases in China. The 20th BC would supply its own planes for combat missions against Japanese targets, by flying bombs and extra gas across the Himalayan Mountains to bases in China. To accumulate enough of each to complete one combat mission, a B-29 would have to take about seven trips across the mountains.

*Chapter 3*

# Ready or Not, the 58th Bombardment Wing Heads for India

In late November 1943, the Matter-horn plan was approved; Generalissimo Chiang Kai-shek promised to build bases in China, and the British agreed to provide bases in India. The decision to use the B-29s against Japan was never in real doubt, but there was much haggling when it came to how they should be used.

As the B-29s moved closer to overseas debarkation, theater commanders clamored for a piece of the action. Gen. Douglas Mac Arthur thought all the B-29s should be placed under his command, but others wanted to divide the lot. Gen. Claire Chennault, 14th AF commander in China, all but demanded that some of the Superfortresses be sent to him. Generalissimo Chiang Kai-shek wanted some and so did British Admiral Lord Louis Mountbatten. Even the US Navy wanted some for long-range reconnaissance flights.

**Birth of the 20th Air Force**

General Arnold and the Air War Plans Division found all of the requests for B-29s totally unsatisfactory. Brig. Gen. Haywood S. Hansell, Jr., recalls his part in these developments: "As a member of the Joint Plans Com-

*Every crew was anxious to have its bomber named and illustrated properly. This B-29 flew with the 468th BG, 73rd BW, Saipan. Ken Rust*

mittee, I got permission from General Arnold to approach Adm. Ernest Joseph King with a proposal for unified command of the B-29s.

"I pointed out to Admiral King a similarity between the command problem of the B-29s and that of the US fleet units who were temporarily based in the various ports, but the operational command of those fleet units resided not at the local base level, but at the top echelon of the Navy. Admiral King was a member of the Joint Chiefs of Staff (JCS) and commanded the US fleets, regardless of where their components were located. Base area commanders were responsible for the administrative and logistical support of fleet units and for the defense of the bases, but they did not have operational command. Unity of command of combat units was needed in the area of concerted combat.

"'The B-29 command problem was very similar,' I told the Admiral. 'Would it not be reasonable to solve it in a similar manner by providing unity of command at the highest level, and charging base commanders with administrative and logistical support and base defense? Top command could be vested in the JCS, with General Arnold as executive agent and commander of the B-29 force. Theater commanders could be charged with support, but not operational command.' Admiral King

said simply, 'I could find such an agreement acceptable.'

"Gen. George C. Marshall agreed. Thus was born the 20th Air Force, with Gen. Hap Arnold as its commander. The date was April 4, 1944."

Although the decision to concentrate the B-29s under JCS control made possible the development of the concerted bomber offensive against Japan, it did not mark the close of the argument from the theater field commanders. They continued their efforts to gain control of the B-29 units in their own areas. General MacArthur's headquarters was especially insistent and coupled its requests with personal letters from Gen. George Kenney to Arnold contending that B-29 operations out of the Mariana Islands against the Japanese home islands were militarily and technically unfeasible. At this time, plans had been formulated for the Navy, with Marine and Army troops, to invade the Marianas and to prepare one of the islands, Saipan, with a suitable base from which B-29 combat missions could be launched against targets in Japan.

With the activation of the 20th AF to operate under one commander and reporting only to the JCS, General Arnold, the new 20th AF commander, named General Hansell his chief of staff, responsible for the day-to-day activities of the 20th BC. He was assist-

*The 20th AF patch insignia.*

ed by Operation Deputy Col. Cecil Combs.

B-29 combat training continued at the Kansas bases as 1943 faded into history. There were still many bugs to be ironed out, as the battles continued. About 600 Boeing employees from the Wichita plant were sent to the B-29 bases in Kansas to try to solve the problems before the airplanes were sent overseas. Crews trained for combat flying B-17s. The bitterly cold Kansas winter was no help; mechanics had to work outside in freezing weather, because the hangars were not large enough for the B-29s. In the meantime, by December, the Bell plant in Georgia and the Renton plant were turning out B-29s ready to be modified, and the Omaha plant would be ready to start up by mid-1944.

## General Wolfe Goes to India

In addition to training problems plaguing the B-29 program, General Arnold was deeply concerned with the quality and progress of bases being prepared in India and China. As 1943 ended and with President Roosevelt

breathing down his neck, he ordered General Wolfe to round up his 20th BC staff and check those bases. Wolfe arrived in India in January, and in early February reported that he had met with Generals Chennault and Stilwell and members of their staffs, as well as other key figures.

In India, existing airfields the British had used were brought up to B-29 standards. The southern Bengal area was chosen for the base area, because it was fairly safe from Japanese attacks and not far from port facilities at Calcutta. Wolfe decided on the Ganges plains about 70mi west of Calcutta to build the four bases, one each at Kharagpur, Chakulia, Piardoba, and Dudkhundi, and Kharagpur for his headquarters.

The Chinese bases were built in the Chengtu area, mostly using thousands of peasants who broke up stones and transported them by hand to build the runways. Washington accused the Chinese of greatly overcharging for this work, but they got the work done.

When the Dudkhundi base was finished and ready to accept the 444th BG, the personnel saw little improvements over the base they left. Years later, one of the aircraft commanders

of Colonel Harvey's group, Winton R. Close, had this tongue-in-cheek assessment of conditions at Dudkhundi: "In 1944, Dudkhundi was a little, rural village about 40mi northwest of Calcutta, India. It was not a very attractive place. In the dry season, it was flat, ugly, dirty, dusty, and hot. During the monsoon season, it was flat, ugly, dirty, and muddy. During the months of April through August—part of the dry season—it would become so hot in the middle of the day that one could not touch the aluminum skin of the B-29 without getting burned.

"It was not a nice place at all. The water supply was suspect, so we drank slightly diluted chlorine from Lister bags. There was no ice. There was no beer. The only distilled liquor came from Calcutta. Its brand name was Carew's. We called it Carew's Booze for combat crews. It came in three flavors: gin, rum, and whiskey. All three tasted exactly the same. The only difference was the coloring used in each: no color for gin, a light tinge of yellow for rum, and a sort of dark tan for whiskey."

Colonel Carmichael and his 462nd BG settled at Piardoba, and both the 468th BG and the 20th BC headquartered at Kharagpur. Each of the four groups of the 58th BW were now in India and anxious to get on with the task of bombing Japanese targets. They were assigned forward bases in China, from which the mission against Japan proper and other targets on the Chinese mainland, would originate. The 40th BG would operate out of Hsinching, China, the 444th BG from Kwanghan, the 462nd BG from Kiunglai, and the 468th BG from Pengshan.

When new combat crew members got their first look at the giant B-29 Superfortress, they were amazed at its size. It was a beautiful airplane. Weighing in at about 100,000lb empty, its gross load with fuel and bombs, plus the crew, increased to almost 140,000lb on missions to Japan during the low-altitude fire raids. This was about 20,000lb more than original specifications called for. The original design was for a total gross load of 120,000lb.

The airplane's wingspan was just short of 142ft from wing tip to wing tip, and from nose to tail, it measured 99ft. There were four remote-con-

trolled gun turrets, one forward on top of the fuselage and aft on top, with the same alignment on the bottom of its fuselage. Each turret had two .50cal air-cooled machine guns. The tail gunner's position also had twin .50s and originally contained a 20mm cannon (later removed). Broomsticks were installed after the cannon was removed, to make it appear to an attacking fighter that the cannon was still there. Two extra .50cal guns were later incorporated into the top forward turret. During World War II, 3,965 B-29s were built at an average of $600,000 each.

Denny D. Pidhayny, historian and recording secretary of the 58th Bomb Wing Association, quotes General Arnold in a fascinating story of how one of the most famous B-29s of World War II got its name: "On January 1, 1944, I was going through the Boeing Airplane Plant at Wichita, Kansas (where the giant new airplanes were being produced), looking over the B-29s as they were assembled. When they told me how many B-29s they planned to complete that month, I walked back down the line and picked an unfinished aircraft just a little beyond that goal. I wrote my name across the fuselage and said, 'This is the plane I want this month.' The Superfortress I wrote my name on became known as the *General H. H. Arnold Special.*

"Needless to say, the Boeing people met that goal and shortly thereafter, Gen. [William S.] Knudsen, in an impressive ceremony, accepted the plane for the government. The crew that came to fly the plane to combat became known to everybody at the Boeing plant, and when the *Special* reached the Far East, the factory employees followed with pride each mission as closely as they could.

"Assigned to the 468th BG, 58th BW, which deployed to bases in India to begin combat operations against the Japanese via forward bases in China, the *General H. H. Arnold Special* began its sixteen-mission combat tour of duty on June 5, 1944. The mission was the first shakedown B-29 mission in combat. The target was the railway shops at Bangkok, Thailand.

"Mission number sixteen, and the final one for the *General H. H. Arnold Special*, took place on November 11, 1944. Flying from a forward base in the Chengtu area, the target was the Omura Aircraft Factory on Kyushu, one of Japan's home islands. While over the target, the pilot reported that

*A Superfortress in India. Note the guard at the front of the plane.* Josh Curtis

his airplane was low on gas. That was his last message.

"Later, intelligence learned the crew landed the *Special* at the Vladivostok Naval Air Station in Siberia. They were escorted on the last leg of their flight by ten Russian fighter planes, and then interned until their release by Iran on February 2, 1945."

General Arnold's promise to President Roosevelt that the B-29s would be headed to India by March 1, 1944, fell short this time by fewer than three weeks. Col. Frank Cook, a former Wright Field production engineering officer, took the first B-29, one of the original fourteen YB-29s built at Boeing's Wichita plant, off on a mission planned to confuse the Axis intelligence spy-ring en route to a newly enlarged base in India. The idea was to make it appear that the giant new bomber would be used in the European theater, rather than against the Japanese. Colonel Cook's flight plan took him on a criss-cross flight across the Atlantic. Within an hour after landing in England, a German reconnaissance plane recorded the arrival.

*A mechanic removes the cowling on the huge R-3350 radial engine.* Chuck Spieth

*A formation of 462nd BG B-29s on their way to a target.* Marshall

Neither the Germans nor Japanese were fooled by the ploy. They knew about the development of the long-range B-29, and the Japanese had long since determined that the Superfortresses would be stationed at the larger bases in India and in China, from which they would attempt to attack Japanese targets. The airplane was inspected by Generals Eisenhower and Doolittle, before Cook took off for India. He landed at the Karagpur base on April 6. His B-29 was not the first, but the second, B-29 to reach India.

## First to Reach Bases in India

Brig. Gen. Blondie Saunders and Col. Jake Harman departed Kansas on March 25, leading a stream of brand-new B-29s to their overseas bases in India. Their first stop was Presque Isle, and from there they flew to Gander Lake, Newfoundland. Each leg of the journey into the unknown was briefed before departure to the next destination, which in itself was confusing to some of the crew members. After Gander Lake came Marrakech, French Morocco, then Cairo, Egypt, and on to Karachi. Leaving Karachi, Saunders and Harman landed at the Chakulia base on April 2, 1944. Theirs was the first B-29 to reach the theater from which they would begin combat against Japan. General Wolfe and aides were on hand to greet them.

Saunders also pioneered the route over the Himalayan Mountains to the forward base of Kwanghan at Cheng-tu, China. He was met by Chinese dignitaries and Maj. Gen. Claire Chennault, commander of the US 14th AF, which was based in China. More than 75,000 Chinese laborers were also there when the Superfortress landed, all shouting "Ding haó," or "Congratulations." Crews from the 40th BG were among the first arrivals and, as commander of the 40th BG, Colonel Harman assumed command of the advance echelon.

The climate change from a cold environment to the suffocatingly hot and dry desert played havoc with the troubled R-3350 engines. At one point during the deployment, after several planes were lost due to engine failures, General Wolfe wired General Arnold and insisted that a better engine cooling system still had to be developed before the B-29s could possibly be combat ready. At this point, all B-29s were grounded en route to overseas bases and more field modifications were made on cowl flaps and crossover oil tubes were installed from the intake to the rocker box of the top cylinders on both rows of the twin engines. After this modification, the flights resumed, and by May 8, 130 B-29s had arrived at the Indian bases.

Since the Dudkhundi base was not yet ready to receive it, the 444th BG was routed temporarily to another British base at Charra, where steel matting was used to extend the runways for the B-29s. The Group arrived at Charra on April 12.

### First Enemy Attack, First Injury

One of the major concerns General Wolfe had with his attack force now at bases in India lay with getting supplies across the Himalayas to the forward bases in China. Since no transport planes were available, the solution was to use the B-29s to fly the extra fuel and bombs over the "Hump" and store them at their forward bases until enough supplies were accumulated for a bombing raid on a Japanese target.

It was during one of these Hump supply trips that the B-29s' first attack by Japanese fighters and the first B-29 crew member injury took place. On April 26, 1944, shortly after the B-29s started arriving in the CBI theater and two days after the India-to-China supply run was initiated, the Superfortress piloted by Maj. Charles Hansen and transporting fuel was attacked by six Japanese Oscars. After staying out of range for 15 or 20min, one of the enemy planes suddenly whipped out of formation and twisted toward the B-29. During the attack, Sgt. Walter W. Gilonske was injured, becoming the first B-29 crewman in World War II to receive injuries from an enemy attack.

The enemy attack lasted about 25min before the Japanese broke off.

*A weapons carrier loaded with 2,000lb high-explosive bombs.* Chuck Spieth

One of the airplanes left the scene smoking as a result of fire from the tail gunner's position. Major Hansen and his crew were credited with two historical "firsts" in the B-29 offensive against Japan.

Bill Rooney, who edits the quarterly publication *Memories* for the 40th BG, tells an interesting story of President Roosevelt's introduction to the Boeing B-29 Superfortress: "On February 20, 1944, Col. Walter Lucas [aircraft commander in the 40th BG] and his crew, plus two crew chiefs, were dispatched to Washington, DC, in B-29 no. 42-6303. They were to land at Bolling Field. As far as can be determined, no reason was given to the crew for making the flight. Bolling Field, at that time, had four runways, the longest of which was 6,000ft. Colonel Lucas landed the airplane and was met by none other than Gen. H. H. Arnold himself. It was learned then that the purpose of the flight was to show the B-29 to President Roosevelt.

[Considering that the cost of the B-29 project was more than the atomic bomb project—$3 billion compared to $2 billion—this was a significant occasion.]

"General Arnold met each member of the crew and had each one brief him on his duties. The following day, February 21, between 4:00 and 4:30pm, the President came to Bolling Field and visited the plane. His chauffeur drove the limousine to the front of the plane. The President did not leave the car, but he gave the giant bomber a close scrutiny. Accompanying the President were his daughter, Anna, and her two children, Eleanor and Curtis. They did get out of the car and inspected the plane. The President flashed his famous smile at the crew members as he left."

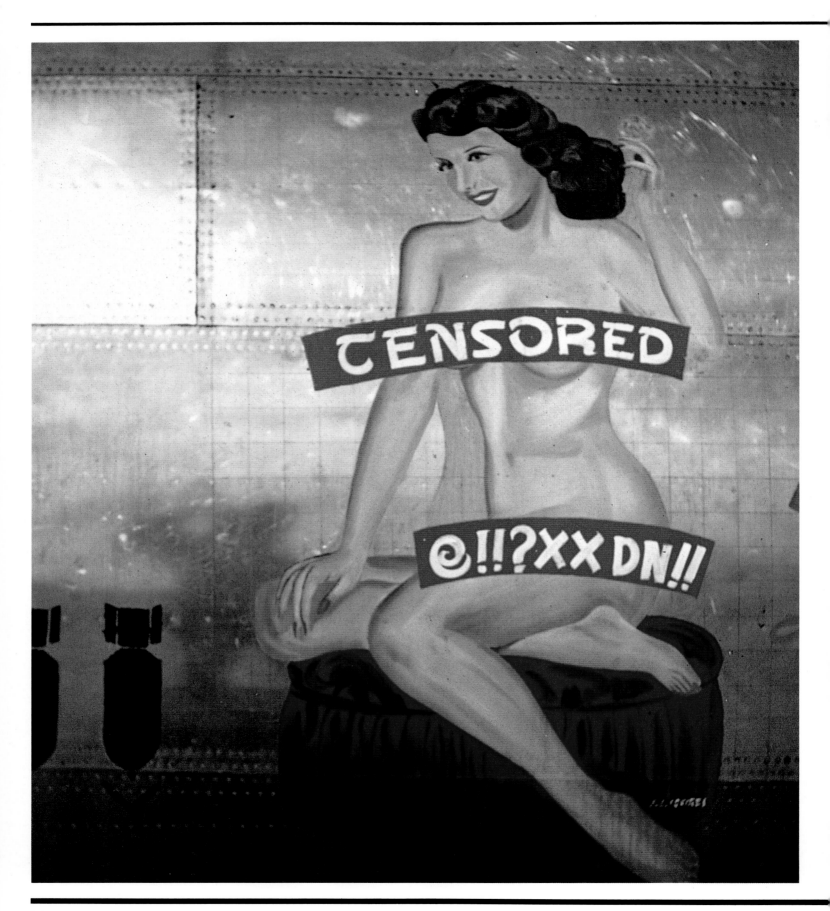

*Chapter 4*

# 20th Bomber Command Poised for Combat

With 120 Superfortresses in India by May 8, 1944, ready and anxious to get the show started, General Wolfe and his staff wasted no time preparing plans for the first strike against Japanese targets.

The B-29s, each with an extra engine aboard, had made the long trip from the States with some difficulty, losing five planes en route, but otherwise arriving in fair condition. There had been a few cases where plexiglass bubble blisters protecting gunners operating remote-controlled gun turrets blew out due to climatic changes. The engine overheating problem was not yet conquered.

Ground personnel were already in place when the combat crews arrived, and the crew complement had been standardized in all four groups, each with four squadrons. (The 58th BW was the only wing to have four squadrons per group.) By October 1944, three squadrons became standard.

As the 58th BW prepared for its first mission, a major decision had been made to change plans for the 73rd BW, now training at the vacated Kansas bases. The 73rd would be sent to Saipan as the initial wing of the

*Appropriately named* Censored. *This aircraft flew with the 444th BG, 58th BW, Tinian Island.* Ken Rust

21st BC. American forces planned to attack and capture Saipan, located in the Pacific about 1,500mi south of Tokyo, by July 1944.

The crew complement in the B-29s consisted of eleven men. Five were officers—the aircraft commander, pilot, bombardier, navigator, and flight engineer—and six were enlisted men—the central fire control gunner, left and right gunners, tail gunner, radio operator, and radar operator. This crew configuration was the same in the 73rd BW. By mid-1944, the flight engineer ranks had been opened to enlisted men. Some of these men were among those who had replaced the pilot-flight engineer officers back in 1943. Also, some of these enlisted men were offered a commission, and a few received commissions after having been given the rank of flight officer. Later in the war, because of the highly classified electronic equipment, such as high-tech radar and the new navigational aid Loran, the crews had one or two more officers.

## First B-29 Raid Was to Bangkok

The 58th BW commander, Brig. Gen. Blondie Saunders, led the first B-29 combat mission against a Japanese target on June 5, 1944, one day before another memorable occasion, that of the second front invasion of Europe by Allied forces led by Allied Supreme Commander "Ike" Eisenhower. Sched-

uled for a strike—or a "shakedown mission," as some called it—against the Makasan Railway Yards at Bangkok, Thailand were 112 B-29s, ninety-eight of which proceeded toward the target; only seventy-seven made it to the target area.

The mission, with a nighttime takeoff, involved a 2,261mi round trip, the longest bombing mission yet of World War II. It was a daylight attack from 23,000ft altitude. Only forty-eight planes were able to bomb the target, and five of the bombers were lost to mechanical problems. None were lost to enemy action.

The nighttime takeoffs really woke up the base. One-hundred or more B-29s taking off, which lasted almost 90min, literally shook the earth, as witnessed by Sgt. Mary Thomas of the Red Cross, stationed with the 22nd Air Depot, 20th BC, at Kharagpur. She remembers how it was when the big bombers woke her up, to go on a prowl: "The 'basha' where the Red Cross girls lived was down near the end of the 2mi-long runway, and when they began revving up the engines on the B-29s, not only could you hear the sound, but the ground reverberated as well.

"I would grab my flashlight, tie a scarf around my head, and run out between the buildings, hoping the sound of my boots would scare away the snakes. I didn't have time to worry about the panthers they said lived in

*Bombs spew from the bomb bays of the 497th BG over a target in Japan.* Chuck Spieth

the nearby jungles. I just wanted to get to the place where the big silver planes stopped before they turned out on the runway. I could see the aircraft coming one behind the other down the taxi strip as they left the herring-boned side ramps.

"Where men were still working on planes, there were big, hazy patches of light from the lamps mounted on top of tall metal stands that could be wheeled to where they were needed, but as the planes approached the end

of the runway, it was all dark except for the little lights on their fuselages. From where I stood, the blisters were all dark. I couldn't see the faces of the crew members, but I knew they were there.

"I did as the men had asked after they learned I always came out to watch the night takeoff. I held the flashlight under my chin and made the "Ding Hao" sign with my right hand, my thumb pointing up. Some-times, the gunners would reply by making a cross with their lights inside the blisters. While the pilots checked the magnetos, I walked around under the plane and down the other side, waving to the right gunner, as well.

Then I'd dash under the tail and back to the outside edge of the strip as the huge plane turned right onto the run-way. I could feel the engines roar, and then she was off—moving slowly at first because she was so heavy with full fuel tanks, a heavy bomb load, and a precious cargo of men. The runway was long, over 2mi. As an aid to the pilots, a huge magenta-colored light was pointed skyward at the far end so they could judge how much runway they had left. The planes had to be airborne by the time they crossed the colored beam or they'd never make it off the ground. It was scary and I prayed hard until I saw the last plane—like a silver-grey dragonfly, its wings headed with tiny lights—lift into the night sky and disappear.

"Then I would turn as the next big bomber lumbered into place, flick on my flashlight, and repeat my ritual for its crew. I didn't know all their names; there were so many that we called them by their rank. Sergeant, mostly, because there seemed to be very few privates or corporals in such a specialized operation. I knew them by the names of the planes they flew in. We'd say, he's from *Miss Shorty*, or *Lassie*, or the *Mary K*, or the *Raiden Maiden*. I admired them and loved them because they were men like my brother, Tom, who was flying a Navy Liberator in the Pacific."

## Action in the Pacific

As the 58th BW geared up for the first B-29 strike against the Japanese homeland, things were beginning to happen in the Pacific that would have great bearings on the B-29 program as a whole. At about 4:30pm on June 15, 1944, General Saunders, flying with 468th BG commander, Col. Howard Engler, took off from their forward base in China, heading for Kyushu, Japan. It was a night strike against what was billed as "the Pittsburgh of Japan," the Imperial Iron and Steel Works at Yawata, located on the southern-most home island of Kyushu.

Sixty-eight B-29s were airborne for the mission, but aborts stopped all but forty-seven from making it to the target area. The results of the raid were not too impressive, but the strike against Yawata had psychological impact. Not since the Jimmy Doolittle raid of April 18, 1942, had an enemy airplane darkened the skies above a Japanese home island, and it was the first time B-29s had made such an attack.

The other important development of June 15 was the announcement that a giant Navy task force had landed a Marine invasion force on Saipan. The purpose of this invasion was to secure the island and build a B-29 base from which an all-out assault against the entire main Japanese home islands could begin.

Back in the States, the second B-29 wing, the 73rd BW, had completed its third month of combat training at the same bases in Kansas the 58th

*British Admiral Lord Louis Mountbatten, the Southeast Asia theater commander, and Brig. Gen. Roger Ramey prepare to inspect the 40th BG in India. Josh Curtis*

BW had vacated when it left for India in April. Like the 58th BW, the 73rd was having to use old B-17s to train with because factories could not supply enough B-29s.

The AN/APQ-13 radar unit in each of the B-29s was so new that very few aircraft commanders, pilots, or even navigators had much faith in it. Each crew had a trained radar operator aboard, but he had a hard time convincing his crew that they should rely on the unit more heavily. Sgt. Francis Boyer, a radar operator in the 462nd BG based at Piardoba, recalls how his crew members became thoroughly convinced of the merits of the radar set: "Once on a mission to Formosa from our India base," he recalls, "we got lost. One engine failed before reaching the target, and then on our way home, a second engine decided to quit. Our pilot told us to start throwing out everything we could pry loose to lighten the plane, so we could try to gain some altitude. I asked him, 'How about the radar set?' He came back with, 'No! Anything but the radar, that's our only hope of reaching base safely!' So it was left up to me as the radar operator to guide us through the mountain passes.

"We were very close to bailing out when we finally located an airfield not very far north of our own base. It was a very dark night and, unfortunately, all the lights on the runways were

turned off because the base was under a Jap air-raid attack. We finally got in touch with the tower and told them about our desperate situation, and they turned the lights on long enough for us to scoot in for a hair-raising landing. But any landing you can walk away from is a good one, so the saying went. Our CFC gunner risked breaking his legs by leaping from the side door before the ladder was lowered, a distance of over 10ft from the ground. He immediately bent down and kissed the ground.

"After that mission, our entire crew's faith in the new-fangled radar unit was strictly enhanced!"

## First B-29 Mine-Laying Mission

The Boeing B-29 Superfortress was built specifically for high-altitude precision bombing, with hopes of destroying the Japanese will to continue the war. As hostilities progressed, however, bombing altitudes fluctuated from tree-top level to more than 6mi high. The types of weaponry also varied.

A drastic change from the normal task of the B-29s took place on the night of August 10, 1944, when four-

A 498th BG B-29 rests on its hardstand at Saipan. Speith

teen Superfortresses from the 462nd BG, led by Col. Richard Carmichael, took off to lay mines in the Moesi River at Palembang, Sumatra. This was responsible for a major change in the air war against Japan.

The Palembang mission was part of a three-pronged strike at Japanese targets. Fifty-six B-29s from the 58th BW participated in the mission. Thirty-nine airplanes hit the Pladjoe Oil Refinery complex. One plane was lost. Eight of the mine layers, each plane carrying two mines, made it to their target area, and dropped the mines from altitudes of 100 to 1,000ft. The mission would be the longest made by B-29s in the CBI theater, more than 4,200mi nonstop. Time in the air averaged 19hr. The mission was so long that it was staged from a British base at China Bay near Trincomalee, Ceylon (now known as Sri Lanka). .

During this double-barreled attack, a strike force of B-29s struck Nagasaki, one of the home islands of Japan, located in Kyushu. One plane from this force was also lost.

The mine-laying mission illustrates the cooperation established by

the Allies working together to defeat Japan. This story of how the B-29s became involved in mine warfare is told, in part, by one of the Navy's experts in the field, R. Adm. K. L. Veth, US Navy (Ret.).

In 1944, Admiral Veth, then a lieutenant commander in the Naval Mine Warfare Section, was assigned to Admiral Lord Louis Mountbatten's Southeast Asia Command. When the decision was made to use B-29s to drop mines, Veth was loaned to the 20th BC to teach B-29 personnel about mine warfare.

In a speech to the 58th BW Association members several years ago, Veth had this to say about the B-29 mining effort: "The post-war analysis revealed an interesting story. The B-29 mining effort against the Japanese homeland consisted of some 1,528 sorties, or 5.7% of the entire B-29 strike force against Japan. Over 12,000 mines were dropped in Japanese waters. These mines, combined with another 13,000 laid by aircraft, submarines, and ships in the so-called outer zone of Malaysia, Indochina, and Pacific islands, had rather phenomenal results.

"In the last six months of the war, these mines sunk and damaged more Japanese shipping than all other forms of attacks put together—that in-

cluded all of the submarines, all the Navy ships' gunfire, and all the Navy and USAAF bombing attacks on shipping during the six months' period. Their combined results were less than the results of the mining attacks, most of which was accomplished by the B-29s.

"The code name 'Operation Starvation' was a most appropriate one. Near the end of the war, a group of Japanese industrialists made a report to the Japanese military that, if the war continued for another year, seven million Japanese would die of starvation. By the summer of 1945, the average calorie intake of each Japanese was less than half that of each American. In fact, it was only about 1,400 calories a day, which is what most doctors consider a weight-losing diet.

"An example to illustrate how desperate the Japanese were for rice. In order to get rice supplies from Korea to Japan with no ships, they were forced to partially fill barrels with rice, dump them in the ocean off Korea, and let them drift by ocean current to the west coast of Japan.

"Monthly shipping through the vital Shimonoseki Straits was reduced from over 500,000 tons in March 1944 to a trickle of only 5,000 tons by August of 1945. Much of the decrease was a direct result of B-29 mining."

In speaking of the overall effect the mine laying effort of the B-29s had on Japan, pertained not only to the later dropping of mines by the 58th BW planes on the dry-docks at Singapore, which was in support of the Philippine Sea war. Other mining missions by the 58th BW were to Saigon, Jahoce Straits, Shanghai and Yangtze. The 313th Bomb Wing's stepped up mining efforts with excellent results.

The second element of the three-pronged strike at Japanese targets was the mine drop on the Moesi River. Ed Perry, Group Navigator for the 462nd Group and sitting in the lead ship with Group Commander Carmichael, had this to say about that historical mission: "The fourteen crews from the 462nd Group were integral, experienced crews. The only substitutions were aboard our aircraft—where Col. Dick Carmichael flew as aircraft commander and mission leader and I replaced the navigator. The normal crew commander [Maj. Conrad Colander] flew co-pilot and Commander Veth flew as observer.

"The plan had called for release of the mines in the river using radar if necessary. However, as we approached the IP, we could see that conditions were very good for visual release. There was a bright, full moon at about 11 o'clock, which reflected off the river surface. Tall trees along the river really highlighted the water surface, with the trees being quite dark and the river surface shimmering from the rays of the moon. Our release points were the furthest down river, therefore, the one closest to the aiming points being attacked by the bombers. Before our release, we could see bombs going off at about 2 o'clock. We could see anti-aircraft fire and searchlights across the area. "Red," our bombardier, and the gunners did some low-level strafing as we went upstream to our release points. Since we were the first low-level aircraft along the river, we had the element of surprise in our favor.

"As we approached the scheduled release for our two mines, we saw a large ship, presumably a tanker, in the channel. Red released our mine before we reached the ship, strafed the ship as we passed overhead, at not more than 350ft altitude, and released the second mine just beyond the ship. The tail gunner reported that both mines entered the channel. At this point, we broke left away from the aiming points for the B-29s dropping the bombs, and started our climb out."

Only eight of the fourteen aircraft loaded with mines reached the target, but all crews made it back to their home base. Thirty-nine of the forty-one aircraft carrying bombs made it to the target, but one plane crew failed to return to home base.

The logistical problem of getting gasoline and bombs to China with which to fly missions out of that forward area to targets in Japan were formidable beyond belief. Washington leaders put the blame, evidently, on the leadership in the field, and General Wolfe, who had shouldered one of the heaviest responsibilities of the B-29 project from its beginning up through the early stages of combat,

*Superfortress being fueled up. These huge bombers carried as much as 8,000gal on long missions.* Speith

would shoulder the blame for the early unsatisfactory results.

Mechanical problems and bad weather teamed up at times, forcing crews flying over the Hump from India to the forward bases in China to bail out over the treacherous Himalayas. Some were more fortunate than others and lived to tell of the experience. Stubbs Roberts, flight engineer on the John Sims crew in the 468th BG, thinks he established a record in B-29 bail-outs: "Twice, I had to hit the silk because of mechanical trouble. Each time with a different crew, my bails took place on both sides of the Hump. Our first two attempts to fly safely over the world's tallest mountains with my regular crew ended in a bail-out when two engines failed just as we entered the crest of the mountains. We turned around to return to our base in India, but when another engine failed, Sims gave the bail-out signal. We all were lucky enough to make it out of the plane and eventually make it back to our base at Kharagpur.

"My second encounter at looking up at a silk canopy of a parachute came on a supply run to Pengshan. Fate had placed me in the flight engineer's seat flying with another crew.

Jim Patillo's flight engineer reported to sick call the morning of this particular flight, so operations assigned me to fill in for him. This time, the flight went well until we started our descent into A-17, our destination at Pengshan, China. Suddenly, during the descent, propellers on two engines ran away, and the pilot could hardly control the plane. He finally passed the bail-out word, now becoming a familiar word to me. The entire crew made it out of the plane, but we lost the co-pilot and one of the gunners.

"We were eventually picked up by friendly Chinese civilians, and were treated like heroes. After spending a couple of nights in a small village, we were escorted by Chinese soldiers, transporting us by boat and cart to Pengshan. By this time, I was beginning to wonder what kind of card fate was holding for me."

Nineteen forty-four was an eventful year for changes in command. In the spring, General Hansell was put in charge of the 21st BC, relieved as chief

*A lone Superfortress over the Indian countryside.* Josh Curtis

of staff of the 20th AF by Brig. Gen. Lauris Norstad. And on August 29, 1944, cigar-smoking Maj. Gen. Curtis E. LeMay was named to replace General Wolfe as commander of the 20th BC. As the youngest major general in the US Army at the age of thirty-eight, LeMay had earned quite a reputation as commander of a B-17 Flying Fortress air division in Europe. He was a tough, Patton-type commander, who knew how to get things done.

It didn't take LeMay long to learn that he had stepped up to the plate in an entirely different ball game. The difference between the European air war and the new one he inherited was like going from daylight to nighttime. LeMay came aboard, full of confidence, however, and was equal to the task. He immediately stepped up the frequency of B-29 missions and intensified the training of combat crews. At the same time, he cut back the number of missions out of China in favor of such missions as those to Singapore and other targets flown from base in India where logistical support was manageable.

Some of the crews on the early missions in the CBI theater were fortunate enough to find British airstrips in the area on which to make emergency landings. Bill Garland, aircraft commander of *Ready Betty* in the 468th BG, describes such an emergency landing he and his crew made in Burma: "One day, we were returning from Sumatra and were low on fuel. So I decided to attempt a landing on an improvised dirt P-38 strip at Akyab, Burma. The airstrip had been captured by British troops only three days earlier. After landing, we walked over to talk to some British soldiers who were cooking dinner in a large black pot suspended over an open fire on a wooden tripod. The scene reminded us of the comic cartoon of the Katzenjammer Kids.

"Since we needed gas to get back to our base, we did a little bartering with the soldiers. We gave them a few crates of K-rations we had stashed in the back of our B-29, and they responded by giving us many 5gal tins of gasoline, which we poured into our fuel tanks by hand. We thanked them and made a hair-raising takeoff from the short air strip, and returned to our base in China."

## B-29s Converted for Photo Reconnaissance

Photo reconnaissance had not reached its zenith during initial 20th BC operations in the CBI theater. As early as March 1944, the Air Material Command in Washington had directed the Air Technical Service Command, in cooperation with Boeing Co. and Fairchild, to design a photo-reconnaissance version of the B-29. On April 7, 1944, requirement deadlines were set for the modification program, which was designated Project 98115. Initially, twelve airplanes were allocated for the project, all of which were to be completed by August 1; the prototype, to be called F-13, was to be finished by June 1.

It was apparent, because of delays, that the F-13s would not be operational when the 58th BW was ready for the first bombing raid against Bangkok, June 1, so the 21st BC's maintenance division was ordered to convert a B-29 into a photo-reconnaissance aircraft for temporary use in the 58th BW. These aircraft, called FB-29s and nicknamed "Photo Joes," would fill the bill for camera work and some were even equipped with radar countermeasures.

The first converted FB-29 was sent to the 444th BG's forward base at Chengtu, China, on June 15, 1944, which was the day of the first B-29 strike against Japan proper, at Yawata. The crew was scheduled for photo missions that same day, but the airplane crashed on takeoff and the entire crew was lost. The second FB-29, which was assigned to the 468th BG's forward base at Jsinching, China, was also lost after seven photo missions to obtain information for the Army and Navy prior to the Philippine landings in October. One of the most successful FB-29s was a converted B-29 belonging to the 40th BG. It made several post-attack photo missions to Anshan, North China; Palembang, Sumatra; and at Nagasaki and Sasebo, Kyushu. During September 1944, this FB-29 was ordered to cover specific points of interest in Okinawa in conjunction with future carrier strikes by the Navy.

In October 1944, all aircraft assigned to photo work, which included the FB-29s and some regular B-29s that had not been fully converted, were organized into a single unit called the Photo-Reconnaissance Detachment, 20th BC. Maj. Harry B.

Allen was named detachment commander, its headquarters was at the 40th BG forward base of Hsinching, and its airplanes were kept at their home stations of Chengtu, Pengshan, and Hsinching.

The 3rd Photo-Reconnaissance Squadron (PRS), which had trained at Salina, Kansas, was being deployed to Saipan to work with the 21st BC in October. During October, General Hansell ordered some of the F-13s to China for the 20th BC. By the end of the month, four of these planes had reached China and began operations as the 1st PRS.

During World War II, men with special analytical skills served with an organization known as the USAAF Operations Analysis Committee. They served mostly in a civilian capacity, but usually were given a field-grade rank or higher.

As an example of how Operations Analysis worked, consider this request made by the 20th BC. In 1943, after the B-29 combat operations got underway in the CBI theater, the 20th BC asked the Operations Analysis Committee if they could furnish a gunnery expert to investigate combat losses of the B-29s. Alex E. S. Green, who had considerable experience in conducting air-to-air gunnery, was chosen to go to the combat theater to analyze problems in the B-29 gunnery system and offer suggestions for better performance.

The following is his report on how the B-29 gunnery system was improved: "After several weeks of briefing and study of the B-29's gunnery system and its combat problems at Wright Field, Elgin Field, and the Pentagon, I flew by Air Transport Command (ATC) to the Kharagpur, India, headquarters of the 20th BC. My first trip over the 'Hump' to our advanced base in Chengtu, China, was in a B-29 with General LeMay as the command pilot. My purpose was to gather information from the gunnery officers, intelligence officers, and crews that had witnessed the loss of other planes in their formations. After six weeks involving a second trip to

Dina Might *was a lead plane, as designated by the yellow and black stripes around the tail. Two crew member sit atop the bomb load of twenty-four 500lb bombs.* Teed/Josh Curtis

Chengtu, my analysis showed that we had shot down seventy fighters for each B-29 lost in attacks from the rear, whereas we shot down only three fighters for each B-29 lost in attacks from the front [6]. These results were in direct contradiction to the results of a massive state-side simulated combat study carried out near Alamogordo, New Mexico, which had concluded that the B-29 would be most vulnerable to rear attacks. Nevertheless, the gunnery and intelligence officers endorsed my analysis, and General LeMay modified our formations to bring greater firepower against frontal attacks. I also proposed a simplified way of using the front gunsight to compensate for the short engagement time and this anticipated 'vulnerability' to frontal attacks. By January 1945, the problem was contained."

*Airborn flew with the 444th BG, 58th BW,
Tinian Island.* Ken Rust

*Chapter 5*

# 21st Bomber Command Absorbs 73rd Wing

Early organizational plans for the 20th AF called for the 1st BC to have two wings, the 58th and the 73rd, both slated for India with advance bases in China, from which the bombing of Japan would originate. Along with a series of policy changes, only one wing, the 58th, was assigned to the 20th BC.

Original plans called for the 20th AF to have, eventually, three or four bomber commands: the 20th BC in India-China; the 21st BC in the Marianas; the 22nd BC in the Philippines, Formosa, or Okinawa; and perhaps the 23rd BC in Alaska. The total strength of the 20th AF would be 1,000–1,500 operational B-29s and additional escort fighters.

Hampered by the horrible logistical problems of flying bombs and gasoline across the Hump to the forward bases in China, a decision was made in 1943 to step up the invasion of the Marianas, and launch B-29 bombing attacks from at least three islands in that group as early as possible. This decision did not set well with General MacArthur, because he thought the best way to get to Japan was to go through the Philippines.

On November 28, 1943, the 73rd BW, VH, was inaugurated at Salina, Kansas, with Col. Thomas H. Chapman as first wing commander. In December 1943, the Wing did nothing but accumulate personnel, mostly

overages from the 58th BW and the 20th BC. Most of these men were overseas veterans—specialists, pilots, bombardiers, flight engineers, navigators—and were assigned to the 2nd AF, which would be charged with combat operational training of the 73rd BW personnel. They waited up to four months at the collecting point—Clovis, New Mexico, Air Base—for the 58th BW to vacate the four bases at Pratt, Great Bend, Victoria, and Salina.

*The sugar mill at Saipan after bombardment by Navy, before the island was invaded.* Speith

## 21st Bomber Command Activated

The 21st BC was activated at Smokey Hill on March 1, 1944. Brig. Gen. Emmett ("Rosey") O'Donnell assumed command of the 73rd BW on March 15, and by March 27, wing

The Twentieth Century Limited *flew with the 881 BS, 500th BG. This aircraft arrived at Saipan in early December 1944. It was commanded by Capt. Tull K. McGuire and flew fifty-one missions, surviving the war. McGuire and crew were lost when they ditched another aircraft, Z-Square-13, after bombing Tokyo.* Hurth Thompkins

headquarters moved to Colorado Springs, Colorado, also home to the 2nd AF. Later, the 21st BC would move to Peterson Field in Colorado Springs, Colorado, to be near the new headquarters of its 73rd BW.

All four of the 73rd BW's groups were activated by General Order No. 176 that activated the wing headquarters. These groups were the 497th BG at Biggs Field in El Paso, Texas; the 498th BG at Clovis Army Air Field in New Mexico; the 499th BG at Davis-Monthan Field in Tucson, Arizona; and the 500th BG at Gowan Field in Boise, Idaho.

Each of the groups originally had four squadrons and a photo lab, but before training got underway, the number of squadrons was reduced to three for each group. The groups would train with the 58th BW until it left for India.

General Hansell understood the enormous pressure the 21st BC was under to perform. "One major slip," he said, "and the critics would have had their way—the 20th AF would have been dismembered and parceled out to the various theaters."

When the 58th BW moved out of their bases for India in early April 1944, the 497th BG, under the command of Col. Stewart P. Wright, went to Pratt; Col. Wiley D. Ganey, in command of the 498th, went to Great Bend; the 499th BG, under Col. Samuel R. Harris, moved to Salina; and Col. Richard T. King, Jr., in command of the 500th BG, went to Victoria. Combat training began immediately, even though there was an extreme scarcity of B-29s to train with. Like the 58th BW crews before them, the 73rd BW crews were trained primarily on old B-17s.

On June 1, 1944, the 2nd AF Headquarters announced the assignment of four experienced service groups, then stationed at Tinker Field,

Oklahoma, to service the 73rd BW planes at its overseas base. They were the Sixty-fifth, Ninety-first, 303rd, and 330th. The service groups would remain at Tinker Field until time to depart for overseas.

Other support units were being integrated into the 21st BC as extensive combat training got underway. In April 1944, the 3rd Combat Mapping Squadron (CMS) was ordered from its assignment in North Africa to return to the United States for reorganization and training, equipped with the F-13s. The unit arrived at Smokey Hill Army Air Field, to begin training for B-29 support activities.

### 73rd Wing Combat Training

Combat crew members arriving at their bases in Kansas during April immediately got assignments, met their aircraft commander and other crew members, and happily began flight training as a tight-knit unit.

With a shortage of B-29s to train with, each squadron having only one or two B-29s, old B-17s were used to accomplish some of the training missions. All types of combat-oriented missions were included in the required quota before overseas deployment

Each crew was required to complete a certain number of long-range, mostly over water, missions. With several 100lb bombs aboard, a long-range mission would be scheduled to fly from a Kansas base to the Gulf Coast, south of Houston, Texas, continue at about 3,000ft altitude over water for about 200mi, climb to an altitude of 20,000ft, drop the bombs on a designated little island in the Gulf of Mexico, then proceed to a spot just south of Cuba. Since the United States had the Batista Field USAAF Base in Cuba, the crew was authorized to make an emergency landing there—but only if the airplane was having trouble.

Warren G. Moses, a flight engineer with the 874th BS, 499th BG, 73rd BW, training at Great Bend, Kansas, related an interesting account of the time his crew had to land in Cuba. Kansas was one of two remaining "dry" states, as everyone knew. Moses was the chief monitor of the Superfortress engines, and he was supposed to be the most knowledgeable man aboard to determine the safety factors and performance of the plane. Crew members were always kidding him about not finding something wrong with the airplane, especially on some of the more interesting cross-country training flights—perhaps requiring an emergency landing at a fun-filled town. Even before they took off on the Cuba mission, it was almost a unanimous belief among members of the crew that something would happen to the plane on this trip, causing an emergency landing at Batista Field, with at least an overnight stay and a night on the town of Havana.

"As we flew along," according to Moses, "the intercom was filled with speculative chatter regarding the possibility of landing in Cuba. Like an answer to our prayers, the fuel pressure on our no. 3 engine began to fall off as we began our climb to 20,000ft. I increased the boost, but the pressure continued to drop and the engine began to overheat. It soon became evident that we would have to shut the engine down, so, gleefully, we throttled the engine back, dropped our bombs on the designated target, and headed for Batista Field.

"We didn't make it into Havana that night, but we got our kicks at the Officers' Club on Batista Field. We had a great evening at the Club, enjoying cheap drinks and good tropical food. Then we found out that we could buy liquor by the bottle at the Club at tax-free prices, which came out to about a dollar a bottle. The Club okayed my check, so we proceeded to buy twenty-three cases of scotch, bourbon, and a marvelous Cuban rum, Ron Anejo, which the locals told us was better than scotch. We figured we'd make a lot of long-standing friends when we returned to Kansas with our new-found loot.

"They checked our 'faulty' engine out real good and told me, as if I didn't already know, it was OK and ready to go. Before leaving, however, we got a message from none other than the commanding general of the Caribbean Command, Lt. Gen. George H. Brett, who said he'd sure like to look over the B-29. He had never seen one before, so we took him up for a short hop and he seemed overjoyed.

"After flying the General around the island for about an hour, we land-

Flak Maid—*not bad. This aircraft flew with the 444th BG, 58th BW, Tinian Island.* Ken Rust

ed and soon departed for our home base at Great Bend, Kansas, our contraband well covered and lashed down in the rear of the plane.

"As we neared the Florida coastline, I suddenly felt the all-too-familiar 't-hump' on my throttle handle, the sound of an engine swallowing a valve, and I yelled to Jack Reed, our pilot, to feather the no. 3 engine. This time it was for real. We immediately decided not to try to fly the remaining 1,500mi on three engines, so we landed at Boca Raton, Florida.

"We were, of course, instant celebrities because no B-29 had been seen there before. Since we had arrived from Cuba, the US Customs Inspector was also on hand to greet us. Jack immediately got to the base commanding officer and impressed on him the 'secret' nature of our aircraft. The commanding officer quickly surrounded our plane with MPs, who were instructed to allow no one near it except the crew members. The Customs Inspector was not permitted to go on board, much to our vast relief, because no duty had been paid on the booze."

The B-29 remained on a sort of classified status up through the months the 73rd was in combat operational training. When crews had to make forced landings anywhere in the United States, orders were that they should try to make it to a military air

base and before landing request that a military police detachment be available to guard the aircraft to prevent anyone from entering it. On any given cross-country, pilots were given locations of airfields with runways long enough to accommodate the huge B-29.

This author and crew had to make such an emergency landing at Dalhart, Texas, after an over-water trip to Cuba. We were somewhere over west Texas at about 27,000ft altitude when we experienced oil pressure problems in one of the engines. Aircraft commander John Cox looked up the nearest base we could land at, and it happened to be Dalhart. It so happened that the air base had been vacated, with the exception of the permanent base personnel, awaiting the arrival of a B-29 group scheduled to start training there. We called the tower, told them of our need to land there, and asked them to have an MP detachment to guard the plane while were there. We flew around for over a half-hour trying to use up some excess fuel before landing. After landing and taxiing up toward the ramp, we could tell there was a huge crowd lined up by the fence near the parking area. I

Sky Blues *flew from Tinian Island with the 444th BG, 58th BW.* Ken Rust

think every person left on the base was out there to see the Superfortress for the first time. Our chests swelled with pride as we dismounted and looked over toward the people standing there, agog. It was as if we came in on an alien ship from outer space.

At Salina, where I trained with the 878th BS, 499th BG, our group commander, Col. Sam Harris, and his squadron commanders came up with a well-received idea to encourage crews to stay abreast with the training schedules. Each week, squadron Operations would determine which two crews had done well during the week and award them with a B-17 for a cross-country flight anywhere in the United States. This innovative idea gave us something to shoot for. Some of these trips were designated "whiskey runs," and the crew was instructed to negotiate with a liquor wholesaler out there somewhere and bring back a planeload of alcoholic beverages to replenish the supply for the fellows who had put up money with their order.

## Saipan Invasion

As B-29 training continued in Kansas at mid-summer, US Marines and Army units began the struggle to capture the island of Saipan, which would become the home of the 73rd BW. Adm. Chester Nimitz's Pacific Fleet put the Marines ashore after one of the heaviest battleship and aerial bombardments of the war.

On June 15, 1944, the Marines led the assault, followed by the Army. More than 30,000 American Marines and soldiers were involved in a battle that lasted until July 4. The cost to capture the island was high, with 47 percent of the invading force killed or wounded in one of the bloodiest battles of World War II.

## The 3rd Photo-Reconnaissance Squadron

The 3rd CMS, like the 73rd BW, was attached to the 2nd AF for operational training, and it, too, had to use old B-17s for initial training. The unit was redesignated the 3rd PRS, VH, on May 19, 1944, and later that month, was divided into three flights, each with four aircraft and six crew. Lt. Col. Patrick B. McCarthy was named commander of the 3rd PRS, and Capt. Ralph D. Steakley was named its operations officer. On August 22, 1944, the prototype F-13, a modified B-29 built by Boeing, was delivered to the 3rd PRS in training at Salina.

A modification center was established at Denver to modify B-29s to F-13 configuration. This airplane was a stripped-down version, minus gun turrets, except in the tail section, and test flights indicated that the F-13's range was longer than the B-29's by at least 500mi.

The 3rd PRS's ground echelon left for Saipan to prepare for the acceptance of the aircraft and flying personnel in August. While still awaiting delivery of combat-ready F-13s, it was decided to stage the squadron out of Will Rogers Field in Oklahoma. It would be October 4, 1944, before the unit received its first production F-13. Within two weeks, two planes were ready for deployment to Saipan.

## General LeMay's First B-29 Mission

Within a month after Gen. Curtis LeMay assumed command of the 20th BC, in August 1944, he received permission from the 20th AF Headquarters in Washington to go on a B-29 combat mission. The mission he chose to observe was a daylight strike against Anshan, Manchuria, scheduled for September 8.

Lt. Col. James I. Cornett, commander of the 44th BS of the 40th BG, would lead the strike, in which 108 B-29s were participating. Cornett had no inkling that he would be carrying a "special passenger." He explains how he tried to wiggle out of this assignment, to no avail: "Shortly after landing at Chengtu, I was summoned to Col. 'Butch' Blanchard, our group commander. With a straight face, Butch handed me a piece of paper containing a message from the 20th BC which essentially said, 'Lt. Col. James I. Cornett is directed to take General LeMay on the forthcoming mission. He will not abort a takeoff nor the en route flight. He will bomb the primary target and return General LeMay safely to the base of takeoff.'

"My opposition to the idea met on the deaf ears of Colonel Blanchard, however, so we were stuck with the task of getting the head man of the entire Bomber Command to and from a tough target, unscathed.

"We experienced some pretty heavy flak after leaving the target, and two of our crewmen, the radio operator and the CFC gunner, were hit. The next thing I knew after we re-

ceived the report from the rear of the plane, LeMay, minus his parachute, was slithering through the tunnel to go aft and assist in caring for the injured gunner. Luckily, we got him back to Chengtu safely!"

Ira Matthews, now deceased, who was an aircraft commander of the 40th BG, based at Chakulia, India, told a story about the time his 45th BS attacked a Japanese air depot at Mukden, Manchuria, in November 1944: "It was a daylight raid at about 24,000ft altitude and, suddenly, a small speck in the sky progressively grew larger and larger, and low and behold, the speck turned out to be a strange-looking aircraft, a pre-Pearl

Harbor, fixed-gear Japanese Nakajima 97.

"At debriefing, almost all of our conversation centered on the Nakajima 97, or 'Nate' as we called them. The intelligence officer took the reports into our group operations section. Soon he returned, with an amused expression on his face. He informed us that a total of seventeen claims had been reported by eight bombardiers, eight upper gunners, and one tail gunner.

"For several days afterwards, we ragged our bombardier and upper gunner on how our crew chief was going to stick 2/17th of a downed enemy fighter decal on our plane's nose."

Heat's On *flew with the 498th BG, 73rd BW, Saipan. This was one of the first B-29s to have its underside painted black when the low-level raids against Japanese cities began. Only a few planes based in Saipan were painted black.* Warren Thompson

*Chapter 6*

# General Hansell Leads 73rd Wing to Saipan

July and August 1944 were crucial months for Hap Arnold's infant 20th AF, especially the newly activated 21st BC. Curtis LeMay's 20th BC personnel in the CBI theater were picking up more experience and a lot more confidence. They were also showing improved results with the Superfortress. A double-barreled assault against Tinian Island just 3mi across the channel from Saipan was carried out by the Marines on July 24, after an assault took place at Guam, 125mi to the south, two days earlier. Tinian Island was declared secure August 2, and Guam, the major island of the Marianas group and a US possession captured early in the war by Japan, was secured later that month.

As fighting continued on each of the islands, engineers and Seabees were being put ashore with equipment to build runways and hardstands for the B-29s.

While the combat crews of the 73rd BW were about halfway through their combat operational training at Kansas bases in August, ground personnel, including the mechanics, the cooks, the clerks, the armorers and medical units were brought to Saipan

*Miss Judy takes a whack at Tojo in this creative piece of nose art. This B-29 flew with the 462nd BG, 58th BW, Tinian.* Warren Thompson

by transport ships, commonly known as Liberty Ships. They all helped build maintenance facilities, supply dumps, and their own living quarters. At first, tents were set up for living, but later, work began on assembling metal Quonset huts for the flying personnel yet to arrive. Personnel of the 73rd BW Headquarters arrived on the island September 7, ready to set up business.

In the meantime, two more wings, the 313th and the 314th, were in operational training and would occupy the bases at Tinian and Guam. The 313th BW would arrive in December and January at North Field, and would be the third wing to become operational, followed by the 314th BW at Guam.

Trennis Beers, a medic attached to headquarters of the 498th BG, remembers his advance party trip to Saipan: "We rocked and rolled aboard the S.S. *Exchange* across the Pacific Ocean before debarking after a twenty-seven-day trip to Saipan.

"For most of us, it was our first encounter with an ocean-going vessel, and unlike the 'South Seas Cruises' we had always read about, we had heard how boring a troop transport trip always was. To me, the trip wasn't too bad; the one exception was the food. It was terrible. At breakfast one morning, a cook slapped a pile of green spinach on my tray. Now, even if you were not seasick, that stuff was

enough to make your stomach do flip-flops.

"As we were being loaded on trucks, upon arrival, to be taken to our designated area, I asked one of the drivers, 'What the heck is that terrible odor I smell?'

"'Dead Japs!' he said.

"Right then I knew we were in a combat zone, and not on this Pacific Island for recreational purposes."

With the capture of Saipan and Tinian and the recapture of Guam, the Japanese leaders suddenly found themselves in severe shock. Prince Higashi-Kuni, a member of the Supreme War Council and Commander-in-Chief of Home Defense Headquarters in Tokyo, testified after the war that they realized the B-29 was an exceptional airplane after the B-29 Superfortresses began bombing Kyushu from China, knew that they had no means to defend themselves. When Saipan fell, one of the best known Axis villains, Hideki Tojo, the Japanese Premier and former War Minister, resigned. Still in command, the military made plans to attack the airfield on Saipan, which they knew would be built soon.

## Airfield Construction

The US Navy played a major part in getting the B-29s of the 20th AF in position to begin the air assault against the Japanese home islands. As the Central Pacific theater comman-

*Maj. Jack Catton, pointing, describes the nose compartment of a Superfortress to Admiral King (left), commander of US fleets, as General Hansell, center, looks on. The picture was taken in Hawaii about October 10, 1944, prior to departure to Saipan. Speith*

*Lt. Col. Robert Morgan, center, standing, and crew of* Dauntless Dotty. *Morgan and General O'Donnell led the first B-29 mission against Japan on November 24, 1944.* Speith

der, Adm. Chester Nimitz was responsible for all logistical and administrative military activities in the area. He and his staff planned the assault on the Marianas, after exhaustive preparations for the amphibious assaults. Nimitz was responsible for formulating plans for constructing airfields large enough to handle the huge Superfortresses. He was also charged with moving the air units from the States, stockpiling fuel and ammunition, and providing logistical and administrative services for the 20th AF wings that would eventually occupy the bases at Saipan, Tinian, and Guam.

To accommodate five wings, each consisting of four groups, it was decided to build a separate base large enough for each wing. Twin 8,500ft runways at each base were constructed. The Army engineers constructed one field at Saipan and two fields on Guam, and the Navy Seabees built two bases on Tinian.

Completion of the bases on Tinian and Guam were delayed at least a month each because of "mop up" activities against the enemy. Further delay in preparing bases on these two islands occurred when Nimitz decided in August 1944, soon after Guam was captured, that he would use that island as a base for the Pacific Fleet. Construction on B-29 bases was drastically curtailed because priority went to the naval base installations and harbor facilities, much to the displeasure of the 20th AF leaders.

Construction of the air base at Saipan was not delayed, however. As soon as the Japanese airfield at the southern end of the island was captured, it was renamed Isley Field in memory of a naval aviator who was killed during one of the first air strikes on the island. The 804th Army Engineer Battalion was the first construction unit to reach Saipan, and they immediately began work on the field by enlarging and lengthening the runway to accommodate the B-29s.

William F. Roos, a construction engineer with the 804th Army Engineer Battalion, relates some of the enormous obstacles that had to be overcome before the runways could be built: "As the enemy was forced back toward the north of Saipan, we knew we had to accomplish three tasks in short order. First, we had to build docks so we could unload our construction equipment and supplies; second, we had to build the roads to get the equipment from the docks to the airfield site; and finally, we had to build the airfield for the B-29s.

"When work began on the B-29 runway at Isley, we found that the topsoil, rather than being about 2ft deep, as forecast, was only a few inches deep. Beneath this thin layer of soil was hard, coral rock that had to be blasted and hacked away a bit at a time. Working on a 24hr basis, engineers were beset by all manner of other difficulties, including enemy air raids at night, during the first few weeks, which caused all work to stop because of the necessary blackouts."

Isley Field was laid out to run, more or less, west to east, and the runway took up almost the entire width of the southern portion of the island. A huge portion of the southernmost mountain was blasted and from it crushed coral rock was used for the base of the runway, and hardstands where the B-29s were to park. An on-site asphalt plant made the asphalt to finish a smooth surfaced runway.

In spite of the overbearing difficulties experienced in blasting and leveling the huge air base, Isley Field was ready to receive the first B-29 on October 12, 1944. The second runway was ready for use on December 15.

North Field, on Tinian, was ready to receive the 313th BW by late December; North Field on Guam was ready for the 314th in January 1945; West Field on Tinian was ready for the transfer of the 58th BW from India-China in April 1945; and by June, the 315th settled in at Northwest Field on Guam. The building of these five air bases, under extreme difficulties, was one of the major accomplishments of World War II.

Gen. "Possum" Hansell, as commander of the 21st BC, was ready to lead his command to Saipan by the first week of October 1944. At this time, the command consisted of the 73rd BW with its four BGs, and he knew the combat crews that would follow to begin the all-out air assault on the Japanese homeland, didn't have enough experience flying in the B-29s.

When time came to move the first units to Saipan, the crews averaged fewer than 100hr of total flying time in the B-29, and the average high-altitude formation flying experience was fewer than 12hr. The engines of the B-29 were still swallowing valves and catching fire. The magnesium crankcases burned with a fury that defied all extinguishing efforts. In addition, gunsight blisters were either blowing out at high altitude or frosting up so badly that it was impossible to see through them. This problem was fixed, however, by extending warm air to them.

In his last meeting with Generals Arnold and Marshall in Washington, in mid-September, Hansell renewed his pledge to attack Japan in November. Leaving the States on October 5, flying a B-29 nicknamed *Joltin' Josie, the Pacific Pioneer*, Hansell headed for Saipan and started the flow which would ultimately become massive. He recalls that flight: "I flew with a crew from the 73rd BW commanded by a bright and capable young major named Jack Catton, who retired in 1979 as a four-star general. Catton and I alternated in the pilot position; I took it from Sacramento to Hawaii; he took it to Kwajalein; and I flew the last lap to Saipan. We took off from

*Bird Island, on the northeastern coast of Saipan.* Bill Rooney

Mather Field near Sacramento. The original design gross weight of the B-29 was 120,000lb. Wright Field reluctantly permitted an overload weight of 128,000lb. With our spare engine in the bomb bay, and the various kits we carried, we weighed in at about 130,000lb.

"When we arrived at Saipan and circled over the island, we could see the crowd of people gathered at Isley Field. We landed and taxied up to the parking area, and the crowd rushed toward the plane to see the first B-29 to reach the Marianas, and possibly the first B-29 they had seen, period. When I climbed down from the plane, a microphone was handed to me by a reporter. I spoke firmly into the mike expressing my feelings: 'When we've done a little fighting, we'll do a little more talking!' The date was October 12, 1944."

The race for the Marianas really exploded after Hansell's flight. For some, the three-legged flight to Saipan became a hair-raising experience, while others claimed the trip was a "piece of cake." LeRoy Florence, pilot on the Cecil Scarborough crew, 499th BG, tells of their trials and tribulations on the first leg of the flight: "There were quite a number of crews taking off for Hawaii en route to Saipan the day we left Mather Field, and considerable discussion about which crew had the fastest and best B-29. Wagers were laid, with several crews participating, and the crew landing first at John Rogers Field would get the pot. We felt we had the race about won as we made our power

approach toward Diamond Head. Blocking our path as we neared our destination, however, was the Pacific Ocean's ferocious friend, a huge thunderhead. We barreled right into it and 'bam' our radar went out; so did the VHF radio. We had no choice but to pull up right into the middle of the storm. Naturally, the LF radio was not much good in all that lightening.

"While wandering around for what seemed like days, we made several descents with the idea of bailing out or ditching on our minds. We were running very low on fuel.

"We chickened out each time and pulled back up again into the middle of the storm. When the thunderhead began to subside a little, some fighter planes from nearby Hickam Field came up to try to find us. They did, to our great relief, and led us to a hole over the base where we made a Split-S, found the field, and made a smooth landing.

"To the best of my knowledge, all bets were off, and we were left in wonderment thinking if this was going to be a normal Pacific flight in days ahead."

This author had a sort of unusual, and exciting, thing happen to him on his way across the Pacific. I was pilot on the Cox crew (no. 25) in the 878th BS, 499th BG, 73rd BW. Our departure date from Mather Field, California, was November 11, 1944. I had a feeling the departure date itself held

*Gen. Emmett ("Rosey") O'Donnell, left, confers with officers near 73rd BW headquarters on Saipan.* USAAF Photo

*B-29s taxi out to takeoff positions on Runway B at Isley Field, Saipan. V-Square-44 of the 879th BS, 499th BG is aligned with the runway and awaits the signal for takeoff.* Hurth Thompkins

something of a omen. From my earliest childhood memories, I associated November 11 as a day of eternal peace, because on that date I had been taught, the war to end all wars ended, and not just a few people, but everybody, I thought, celebrated that date with some kind of reverence. But here we were about to depart for another World War on this Armistice Day.

We arrived at Mather, our port of debarkation, the day before from our staging base at Herrington, Kansas, where we received our brand-new Boeing B-29 Superfortress, and after several shakedown flights to swing the compass, check the engines, etc., we awoke that morning, long before dawn, ready to go to war.

After takeoff, we immediately entered a light overcast which had turned into a thick soup by the time we reached altitude. The lightning danced across our plexiglass nose and the thunder made its appearance known, even above the roar of our four engines. We hoped, and some of us silently prayed, that our new V-Square-27 B-29 was well bonded. Because if it wasn't, there was a strong chance that a bolt of lightening would do us in. Lucky for us, the only damage from our being struck by lightning once or twice in that thunderstorm was the destruction of our trailing radio antenna.

Excitement was building as we landed at John Rogers Field. Big, beautiful, silver B-29s were departing for the second leg en route to Saipan, while others were arriving from the mainland. It was an exciting time for all of us, and we were getting in the spirit of the times, like the popular saying making the rounds in those days, "Live it up today, for tomorrow you may die!" I suppose my navigator, J. W. ("Jim") O'Donnel, was the first to bring up the subject, so flight engineer John Huckins and I decided that afternoon to take that saying for granted. We decided to go into Honolulu. We were, of course, restricted to the base; supposedly, the brass didn't want us B-29 flyers getting a little tipsy at some bar downtown and spilling the beans to some sleazy Japanese spy as to where we were going, etc.

After settling down in our assigned quarters in the officers' quarters at John Rogers Field that afternoon, O'Donnell blurted out, "Restricted hell!" he said, "I have heard of Honolulu and Waikiki Beach all my life, and being this close to it, I've just got to see it. Who wants to go to town?" Huckins and I were the two volunteers who were willing to put our USAAF careers on the line by overlooking the restriction rules for B-29 crews passing through. We decided to check out the security system at the main gate. Just outside the gate, buses were leaving for Honolulu every few minutes. We assumed the appearance of "permanent personnel" as best we could, showed our ID cards, and walked casually through the gate. The MP glanced at our cards, snapped a salute, and we were off the base. I suppose the MP thought surely none of the B-29 flyers were dumb enough to take such a risky chance. Our main objective was to check out those grass skirts we thought those Island Queens were wearing.

Our first stop downtown was the cocktail lounge overlooking the famous beach at the Royal American Hotel. I remembered the scene from movies, and subconsciously I kept glancing around the room expecting to see Humphrey Bogart or some other big movie star. But the place was filled with service people—more sailors than you could shake a stick at—no movie stars—and no girls in grass skirts. We finished our drinks and wandered out the door onto the white sandy beach made famous by song and movies, and there, too, we faced disappointment—more sailors.

We walked out into the street and moseyed along the best we could, dodging soldiers, sailors, and Marines. Down the street we saw a line reaching nearly a block with service guys waiting to get in. At first we thought it must be a good show, or a fine place to eat. We tapped a guy on the shoulder and asked him what the big line was for. "Well," he said, "they're sweating this line here to get into one of the best whorehouses in Honolulu. The girls are all dolls, and the price is only $5." Being fresh from the States, we were not interested in that venture, and since there was a 9 o'clock curfew, we caught a bus back to John Rogers Field. Our fling was a dud, and it would be our last contact with civilization for a long, long time!

War correspondents were thick as flies at John Rogers Field, all trying to catch rides to Saipan. They were certain, they said, the first big raid on Tokyo would be taking place in just a few days. We, of course, didn't believe that, and told them so. "Half of our 499th BG is still back in the States," we'd tell them, "and they can't bomb Tokyo until we get there!"

Clinton Green, war correspondent for the *New York Times*, asked Commander Cox if he could hitch a ride with us. Of course we all said yes. We figured it would be exciting to have a real live correspondent from a big-time newspaper along with us. Now, if we could do something heroic, like shooting down a stray Jap plane en route to Saipan, he might put our names in a news release.

With Green aboard, we took off the next morning and edged our way

*Shown here is an innovative way to combat hot weather and high winds, while mechanics work on* Fluffy Fuz IV's *engines. Josh Curtis*

*A lead aircraft with the 9th BG, 313th BW, Tinian Island. The black and orange stripes on the vertical stabilizer indicate that it is a lead plane. These special markings made rendezvous much easier for squadron airplanes. Josh Curtis*

toward the international dateline. Our next stop would be a little flat atoll in the middle of a big ocean called Kwajalein. O'Donnel came on the intercom to announce that we could move our watches ahead 24hr. Instead of November 13, it was then November 14. We spent a "combat zone" night at Kwajalein, with a sudden flash flood and we all thought the island was going to sink into the ocean. The next morning, bright and early, we left Kwajalein, but not for long. One of the engines swallowed a valve, and we had to return to the island. Green threatened to leave us and said he was going to try to catch another plane coming through because he was sure the first raid was about to take place. We talked him out of it, telling him it would be bad luck for him to desert us in the middle of the ocean, so he stayed with us and we spent another night on Kwajalein. Our crew chief, Fred Reid, was with us, and he was able to get us underway the next morning.

We made it on to Saipan without further trouble, and just as soon as we parked the plane, Green rushed off to check in with someone to see if he could go on the Tokyo mission. But before he got out of sight, I yelled to him, "I told you they wouldn't go on that bombing mission to Tokyo without crew no. 25!" Green turned and waved at us and wished us well.

We couldn't wait to get to our living area to see what the heck was going on. We couldn't believe what they were saying up on the line about the mission taking place the next day!

*B-29s from the 9th BG head for a target over Japan. Josh Curtis*

This photo of the author's crew was taken at Isley Field, Saipan, on June 8, 1945, one day after they had completed a combat tour of thirty missions against Japan. Standing, left to right: John W. Cox, aircraft commander; the author, pilot; John W. Huckins, flight engineer; James R. O'Donnel, navigator; and Herbert Feldman, bombardier. Kneeling, left to right: Robert Slizuski, radar operator; Alvin Torres, radio operator; Kendal Chance, central fire control gunner; George Koepke, right gunner; Arle Lackey, left gunner; and John Sutherland, tail gunner. Our plane was V-Square-27, the V designating that the plane was part of the 499th BG. Japanese flags on the nose mark the ten confirmed victories scored by the gunners. Tail gunner Sutherland was the leading "ace" in the bomber command, with five victories. The winged ball and spear with the name of the aircraft replaced all "girlie" art in the 73rd BW in April 1945. The first B-29 assigned to the crew was destroyed on the ground in December 1944 during a Japanese retaliation raid against Saipan. The crew's second B-29 was shot down over Tokyo on January 27, 1945, while being flown by another crew. Mary Ann was the third B-29 assigned to the crew and had been named by its ground crew chief in honor of his new baby daughter. When the crew went up to the line to look over the new plane, they decided that it would be a bad-luck omen to change the plane's name, so the name stuck for the rest of crew no. 25's tour of duty. Marshall

*Chapter 7*

# B-29s on the High Road to Tokyo

The war correspondents hitching a ride to Saipan were right. The first B-29 raid on Tokyo originally had been set for November 15, one day before our arrival on Saipan.

General Hansell was anxious to fulfill his pledge to bomb Japan from Saipan in November. The November 15 date was set, because the rate of five B-29 crew arrivals per day assured him that by then, more than eighty Superfortresses would be on hand to participate in the first strike.

Initially, the plans for the first B-29 bombing mission from the Marianas called for a combined strike with the Navy, with carrier-based planes helping to divert some of the Japanese fighter planes away from the B-29s. The planned strike was labeled San Antonio I. Six practice missions—four on the island of Truk and two on Iwo Jima—were made by the 497th, 498th, and 500th BGs; the 499th BG didn't participate because it did not arrive on Saipan in time.

But things didn't work out as anticipated. Late in October, the Japanese fleet set out to do the battle in the Philippine Sea. This action disrupted Pacific plans and Adm. Chester Nimitz notified the Chiefs of Staff that the Navy would be unable to launch an attack on the Japanese home island in conjunction with the 21st BC in November. He recommended that the attack on Tokyo be delayed until the Navy would be in a position to participate. As Hansell saw it, this would have grounded the B-29s indefinitely. He found Nimitz's proposition intolerable. "If the 21st BC could operate only when the Navy was prepared to cooperate," he said, "we might as well disband the 20th AF and put the 21st BC under Admiral Nimitz."

## 3rd Photo Squadron Arrives on Saipan

Fate dealt a kinder hand to 21st BC at Saipan during October. The 3rd PRS finally got its first modified F-13, specially equipped for high-tech photographic work, on October 4, and the second plane arrived shortly thereafter. By this time, the squadron had been assigned to the 21st BC's 73rd BW on Saipan. On October 27, the squadron was ordered to Saipan.

On November 1, 1944, after flying 33hr to Saipan and with only 5hr of rest, operations officer Captain Steakley and his crew headed off for Tokyo in his plane, nicknamed *Tokyo Rose*. They would fly over the city and other selected targets and photograph the area in order to pinpoint target areas. It would be the first American airplane over Tokyo since the Doolittle raid of April 18, 1942.

General Hansell called the mission results phenomenal: "Captain Steakley insisted upon an immediate mission even though they had just arrived from the United States. I advised a rest, but the captain and his crew were insistent. Thank God they were. They found clear skies over Japan—a phenomenon. Called *Tokyo Rose*, his aircraft flew above the Japanese capital at an altitude of 32,000ft, photographing a complex of aircraft and engines plants just west of Tokyo and another on the outskirts of Nagoya. They shot over 7,000 excellent photographs in seventeen sorties before the first strike on Tokyo on November 24. Many of the missions were hampered by bad weather, but enough information on the location of aircraft factories was obtained for the first bombing missions. Copies of the photographs were sent to General Arnold for the JCS and to Admirals Nimitz and William Halsey.

"Mosaics were made, strips laid out, initial points and target approaches selected. Every combat crew was required to trace its photo map, mark landmarks and target runs, and then redraw them from memory—over and over."

With this fantastic bit of luck and expert photographic work, General Hansell was indeed confident that his command was ready to launch the B-29 Superfortress attack on Tokyo and the major targets in the Japanese home islands, even if it meant going it alone.

*The crew of the* Tokyo Rose, *the first B-29 to go over Tokyo on November 1, 1944. Commanded by Capt. Ralph Steakley, the 3rd PRS crew took pictures in Tokyo and other areas to help establish targets for future B-29 strikes. Left to right: Starks, Arnett, Clark, Marvin, Johnson, Hutchins, McCommon, Hart, Burke, Stamaught, and Steakley.* USAAF Photo/Josh Curtis

## Japanese Retaliation Raids on Saipan

On November 3, two days after *Tokyo Rose* roamed for more than an hour over Tokyo, nine twin-engine Betty bombers struck back at the Superfortress base on Saipan. The alert came at 1:30am, and even though very little damage was done to Isley Field or the B-29s, the attack did serve notice that Saipan was not out of range of Japanese bombers. Only five fragmentation bombs were dropped on the runway at Isley Field. One of the planes was shot down near Tinian by antiaircraft guns, and another was downed by a P-61 Black Widow night fighter. That downed plane crashed in the engineers' bivouac area, killing four and seriously wounding six other Americans.

The next retaliation strike against Saipan came on November 7, in two separate attacks. The first came at 1:30am when a low-flying aircraft strafed the runway, causing very little damage. The other came at 4:30am, flying over the field and evidently taking photos. Both aircraft escaped without drawing fire.

## On the Road to Tokyo

As the B-29s continued to arrive at Saipan, this author and his colleagues sat poised for the initial strike on the Land of the Rising Sun. Soon, we thought, as anxiety climbed like a thermometer's reading on a high-fevered patient, we would be on the road to Tokyo. From this spot of land in the middle of the Pacific Ocean, we were 1,500mi to the south. There was no road, only a red ribbon on a briefing map pointing out the route we would take to the target in the western suburbs of one of the largest cities in the world. There would be no road, just water and a few jutting rock piles sticking up out of the water, some with nothing but volcanic ash and rock showing and some with a bit of vegetation. All had strange names, such as Pagan Island and Iwo Jima. Above Iwo, the string of islands were in the Bonin Group, and all had a name ending with Jima, like Ha Ha Jima, Chi Chi Jima, and so on. Our thorn in the ˜ide, as far as enemy aircraft harassment, would come from Pagan Island just north of Saipan and Iwo Jima. The retaliation raids on Saipan came from Iwo Jima, with Pagan Island used as emergency landings.

## Seven Days of Agonized Waiting

Never before in the history of aerial combat had so many men stood by in total frustration as they waited in a "Will we, or will we not?" frame of mind as they contemplated what could or would happen to them or their aircraft on the long, over-water mission.

The raid on Tokyo, with just over 100 B-29s participating, was scheduled for November 17, not two days earlier as Hansell had hoped. As commander of the 21st BC, now poised for its first strike against the heart of Japan, Hansell was experiencing stress he had not been subjected to commanding an air division in Europe. Bad blood was rearing its head between the USAAF and the Navy, all of which could have a bearing on the future of the USAAF's hope for a separate but equal branch of service.

Some of General Arnold's staff expressed grave doubts about launching the initial mission to Tokyo without naval protection. Arnold forwarded the concerns to Hansell and stated his own skepticism, but left the decision up to him. The record would show that Hansell had been warned. In other words, Hansell's USAAF career would be riding on this mission. Even his 73rd BW Commander, General O'Donnell, wrote a letter to him, stating that he, too, had doubts that the mission could be successful without the Navy's help. Instead, he suggested a night raid against a seaport city, which brought this statement from Hansell: "If you are not willing to lead your wing on the planned daylight mission,

General, I will turn the wing over to Roger Ramey, my deputy, who is anxious to lead it." Given this ultimatum, O'Donnell chose to lead the 73rd BW to Tokyo, riding with Maj. Robert Morgan, who had been among the first B-17 pilots to complete a twenty-five-mission tour and bring his entire original crew back to the States to begin a nationwide bond-selling campaign. Hansell had received orders not to go on the mission because, if captured and tortured, he might reveal that the Japanese secret code, known as Ultra had been broken.

Briefing for the mission would be somber and to the point. At least two major weather fronts would be blocking the 3,000mi over-water flight to and from target no. 357, the Nakajima Aircraft Co.'s Musashino Engine Factory located in the northwestern suburbs of Tokyo. One B-29 crew from the 497th BG flew over Tokyo alone on November 10, not to take pictures, but to "test" Japan's fighter strength and to see how aggressive they were. Results of the flight were not too helpful, but it was estimated that at least 3,000 Japanese fighters were in the Tokyo area, and they were expected to be highly aggressive in trying to protect their capital city. Bombing altitude would be 30,000ft, with each

*Results of the Japanese raids on Isley Field, Saipan, in November and December 1944 and January 1945.* Speith

plane carrying 25 tons of bombs. Takeoff was set for 6am, November 17, 1944. The crews would be awakened 2hr before takeoff so that they could eat breakfast and then go to the line and perform pre-flight inspections on their aircraft.

Crews were told there would be air-sea rescue units along the flight path between Saipan and Japan. Five submarines would be deployed north of Iwo Jima, up to just off the coast of Japan, and two destroyers would roam along the path between Saipan and Iwo Jima.

Clinton Green, the *New York Times* war correspondent who had ridden with us from Hawaii and had assured us that the first raid was about ready to go, even back in Hawaii, would be among the twenty-four war correspondents at Saipan who would break the news to the world.

The Navy's air-sea rescue project was good news to the combat crews as they listened with deadly serious attention as instructions of how the rescue of a downed crew would be attempted. Edwin L. Hotchkiss, of wing

*Mechanics had a tough job, constantly having to change those big R-3350 engines when the engines developed troubles.* Josh Curtis

headquarters and assigned to communications and air-sea rescue, illustrates how the operation was supposed to work: "Air-sea rescue was begun by the Navy, particularly the submarines. Lifeguard subs would take up station at established coordinates off well-known points near the Empire. If not harassed by enemy air or surface craft, the sub would remain on surface, homing battle-damaged B-29s to them so that if ditching or bailing out were necessary, they would be there to pick up the crews.

"The call signs of these lifeguard submarines were always made up of words containing as many of the letters 'L' as possible—such as 'Sally's Belly' or 'Nellie's Nipple.' Such call signs had two major advantages: Most Japs pronounced the letter 'L' as if it were an 'R,' thus reducing attempts at voice radio deception because the Nips would come out with something that sounded like 'Sarry's Berry' or Nerrie's Nipper.' The second advantage was that such names recalled to our boys some of the better things of life, things

from which they had been too long separated!

"By war's end, the air-sea rescue units had saved 212 downed B-29 crewmen!"

At the briefing, crews from the 499th BG were told that if they had enough fuel when they returned to Saipan, they were to fly to Guam and land on the landing strip near the harbor (later named Harmon Field). This was a question of logistics: Nobody knew what would happen when 100 B-29s or so, all low on gas trying desperately to reach Isley Field, would converge on the field almost simultaneously.

At Saipan, the early-morning hours of November 17, 1944, brought a message of great disappointment to the combat crews anxiously listening for the wake-up call that would send them on their first mission north to Tokyo. The terse announcement over the squadron PA system blared out over the 73rd BW area: "Attention all personnel participating in today's mission. The missions have been postponed 24hr. I repeat, the mission has been postponed!"

What a let down! How could this be? Every man participating in the mission—the cooks preparing the meals, the armorers who had loaded

the bombs on the B-29s, the ground crews, and, of course, the flight crews—were psyched to a point of extreme anxiety to get this initial mission underway. But this would not be the day. This delay was caused by extreme bad weather in the area, but it was only the beginning; the delay message was repeated for a solid week. Three of those mornings, crews actually boarded their aircraft, only to be told, again, that the mission had been delayed. During the agonizing delays, some crew members even thought something or somebody was trying to tell our leaders that bad things would happen if they undertook this mission alone.

November 24 was different from the six previous days. As dawn came to the island that morning, you could feel the excitement which seemed to scream out "This is it!"

One crew member remembers how this day began for his crew: "Before the engine start-up, it is the tail gunner, Sutherland's, duty to start the gasoline auxiliary unit which we call the putt-putt, located in the non-pressurized compartment in the rear of the fuselage. Power from this unit must be switched on to the main electrical circuit line before starting the engines or closing the bomb bay doors, to prevent running the batteries down.

"Sutherland enjoys his lone 'take-off' duty and reports the accomplished fact over the intercom each time in a musical fashion, 'Putt-putt started and on the line, sir,' after which Bombardier Feldman flips a switch and announces, 'Bomb bay doors closed and we are ready to taxi.' The procedure is automatic for crew no. 25. We have practiced it so many times there is no way a foul-up could occur in this phase of our first trip to the Land of the Rising Sun.

"Or is there?

"6:00am—The word is go! No postponement today. It is time to get this show on the road. We are still fidgeting around the plane, talking to the ground crew. There will be at least 20min before we start up. Two groups will proceed us in takeoff.

"Spectators by the hundreds—sailors, Marines, ground personnel from the 73rd BW—people from all over the island have swarmed to Isley

Field and taken up advantageous spots from where they can watch the massive takeoff of the heavily loaded B-29 Superfortresses for this historic mission.

"Across the way, the roar from the engines in the 498th BG has begun and General O'Donnell and Major Morgan, in the lead plane, quickly taxi out to the west end of the runway where the takeoff runs start. There are spotters to direct each plane to the runway at the appropriate time. A flagman and timer will flag each plane off at 60sec intervals.

"The excitement and anxiety is everywhere. You can see it even in the eyes of our ground crewmen. We stand by our plane V-Square-27, in our hardstand near the eastern end of the runway and watch as General O'Donnell lifts off the runway, dips down toward the water of Magicienne Bay to gain airspeed faster, and heads out past Kagman Point before turning north toward Tokyo.

"Cox and I look at each other as we prepare to climb aboard our plane. I think each of us is detecting the feeling of apprehension that we are experiencing.

"Before boarding the plane, I turn to our ground crewmen, and paraphrasing MacArthur's famous remark, exclaim, 'We shall return!'

"Standing by their B-29 ready to board, or already in their positions in their plane, are 111 crews, representing a strike force of 1,221 men from four groups: the 497th, 498th, 499th, and 500th. They are members of the 73rd BW, 21st BC of the 20th AF. They are about to write a new chapter in the history books, by blazing a bombing trail over Tokyo. This is certain to bring a message to the people in the streets of that capitol of the Japanese Empire that the handwriting is on the wall for the warlords of Japan."

The first B-29 raid on Tokyo, in fact the first land-based bombers ever to strike the city, was carried out—not exactly as billed, but like the message sent out after the China-based 58th BW's first mission against a Japanese target a few months before—it was a beginning.

As forecast by the weathermen at the briefing, two massive weather fronts had to be penetrated on the way to Japan, but if there were 3,000 fighters stationed in the Tokyo area, they were either trying to save face or fuel or just plain couldn't estimate the speed of the Superforts at such great heights of 27,000 to 32,000ft.

Ninety-eight B-29s made it to Japan and thirteen of the number that took off for the mission had to abort and return to Saipan. Two aircraft were lost. Gunners from the attacking B-29s claimed seven victories by shooting down that many Japanese fighters, including one victory for my tail gunner, John Sutherland.

The ice had been broken, from here on out, the giant B-29 Superfortresses would earn their keep, and Japan would feel the wrath!

## Chapter 8

# B-29 Assault on Japan Picks up Steam

With one major mission against Tokyo under their belts, combat crews on Saipan gained more confidence in their Superfortresses. They had listened to the constant roar of those powerful engines for almost 15hr, flown into and escaped two major weather fronts, climbed to a bombing altitude of about 30,000ft, glanced down into the volcanic crater of Mount Fuji, and survived the 45min or so of flak and fighter attacks over Japan itself. Most importantly, the B-29 now left little doubt that the 3,000mi trip, mostly over water, was within its capability.

O'Donnell also left little doubt that there would be no lengthy rest stop between missions for the 73rd crews. The 58th BW, with Gen. Curtis LeMay as its commander, was picking up steam in the CBI area, but that was in a different part of the world. Other B-29 wings would come to the Marianas, but until then the 73rd BW would carry the battle to the heart of Japan alone.

Another mission to Tokyo was scheduled for November 27, just three days after the initial strike. This time, eighty-one Superforts participated. They went back to the same target, no. 357, located in the northwestern sub-urbs of Tokyo, with instructions to try and improve on the results on the other end of the line. One B-29 was lost on this mission, but before the returning planes reached Saipan, seventeen Japanese Zekes launched from Iwo Jima and paid Isley Field a visit. They approached Saipan at lower than 50ft, undetected by the island's radar, and played havoc with the remaining B-29s. They thoroughly strafed the field in the 499th BG area, and extensively damaged the planes parked there. One man was killed during the attack and several in the 500th BG's bivouac area were injured. One of the planes was shot down by antiaircraft gunners, and it hit and exploded near one of the shelters.

Not a single Zeke made it back to Iwo Jima. Antiaircraft guns from Saipan and Tinian shot down thirteen of the planes. One was shot down by a P-47 near Pagan Island, another was destroyed by a P-47 as it attempted to land on a makeshift landing strip on Pagan Island, and one ditched because of battle damage.

Most of us that day who didn't go on the Tokyo raid were about convinced that it was safer in the air over Japan than it was on the ground at Saipan.

Under the command of Gen. James H. Davies, the first aircraft of the 313th BW arrived at North Field on December 21, 1944. The four groups—the 6th, 9th, 504th, and 505th—completed three practice missions to Truk and Iwo Jima before joining with the 73rd BW in a 110-plane daylight raid on Koebe on February 4.

## Retaliation Raids

During December 1944, the Japanese continued their retaliation raids on Saipan and Tinian. Even the propagandist, Tokyo Rose continuously beamed her "report" to Saipan daily, including popular Stateside music in an effort to demoralize the troops. The orderly room people would sometimes put her messages on the PA system.

Five retaliation raids took place in December, with sometimes as many as twenty-five planes participating. The one that left an eternal impression on this author was the December 7 raid. I happened to be the officer of the guard that night. We expected a raid because it was the third anniversary of the Pearl Harbor attack, and we thought they might try to hit us in strength. They did. Gunners on our crew were pulling guard duty that night since policy had been set up to use flight crews to help guard the B-29s up on the line.

My duty was to keep a close check in the area where the B-29s were parked in their hardstands, and to remain alert. The general consensus was that there was a strong possibility

*A B-29 from the 498th BG is shown taking off at Isley Field, Saipan.* Dick Field

*A formation of B-29s from the 498th BG, Saipan, passes near Mount Fuji on its way* *to a target in Tokyo.* 73rd BW Photo/ Harold Dreeze

*This Superfortress from the 500th BG failed by a few miles making it back to* *Saipan. The crew were all saved as ditching took place just offshore.* Speith

that the estimated 8,000 Japanese soldiers holed-up in the jungle-like mountainous area of Saipan would attempt to coordinate an attack on the parked B-29s at Isley Field during or after a Japanese air raid.

My last trip up to the line to check the guards and to carry them coffee took place about midnight. I chatted with each of the guards in our 878th BS before going back down the hill to our living area, which was about 2mi from the flight line. The moon was shining in all its glory that night, and the silver Superfortresses, loaded with bombs all ready for an early-morning strike on Iwo Jima, glistened in the moonlight., offering a big enticement for an attack. As I drove down the hill toward our squadron orderly room, I couldn't help but believe there would be an attack that night. The moon was full, the time was right, and if the Japanese military leaders really meant it when they said they would destroy all the B-29s, this would be the night for a big-time raid.

A light was still shining in the orderly room, and I stopped in to see what the boisterous noise was all about. A poker game was in full blossom, and most of the players, including our operation officer, had been nipping the whiskey ration. I walked in with my shoulder-holstered .45 pistol in full view, and with as much authority as a second lieutenant could muster in front of a few majors and captains, I exclaimed, "You bastards better douse the lights, cut the chatter, and find a hiding place. The Japs are coming tonight!" With that fair warning to my fellow officers, I went to my Quonset hut to get a little nap before going back up to the line to relieve the guards.

I dropped off to sleep almost immediately, and the next thing I heard was the booming of antiaircraft guns. It must have been 2:30 or 3:00am when they struck Isley Field. As always, they came in just above the water and, as almost always, were not detected before dropping bombs on the B-29s. This time they were using some incendiary bombs that scattered on the hardstands and under the planes, before the burning started. Never before had I witnessed such a chaotic experience. The antiaircraft batteries

64

The A-2 (intelligence) section of the 73rd BW pose for a group picture on Saipan. Harold Dreeze

were not only shooting their 50cal machine guns at the low-flying planes, but their searchlights lit up the whole island, it seemed. They scanned the sky and swept across our living area down by the seashore. When the fires caused by the little foot-long incendiary bombs that resembled a large stick of dynamite would reach one of the B-29s, the heavily loaded plane would catch fire. Within minutes, those bombs would explode and the 6,000gal of fuel on fire would envelop the plane and area. Saipan rocked and rolled that night and somebody exclaimed, "They're going to sink the island!"

At the sound of the all-clear signal, I rushed up to the line, expecting to see our gunners' bodies scattered everywhere. Instead, we saw parts of

bodies belonging to the crew of a Japanese "Betty" bomber, shot down near where our plane was supposed to be located, scattered across the taxi strip and area. Where our plane had been was nothing but a hole large enough for a small house.

Three B-29s were totally destroyed, three badly damaged and twenty somewhat damaged from flying shrapnel. Our gunners were not injured, but they were badly shaken up. One guard on the line was killed and two were wounded. The antiaircraft guns on Saipan shot down six planes, including one downed by a mine sweeper off shore, and one by an antiaircraft battery on Tinian.

It was a sobering night, especially for the poker players I had warned.

**Tokyo Rose Sends Message**

It was really a scary time on Saipan. One night, this author went to see the movie *To Have or Have Not*. The movie was very good, and just as Lauren Bacall walked to the door of Humphrey Bogart's room, opened it and looked around, and said, "If you need me, just whistle. You know how to whistle, don't you?", the lights went out. You've never heard such loud groans of protest. A colonel with his gas mask slung across his shoulder said, "Let me have everyone's attention. The island is now on blue alert

*The* Pom-Pom Girl *flew with the 315th BW on Guam.* Josh Curtis

*This B-29, V-Square-60, remained afloat 17hr after ditching by the Sy Silvester crew of the 878th BS, 499th BG, Saipan, on December 13, 1944.* Sy Silvester

[like a weather watch; red alert meant the enemy had been sighted en route to the island]. Tokyo Rose said in her latest broadcast that the Japanese Navy was en route to Saipan and that an invasion of Saipan is likely. She says they will destroy all the B-29s and kill all the personnel either by gas or bullets." The colonel gave us orders that every person must have his gas mask with him at all times. Those were sobering words! We'd have to see the movie later to hear Bacall tell Bogart how to whistle.

Having to ditch a B-29 on the way back from a mission, either because it was out of gas or because of damage over the target, was a very real possibility and caused much worry. Of course, there were other reasons for ditching. The navigator had to remain alert at all times so that he would know where the aircraft was. Deviations from course could cause excessive use of fuel, which could cause an engine to run rough or force the pilot to shut the engine down entirely.

Darrell W. Landau, a squadron engineering officer with the 19th BG at Guam, tells how he found the underlying cause of swallowed valves: "When I joined the 19th BG at Guam, the assignment caused me to want to really know why the valves were failing. Having been up all night helping crews change engines, I felt motivated to find out why. Attention was being given to early detection of failures, but not the cause. It soon became obvious that if the oil cooked to carbon, the valve stem would soon wear out and the valve would not seat well and would become hotter and hotter. In time, the head would burn off. But why was the oil cooking? Many must have thought the valves' failure was the cause of the oil cooking. I had the feeling the oil cooked first and then the valve failed.

"Looking up at the engines as I pondered the cause, I became aware of the size and location of the large distributors and prop governor; my gosh, they could block air flow! But the no. 1 cylinder directly behind this obstruction, the only cylinder with a thermal-couple temperature sensor, was not running hot! It was supposed to be the hottest, the worst-case indicator, but that cylinder rarely went out.

"A while later, watching an engine being started, I observed how the air swirled counter-clockwise over the engine. That was it! The hot cylinders were counter-clockwise when observed from the front. Those big mechanical globs on the top front of the engine were designed to block off air flow, especially when the air passage was reduced by the nacelle air duct, which came down sharply so it could house the front exhaust collector ring. The nacelle's cooling air annulus, intended to reduce drag, aggravated the blocking effect.

"When it was necessary to change cylinders, it had always been these hot ones. Once recognized, the cause seemed so obvious. Engine manufacturers had been making radial engines with these parts in this location for years. But the combination of collecting exhaust gas, supercharging for takeoff, large piston sizes relative to frontal area, and extra-high takeoff power setting all added up to exceeding the limits of the design.

"I made a study of how we could hollow certain bolts to get oil into the rocker arms without impairing their function as mounting brackets. I made arrangements to prove this point, but the next day, the war ended. Abruptly the world changed, and all thoughts changed from improving engines to going home.

"Wright Field's solution to cool valve stems had been to convert to fuel injection. To me, this seemed to be a complete unnecessary waste.

"If someone had only found and implemented the above simple solution earlier, there would have been no need for the costly conversion to fuel injection, the tremendous turnover in engines, and the lost operational effectiveness. If this one malfunction and its simple solution had been implemented early, it could perhaps have shortened the war by many weeks. The Japanese were already trying to surrender before the atomic bomb; their surrender might well have been achieved and the A-Bomb might never have been dropped."

## Buddy System

Gerald Robinson, aircraft commander and later commander of the 875th BS, 498th BG, Saipan, remem-

bers an incident in which he and his crew were saved by the buddy system: "We all remember the 'buddy system' that combat crews practiced on the long haul to and from Japan. If you were in trouble and had to leave the formation, someone would drop out and fly along with you to help drive off attacking fighters, report ditching positions, etc. One day, we developed a problem, and a young West Point lieutenant pilot from our squadron dropped back to escort us. We were just off the coast of Japan at an altitude of about 10,000ft, very vulnerable all alone, and the lieutenant gave us our navigational bearing for home. We were in radio contact with each other until we were about opposite Pagan Island, just north of Saipan, our home base. Then we lost contact.

"Several years after the war, I read where they found his wrecked B-29 on the side of the volcanic mountain on Pagan Island. He got us home, but he didn't make it himself. The weather was awful, not much visibility, and I have often wondered how close we came to hitting that same mountain."

## High-Altitude Missions

All 73rd BW missions to Japan in December 1944 were high-altitude

*A 3rd PRS crew prepares to take off for Japan to take pictures of damage done by a major strike there. John Mitchell*

from 27,000–34,400ft. Most of these missions required the installation of a 640gal bomb bay fuel tank, providing enough gasoline to get the planes back home if all went well. The big drawback was that when these tanks were installed, the bomb load had to be reduced, and at these altitudes, it was almost impossible to get good bombing results, mainly because of the excessive wind speeds at above 28,000ft. At first, most missions were set up to go downwind on the bomb run. With wind speeds sometimes reaching up to 200 knots, that meant the aircraft had a ground speed of more than 500mph. This was unheard-of speed for an aircraft in those days and, consequently, the mechanization in the bombsight could not compensate a correct reading—which meant that it was unusual if the bombs hit their targets.

It took excessive amounts of fuel and high engine settings to climb to these very high altitudes. The increased fuel consumption made it more likely that the B-29s would run out of fuel on their return flights, and the high engine settings were more

*The 500th BG theater, where movies and traveling shows are eagerly watched. Bill Rooney*

likely to cause swallowed valves. Bombing from very high altitude meant more ditchings on the way home, and many of the planes that ditched were forced to ditch at night.

One of the most unusual ditchings happened in this author's squadron on December 13. Lt. Sy Silvester ran out of gas and was forced to set down in an unfriendly Pacific Ocean with waves more than 14ft high. It was dark, and Sy lined up with the swells and made a perfect landing. All the crew made it out, although the impact of the plane against the water tossed the bombsight loose from its pedestal, and it crashed through the nose with the bombardier following close behind.

He got only a few scratches, and came to about 20ft ahead of the plane. The crew got the life rafts out of the plane and crawled aboard. The incredible thing about this ditching was the fact that the plane floated for 17hr, and when the crew was picked up by the Navy destroyer, USS *Cummings*, the destroyer had to fire more than 40 rounds of 20mm shells into the plane to sink it.

There is an interesting footnote to Silvester's ditching. The first crew to ditch after the initial November 24, 1944, B-29 raid on Japan was Capt. Francis Murray and crew of the 498th BG on Saipan while returning from a December 3 mission. He and nine members of his crew miraculously survived for eleven days on rafts before being picked up. His crew was aboard the *Cummings* when the Silvester

crew was found. Murray's co-pilot went down with the aircraft. The flight engineer of the Murray crew happened to be Silvester's classmate from Western High in Washington, DC.

Another tragic mishap took place when two B-29s were returning from the Nagoya mission the night of December 13. Lt. Garland Ledbetter and crew had nursed their damaged B-29 back to Saipan, and asked for a straight-in approach to the field. They were also running low on gas. Because of the heavy traffic pattern at Isley Field, they were unable to maneuver into a safely spaced-out position to land without hitting another plane. Ledbetter had no choice but to abort the attempted landing, go around, and try to enter the traffic pattern again. The attempt was fatal. Witnesses said the aircraft, after crossing over the end of the runway and trying to gain altitude, suddenly nose-dived into the Magicienne Bay.

A Navy picket boat whose job it was to hover in the area just off the end of the runway, alert for just such emergencies, was on the scene of the crash within minutes, but there would be no rescue this time. The B-29, with the entire crew aboard, disappeared beneath the surface of one of the deepest water holes in the Pacific Ocean. Not even a piece of scrap metal from the wreckage was ever found.

S/Sgt. Murray Juvelier, of the 498th BG on Saipan, tells of the night they crash-landed at Isley Field after a mission: "We had to crash-land after returning to Saipan from a Nagoya mission, December 18, 1944. Our B-29 was so shot up by Japanese fighters, it broke into three pieces upon landing impact. Several crew members were injured, including me, during the crash, but our aircraft commander, Capt. Wilford Turcotte, brought us back alive.

"I was pinned under some of the debris and knocked unconscious during the crash. When I came to, I yelled for help as loud as I could. I was still in shock, but I remember a voice yelling, 'Let's get out of here before she blows!' The guy doing the yelling pulled me from the wreckage and saved my life!

"On May 12, 1983, I attended my first reunion of the 73rd BW Association in Denver. Thirty-nine years had passed since the crash-landing on Saipan. I had sort of shoved the awful memory of that experience from my mind. Soon after checking into my hotel room, a fellow came up to me, shook my hand, gave me a big hug, and said, 'I guess you made it after all, Murray. There's one thing for sure, if you were as heavy then as you are now, I never would have gotten you out of that plane wreckage!' I was standing face to face, for the first time, with the 'stranger' who rushed to our wrecked plane that night and saved my life. The stranger's name was Robert Evans from another group, whose plane landed at Isley Field just ahead of ours that night. He and other members of his crew were the first to reach our debacle and were responsible for saving our crew."

As the 21st BC, under the leadership of General Hansell, continued its high-altitude strategic bombing of targets in Japan, with not much improvements shown in bombing results, General LeMay, commander of the 20th BC in India, was telling journalists that the B-29 was now out of the experimental stage. He had made some changes in operations, scheduling more targets in such places as Rangoon, Singapore, and Formosa and less targets where it was necessary to launch from the forward bases in China.

LeMay was showing improvements, partially because of this decision, because of the adverse logistical problems of having to fly so many supply and fuel trips over the Hump. By avoiding missions from the China bases, LeMay saved wasted time and effort necessary in flying the Hump several times to stockpile enough bombs and fuel in China to launch a mission to Japan or other nearby Japanese targets.

On a December 18, 1944, test mission, General LeMay sent ninety-four B-29s, loaded with 511 tons of M69 incendiary bombs, to Hankow. This raid was extremely successful, and it along with the successful aerial mining missions of the 20th BC would be a determining factor in the Superfortresses' role in knocking Japan out of World War II.

The 20th AF Headquarters in Washington thought the Hankow incendiary mission was so successful that the chief of staff, General Norstad, directed General Hansell to launch a full-scale incendiary attack on Nagoya with at least 100 B-29s. Hansell was reluctant to change tactics from his high-altitude strategic bombing, and he let General Arnold know his feelings. Lt. Gen. Millard F. Harman, commander of Army Forces in the Pacific Ocean area, also was against changing to incendiary bombing against Japanese home islands. He insisted that the main targets should continue to be war industries, not flimsy houses, declaring that "Burning houses will not beat the Japs."

Incendiary bombs were used against Nagoya on the December 22 raid, but not in compliance with Norstad's request. The target, again, was overcast, and very little damage was inflicted.

As 1944 came to an end, those in Washington were coming to a decision that would change the direction of the war. Some of the high-ranking USAAF officers were very unhappy about the end results of the B-29 efforts in the Pacific.

## Chapter 9

# World War II Countdown Begins

As 1944 sizzled to an end in the Marianas amid Japanese retaliation raids, high-speed winds at high altitude over Japan were causing frustrations at the highest level of command, as well as for the combat crews who were missing targets considerably more often than they were hitting them. After one mission when a whole group of about forty-five planes, having to revert to dropping their cargo by radar, mistook a large lake just north of Tokyo for the target, rumor had it that there were enough dead fish to feed all the hungry people in the city of Tokyo.

As the new year began, there were other winds afloat, other than the puzzling winds over the Japanese Empire. Nobody knew the answer to high speed, but in due time the world would know the high-flying B-29s had discovered what was to be known as the Jet Stream. Also, the new year brought with it a change in the entire 20th AF structure and in the leader of the bomber command.

By year's end, President Roosevelt was demanding to know why the B-29s had not been more productive. Much money and manpower had been

*The author's airplane* Mary Ann, *V-Square-27, 878th BS, 499th BG, 73rd BW, gets an engine run-up by crew chief Fred Reed at Saipan. The name* Mary Ann *was later painted onto the 73rd BW's winged-ball-and-spear insignia.* Marshall

used to build the B-29s, and many lives were lost to capture the Marianas and to build new bases for them. General Arnold knew something had to be done, and as the new year burst upon the scene, he had made his decision. He would replace his friend, Gen. Haywood Hansell, with cigar-smoking, tough, combat-proven Maj. Gen. Curtis LeMay.

General Norstad, chief of staff of the 20th AF, was dispatched to the Marianas to deliver the bad news to Hansell. Norstad arrived at the 21st BC Headquarters, now at Guam, on January 6. General Arnold had a dispatch sent to LeMay in India that day.

When the dispatch ordering LeMay to proceed to Guam arrived at 20th BC at Kharagpur, a young captain by the name of William A. Rooney, who was an S-2 officer on charge-of-quarters duty that night, took the top-secret message and, according to policy, hand-delivered it to LeMay. Rooney shares this exclusive account of his brush with history in handling one of the most important change-of-command orders involving top-ranking commanders during World War II: "In the bomber command headquarters in Kharagpur, the adjutant's office was manned 24hr a day. Night change-of-quarters duty fell to those rear-rank Ruddys of company grade, as myself. They had to have the additional qualification of be-

ing cleared for handling top-secret material. I casually signed for it, and then began to read it as was my privilege. My hands began to shake just a little when I saw at the top of the message that it wasn't from just an old headquarters, but from the War Department.

"Furthermore, the message was stamped top-secret and 4Z, which meant the highest level of security and the highest level of speed of transmission. Just a little shaky, I proceeded to read the message. It was from Gen. George C. Marshall, Army chief of staff, to LeMay, instructing him to move to the Marianas, where he was to take command of the 21st BC for the purpose of prosecuting the war against Japan. The message was of some length, but reading this far prompted me to go no further, but to get this message to the general as fast as I could.

"LeMay was having dinner in the general's mess in a building connected to headquarters by a breezeway. I had never entered these digs, and, as a lowly captain, I was scared to do so now except that I had to get the general's signature acknowledging receipt of the message. I quietly eased up to LeMay's aide who was sitting beside the general. With great politeness, the aide accepted the message, saying something about having received an alerting message earlier in the day.

*Bombs are appropriately decorated before loading for another mission.* USAAF Photo

*This parade took place on Saipan in May 1945 when the 73rd BW turned out in full to show off for visiting dignitaries and to present medals. The covered nose art on the nearby plane has not been replaced by the* wing's symbol, and some high ranking officials in wing headquarters decided that it would be better if the visitors, and especially the newsreels, were not exposed to that particular piece of art. Dick Field

Relieved of my burden, I exited as silently as one of the barefoot Indian houseboys who were serving the meal.

"That message ordering a change of command of the B-29s in the Pacific was a harbinger of a deadly war to come. Arriving on Saipan, LeMay determined early on that the way the war was being waged with the B-29s wasn't going to get the job done. On his own authority, without seeking approval from any higher command, LeMay began low-level, firebomb raids on Tokyo and the other major cities of Japan, thus bringing to the enemy the devastating destruction that was within the plane's capability. The war with Japan turned on that change of command, and my brush with history came about when that message passed through my hands."

LeMay arrived at Guam on January 7 for the meeting that ended with the change of command of the 21st BC. The meeting of the three young generals had to be an uncomfortable situation. All three knew each other well. LeMay had served as a group commander under Hansell in the European war. It was evident that Hansell's reluctance to change his doctrine of high-altitude bombing was the major cause for the change in command.

The change of command would not take place until January 20, 1945, and Hansell would stick with his high-altitude bombing until the end of his tenure. He had fulfilled Norstad's order to conduct a full-blown incendiary raid on Nagoya back in December, but it was launched with ninety-seven B-29s airborne with only sixty planes bombing the primary target. This raid was flown at altitudes of 28,000–31,500ft and didn't receive the hoped-for results. Five B-29s were lost. Tokyo and Nagoya were the next Hansell-ordered missions, both from high altitude, but the results were no better. The mission to Tokyo, January 9 claimed six B-29s, and the Nagoya mission on January 14 claimed five more.

Before the general's final mission on January 19, he had ordered a major reduction in the weight of the aircraft. Steel plates that protected the pilots and one of the bomb bay fuel tanks were removed, reducing the overall

*Bombs loaded and awaiting signal for start-up. Gerald Robinson/Josh Curtis*

weight of the plane about 6,000lb. Whether this weight reduction was the cause for much better bombing results is a matter of conjecture, but the January 19 mission against the Kawasaki Aircraft Plant at Akashi, near Kobe, turned out to be the best mission to Japan so far. Hansell could return to the States with a bit of consolation about his high-altitude strategic bombing, even over Japan. The planes bombed from altitudes of 25,000–27,000ft. The weather was good, and all sixty-two of the B-29s that participated returned to Saipan. The 3rd PRS planes confirmed that it was a good strike, but the knowledge of just how good it was came after the war, when it was learned that 90 percent of the factory was destroyed on that mission.

The 313th BW on Tinian Island continued their shakedown missions during January as replacement crews started arriving in Saipan to fill the gaps left by downed crews. William G. Schmidt, navigator on a replacement crew in the 878th BS, 499th BG, recalls disappointments that faced most replacement crews: "As a replacement crew, we got a rude awakening just a few hours after we set our brand-new B-29 Superfortress down on Isley Field, Saipan, and checked in at squadron headquarters.

"We never set foot again in what we thought was 'our airplane.' Our morale took a nose-dive when we were informed that the B-29 we brought over would be assigned to an older crew—one who had been here longer without an assigned airplane. We wondered what 'good news' we'd get next, especially after we found out the quarters we were assigned had been occupied by men who had gone down over Japan a few days earlier. Now that was a sobering thought—not exactly soothing to our nerves.

"It took a while for replacement crews to get used to filling the shoes of downed buddies, in the eyes of veteran crews. We did our best to fill those shoes, however, and even though we looked pretty forlorn for a while, we finally jelled and then we were looked upon as 'one of them.'"

All the 73rd BW crews flying their B-29s to Saipan made a fueling stop at Kwajalein, a small atoll with just enough room to land and takeoff a heavily loaded B-29. Jack McGregor, an aircraft commander with the 869th BS, 497th BG, had this to say about his stop at the God-forsaken spot of coral rock in the middle of the Pacific Ocean: "About 20mi out of Kwajalein, our refueling stop halfway from Hawaii to Saipan, our future home, we called the control tower for landing instructions. They told us to hold 5mi east of the island at 2,000ft since they had an emergency landing in progress. We circled to watch the unfolding dra-

*A downed flyer is pulled aboard a Navy submarine. Lifeguard subs stayed on station near the B-29 routes. These subs stayed on the surface as much as possible, homing battle-damaged B-29s to them so the sub could rescue the crews. Sy Silvester*

*Two B-29 crews return to Saipan after being rescued by the Navy. Sy Silvester*

ma and noticed a large group of people on the apron just off the single runway. One of my crew members sighted an F4U Corsair doing a 360deg overhead turn and landing. We soon received an 'OK 467, Come on in and land!'

"On our approach to the landing strip, we saw the group of people milling around the Corsair. Finally, a jeep roared off toward the building area. After landing, I asked the 'Kwaj' operation folks if the Corsair pilot had been badly hurt. They laughed and said that this was just the regular afternoon 'Freezing the Ice Cream Flight.' Our entire crew laughed over the incident as we enjoyed ice cream for dinner that night!"

The first mission under LeMay's command of the 21st BC was flown by the 313th BW from Tinian Island. It was also that wing's practice mission in the Pacific. The big change had not occurred yet. The 313th's practice strike on Truk Island, a former Japanese stronghold, was from the usual 25,000–26,000ft altitude. After LeMay took over, there were many practice missions. Most of the nearby bypassed islands, with a few Japanese soldiers hiding in the brush, would feel the wrath of the B-29 bombers on practice missions.

The high-altitude raids would continue through February, with the exception of three air-sea rescue missions by the 313th BW at 3,000ft.

On January 27, 1945, LeMay sent seventy-four B-29s, loaded with all-purpose bombs, to the Nakajima plant in Tokyo, again at the familiar high altitude, and results were not much better than before. One thing was different this time, however. Swarms of Japanese fighters came up to challenge the Superfortresses, and they knocked down nine of the attacking force, the largest number of B-29s lost

in a raid to date. Over 900 enemy attacks were hurled at the B-29s, including some trial runs of ramming tactics. No B-29s were rammed during this mission, but six B-29s were shot down, two ditched from fighter damage, and one crashed on landing back at Saipan.

While the Tokyo debacle was taking place, Brig. Gen. Roger M. Ramey, now commander of the 20th BC in the CBI theater, launched a double-whammy mining mission. Twenty-six B-29s laid mines at Saigon, and fifty Superfortresses dropped their mines on the Port of Singapore. These were the first of the mining missions performed by B-29s of the 20th AF, since the initial mining mission at Palembang, Sumatra, by the 462nd BG, 58th BW.

## Incendiary Strike on Kobe

February 1945 was the month big new decisions were made and long-held anxieties were beginning to fade.

Sensing that the crews' morale had taken a nose-dive after the tough Tokyo raid of January 27, LeMay requested from Washington that missions should be shifted from heavily defended targets in Tokyo and Nagoya. He suggested that the next mission be an incendiary maximum effort against Kobe. Not only would this

74

relieve some of the tension, he hoped, it would help planners determine the effects of large-scale incendiary raids, since they were unable to get sufficient information from the January 14 incendiary raid on Nagoya.

February 4 was to be one of the most important missions, as far as planners were concerned, in determining whether incendiary bombs should be used on large-scale bombing missions against major cities in Japan.

The mission would include 110 B-29s from the now-ready 313th BW with the 73rd BW bombers. Again, it would be a high-altitude mission at 24,000–27,000ft. It would be a daylight raid, carrying a total of 140 tons of incendiary clusters and 13 tons of fragmentation bombs. Aggressive Japanese fighters shot down one bomber and damaged thirty-five more. Another damaged B-29 crashed and burned upon landing at Isley Field.

The results were a big improvement over the Nagoya incendiary trial mission. Pictures taken by the 3rd PRS revealed that more than 2,500,000sq-ft of Kobe's built-up area was destroyed or damaged.

More encouraging news would soon be announced. Already, rumor had it that an invasion of Iwo Jima would soon take place. There was not much doubt that something was about to take place on Iwo Jima. Seventh USAAF B-24s based on Saipan had, for some time, made daily raids on the airstrip on Iwo Jima, as had B-29s from the 73rd BW and now the 313th Wing.

## B-29 Gunners Sink Two Japanese Ships

Arthur Clay, an aircraft commander with the 39th BS, 6th BG on Tinian Island, recalls a run-in with two Japanese surface ships during a Navy assist in a air-sea rescue mission north of Iwo Jima: "With no mission scheduled for my crew that morning of February 14, 1945, I was stripped down to my underwear and getting in a little sack time, when the PA horn blared out, 'Gus Clay, report to operations immediately.' I jumped up, slipped on my clothes and shoes, and, wondering what the heck was up, took off up the street to find out.

B-29s on their way to their target.

"'Get your crew together,' I was told. 'You are to go on an individual plane search mission north of Iwo Jima, complements of the Navy.' A Navy lieutenant was to go with us. Iwo Jima was still in the Japs' hands, and though the mission could be risky for a single B-29 in that area, we accepted the assignment with enthusiasm.

"The Navy had requested assistance for the radar search mission since the area they wanted covered was out of range of the Navy B-24s. The Iwo Jima invasion was coming up soon—thus, the surveillance north of Iwo.

"We made our turn-around at the designated spot, and headed for our base at Tinian Island. The weather, by this time, was getting pretty bad, so I dropped down to about 1,000ft above the water to get under the heavy clouds, when all of a sudden we faced two Jap surface ships dead ahead. They evidently were en route to Iwo Jima. Our Navy observer identified one of the ships as a 7,000-ton freighter, and the other as a 2,500-ton freighter. We contacted one of our submarines we knew to be in the area, who assisted in the rescue of B-29 flyers forced to ditch, to or from bombing missions over Japan.

"Since we had no bombs aboard, I had not even considered trying to 'attack' the ships, and was about to take evasive action to get out of their way, when the ships started firing at us. Turn about was fair play, I thought, so I immediately notified the gunners we were to strafe them. After climbing to about 2,000ft, I turned and made a diving sweep on the larger ship, with our forward guns blazing and the tail gunner taking over after we passed over the ship. Bingo! As we made our turn for another run, we could see explosions on the ship and, encouraged by the first pass, we turned on the small freighter. It, too, became embroiled in flames. We circled and watched as the larger ship began to sink, as did the second ship. After circling the two stricken ships to make sure they were sinking, we relayed the message to the submarine, explaining to the sub commander that their services were not needed. If I had thought to be more romantic, I'd probably have sent this message: 'Sighted two ships, sank same!'"

## 314th Wing Arrives at Guam

February brought more good news. Brig. Gen. Thomas S. Power's 314th BW began arriving at North Field, which had recently been carved out of a dense jungle on the north end of Guam. On February 25, the 314th would join the 313th and 73rd BWs in a 229-plane raid, the largest so far against Japan, in Tokyo's urban area. Only three B-29s were lost.

The four BGs in the 314th BW included the 19th, 29th, 39th, and 330th. The 19th BG was almost wiped out when the Japanese struck Clark Field in the Philippines, on December 8, 1941. It was ironic that this group, which had been reactivated to join the 20th AF, would deliver some of the final blows that would force the Japanese to capitulate.

The countdown had begun!

Moonshine Raiders *flew with the 331st BG,*
*315th BW on Guam.* Gillum/Josh Curtis

## Chapter 10

# More Help Comes to the Pacific

Early on the morning of February 10, 1945, 118 B-29s from the 73rd and 313th BWs left their bases at Saipan and Tinian Island and headed north toward Japan to bomb a very important target at Ota. It would be a high-altitude mission against the plant producing the new twin-engine airplane called Frank. Intelligence had learned that the new aircraft would be capable of attacking the B-29 at very high altitudes, so it was very important that this plant be destroyed.

This author's crew was one of the strike forces heading north for Ota, located about 60mi inland from the coastline and about 100mi north of Tokyo. It would be an upwind bomb run, because mission planners were still leery of Iwo Jima and dog-legged our route around that island. Rumors of an Iwo Jima invasion were being accepted as a fact. Why else would a steady stream of Navy ships keep passing through the channel separating Saipan and Tinian Island and dropping anchor offshore?

The parade of battleships, carriers—some of which were dubbed "baby flat-tops"—destroyers, landing craft, transport ships, and other vessels was second only to the rendezvous of 100 or more B-29s, circling at high altitude until each plane settled into its designated spot in the formation, then heading across the coastline of Japan toward the target for the day. We

knew it wouldn't be long before the extra mileage around Iwo Jima would be eliminated to and from targets in Japan.

The dog-leg around Iwo Jima for the Ota mission wasn't completely out of sight of the pork chop-shaped, 7mi-long volcanic island. Members of the crew chatted for a while as we passed the island, expressing thanks that soon we'd have a place to land, other than water, if damaged during a raid on Japan.

Passing Iwo Jima, we had not yet started our climb to bombing altitude where we would rendezvous just off the coast of Japan, then go in by groups in train. The B-29s always flew in a very loose formation until nearing the coast to avoid having to jockey the throttles, thus saving gas. Keeping a sharp eye out for surrounding B-29s, we happened to notice what looked like a flight of aircraft directly ahead of us and on our level. At first, they resembled small specks, but this was not the case. The specks got larger and larger. I looked at Cox and said: "Do you see what I see?" Then Herb Feldman, our bombardier, yelled, "Those are Jap planes coming this way!" Not too anxious to play Russian roulette with them at this point, we veered slightly to the right and held our course. It was a very curious sight. A Japanese twin-engine bomber we called a Betty was leading a flight of

six fighter planes we recognized as Zekes or Tojos. They passed within 100yd or so to the left of us, the big red balls on their wings and fuselages shining brightly in our eyes. To this point, it had been the closest we'd been face to face with the enemy. A second close encounter was near at hand.

We crossed the coastline, going slightly north to a certain point we called our Initial Point, and being in the no. 3 position (left wing) of the lead element, our flight leader began a gradual turn to the left, heading directly into a bright and blinding sun.

Every B-29 combat crew member knew it was policy to wear an oxygen mask while in the target or danger area. This precaution was necessary to prevent the crew members from loosing consciousness if the pressurized cabin were to receive flak or shell holes large enough to cause the cabin to depressurize.

The oxygen mask was uncomfortable and I always left it dangling on the side of my face, hooked only to one side on my helmet, until I could see it was time to hook-up. This could have been a fatal habit on this day.

I was in the left seat flying the mission, and my radio was tuned to the interplane channel, not the intercom. All of a sudden, a swarm of fighters found us. They came in droves and out of the sun and we could not see

*Two-thousand pounders ready to be loaded for another mission to Japan. Each B-29 could carry a maximum of six of these massive bombs.* Chuck Spieth

them until they came barreling through our formation. Three Tojos slammed in on our nose, flying in close formation. I thought about pulling up to try avoiding their attempt to ram us, but there wasn't time for that. They had already zoomed past us. Next came two planes diving out of the sun, and they just barely missed clipping our wing. I fought the controls of the plane, desperately trying to maintain our position in the formation. The next attacker was a twin-engine Tony. The pilot concentrated his firepower on our flight leader, Cecil Scarborough, successfully knocking out one of his engines, making it shudder and almost go out of control before Scarborough and LeRoy Florence could straighten it up. They lost altitude and slid under the formation. To prevent collision with Scarborough, those of us around him had to maneuver away, which resulted in a scattered formation. Just as we were about to close up the formation, the fighters came again. This time, they hit K. B. Smith's plane, which was flying on the

left wing of the element at this time. He dived out of formation and slid under us. By now, we were sitting ducks out on the left of the whole formation. I worked up a sweat trying to hustle back to close the formation. I would not make it before a three-ship attack came in from 9 o'clock and really plastered us. I knew we were hit, but I didn't realize the extent of the damage we had sustained since I still maintained full control of the airplane. My main objective was to close up the positions in the formation vacated by Scarborough and Smith as fast as I could because we all knew the Japs always concentrated their attacks on stragglers, or ships separated from the formation.

As aircraft commander, Cox was generous in sharing flying time with me, even at the controls over the target. To this day, I kid him about how he could foresee the harder missions because I was always at the controls during them. He was on the intercom calling out oncoming fighters to the gunners, and I was monitoring the interplane command radio channel. I could hear flight engineer John Huckins yelling something, but I was too busy in my struggle to maintain control of the aircraft and close up with the formation to understand what he

was trying to tell me. Finally, he unfastened his safety belt and came over and punched my shoulder, gesturing for me to fasten my oxygen mask. He pointed to the cabin pressure altimeter, which normally had a reading of 8,000ft altitude. It was going wild. I was immediately aware that either the pressurization pump had been damaged or destroyed, or we had large holes in the fuselage. The atmospheric condition within the plane was rapidly equalizing with that outside the plane. I immediately snapped on my mask as we gradually closed the formation and crept toward the target, bucking a strong headwind.

Miraculously, as if a hand from Heaven had reached into our plane to prevent further cabin pressure loss, the indicator stopped its spin at a reading of 12,500ft. We all breathed a little easier since we knew if the pump could maintain that level of cabin pressure, we could survive, even without oxygen. At this time, we were totally unaware of what had happened to the oxygen bottles stored in the rear unpressurized compartment.

Within 12min of successfully bombing the target, we made a 180deg turn and were back over the ocean, aided by an unusually strong tailwind. Navigator Jim O'Donnel did some fast calculations and announced that we had been doing a ground speed of 520mph. I was all wrung out, with not a dry stitch of clothing on my body, even down to my socks—even though the outside thermometer read about 35deg below zero. I looked at Cox and said, "Take it, Cox, I'm pooped."

The drama began to unfurl further as we set our course toward home and out of danger of further fighter attacks. Radar operator Robert Slewsuski discovered that an unexploded 20mm shell had ripped through the fuselage and tore into the invertor, making the radar system inoperable. During the bomb run and fighter attacks, he had been sitting on the floorboard hatch. The shell had lodged only 4in below his rear end!

We depressurized the plane as soon as we thought it safe to do so, so that the tail gunner, John Sutherland, could open hatches to his pressurized compartment and come forward, as he always did after leaving a target. To

get to the forward pressurized compartments, Sutherland had to pass through the rear unpressurized section of the B-29 where, among other things, oxygen tanks were stored. After crawling through the tunnel that connected the central fire control gunners' compartment and the forward section, he announced, "Guess what, some shells exploded in the rear compartment and destroyed all the oxygen bottles. They are all busted up and scattered all over the place!"

Opposition in the skies over Japan was picking up. A new record for the number of B-29s lost on a mission was set on this up-wind Ota mission when twelve Superfortresses were lost. More B-29s would not have made it back from that mission had it not been for several extraordinary accomplish-

ments from some of the flight crews whose planes were heavily damaged.

One of the most incredible feats ever accomplished by a B-29 combat crew took place in Cecil Scarborough's plane after it was heavily damaged during the initial fighter attack as the 499th BG made the turn to the bomb run to Ota. During the attack, the throttle cables that controlled power on the no. 3 and 4 engines were severed, causing them to run at dangerously high levels. The pilots had no way to control them. Lt. Howard Guiot, flight engineer, accomplished what seemed to be an impossibility, enabling the crew to make it back to Saipan and to save the Superfortress for another day. He crawled into the bomb bays to survey the situation and finally found the severed cables. With-

Ernie Pyle's Milkwagon *flew with the 6th BG on Tinian Island.* Josh Curtis

out proper tools or equipment, he could not splice them together. Guiot decided to place another crewman at the open hatch leading into the bomb bays to relay messages between the pilot and himself. There was no way to speak directly by intercom from the bomb bays to the pilot, so the message relay system had to work. It did! He relayed the message to Scarborough that he would attempt to lash the broken cables to a spar, after deciding on a constant power setting for the engines. After a period of trial and error, the task was accomplished.

The big sweat was what was going to happen when attempting to land

*Bomb bay tanks, each holding 640gal of fuel, ready for installation. The bomb bay tanks were used for high-altitude missions only. At 25,000–30,000ft altitude and above, two of the tanks were used, filling one of the bomb bays and cutting the bomb load in half. The tanks were not dropped during flight; they were reused on later missions.* Chuck Spieth

back at Isley Field. The pilot and engineer, after a conference, decided on a plan and hoped it would work. As they neared Saipan, Guiot crawled back into the bomb bays, unleashed the cables, and on final approach to the runway, manipulated them on signals from Scarborough. The landing was not picture-perfect, but it was most incredible.

## Date Set for Iwo Jima Invasion
The performance of the B-29 continued to improve in February in both the Pacific and in the CBI theater. During the month, two 100-plus–plane missions were flown to Singapore. Others were made to Saigon, Bangkok, Mingaladon, and Kuala Lumpur.

Big changes were about to take place in the Pacific, as General LeMay had promised. Adm. Chester Nimitz's office had already set the date for the Iwo Jima invasion: February 19. Excitement on Saipan and Tinian Island

grew as the ships that had recently come there left port and headed out to sea. B-29 crews were overjoyed because this Navy and Marine operation was being done, among other reasons, to directly benefit the B-29s with a place to land if running low of fuel or damaged.

Seventh AF B-24s and B-29s had dropped so many bombs on Iwo Jima since the Japanese retaliation raids on Isley Field in November that the general consensus was that the Marines should be able to capture the island in a week or two. They were mistaken. They didn't realize how a Japanese soldier would react when his back was to the wall and his country and Emperor were at stake.

Before the invasion, the plan was to pulverize the island with the heaviest bombardment the battleships could lay down for three days, before the first landing craft headed for shore.

On the morning of February 19, the 73rd and 313th BWs sent 150 B-29s to target no. 357 in Tokyo. My crew was one of the strike force, and again we passed near enough to see what was going on at Iwo Jima. We could see the flashes from the big guns that were filling the air with the largest shells the Navy had. It was, indeed, a strange feeling to know that within a very short time the Marines would be going ashore. My heart went

out for them, but what a relief it would be once that little piece of coral rock and volcanic ash was secured.

The 313th BW's four groups were coming of age quickly. With several practice and air-sea rescue missions under their belt, this was their fourth major mission. Six B-29s were lost.

Another raid on Tokyo, this one on February 25, would be the 21st BC's first three-wing mission. Gen. Thomas S. Power, commander of the 314th BW, was now settled in at North Field on Guam and ready to join the 73rd and 313th BWs in a 229-plane attack. This was one of the last high-altitude, regular missions against Japan. Three planes were lost.

Victor H. King, commanding officer of Consolidated Air Service Groups on Tinian Island, remembers an incident during takeoff for an aerial mining mission from North Field: "Early one spring morning in 1945, a B-29 rolled down the runway at North Field on Tinian Island, loaded with aerial mines to be dropped in the Shimonoseki Straits.

"Prior to liftoff, the pilot encountered a 'no-go' situation. However, he was beyond the point where he could safely abort. He tried desperately to bring the heavily loaded airplane to a halt, but to no avail. Brakes smoking, it ran off the end of the runway, across the overrun, and down a deep slope, and exploded.

"All aboard were blown to bits, except the tail gunner. Sensing that the plane was going to crash, he jettisoned his emergency hatch and dropped onto the runway overrun. Miraculously, he was not injured by the fall. But, as he ran for safety, the explosion blew pieces of a propeller blade in his direction. One of these sliced off a big chunk of his buttocks. He was rushed to the emergency medical unit on the field, where he encountered one of his buddies.

"As he lay with his rear end propped up on the treatment table, his pal exclaimed, 'Boy! That prop sure did a job on you!'

"'That was no prop,' the tail gunner replied. 'That was the Grim Reaper's scythe!'"

The month of March would be the turning point in the war for the B-29s, as three wings were now in operation, one each on Saipan, Tinian Island, and Guam. But a decision had been made to shut down the CBI Superfortress operation and transfer the entire 20th BC to West Field on Tinian Island. Also, the 20th BC would merge with the 21st BC, headquartered at Guam. The 58th BW, which was the total strength of the 20th BC, would be the fourth wing now under command of General LeMay's 21st BC. The March 29–30 mission to Singapore, with a twenty-nine B-29 strike force, would be the last mission flown from bases in India, as well as the last mission flown by the 20th BC.

From June 5, 1944, to March 30, 1945, the 58th BW, 20th BC, flew forty-nine combat missions from the CBI theater. The missions involved 3,058 sorties in which 11,477 tons of explosives were dropped in Japan proper, Sumatra, North China, and Formosa. They had given support to British Admiral Lord Louis Mountbatten, General MacArthur, and the US Navy during the Battle of the Philippine Sea. They had experimented successfully with incendiary bombs, which was a factor in later decisions by the USAAF Operations Analysis Committee, and later the Joint Target Group, to firebomb major cities in Japan. In addition, the crews of the 58th BW had spear-headed the usage of mines with some very successful aerial mining missions, which were the forerunners of Operation Starvation, the mine-laying in home ports of Japan that eventually developed into a total blockade into and out of Japanese ports.

On March 30, 1945, the entire 20th BC and 58th BW were deployed from bases in India and China to Tinian Island, to join in the big push against the Japanese home islands and merge with the 21st BC.

General LeMay had other surprising changes to spring. After the March 4 192-plane raid, he shut down combat missions for five full days. Rumor had

it that the reason for no scheduled missions during this period was to give mechanics time to try to get all B-29s flying and in tip-top shape for something special. The something special was enough to roll the rumors out in high gear. Most of the crews had been individually practicing dropping 500lb incendiary clusters, one at a time, on one of the nearby islands. This gave food for a lot of thought. At the top of the rumor list was the idea that LeMay was going to send all the planes up to Japan, loaded with aerial mines, and from very low altitude, plant the mines in Tokyo Bay and other shipping ports. This idea was completely demoralizing, conjuring up visions of flying into steel cables, being held up by balloons, and having wings clipped.

During that five-day stand-down, combat crews had plenty time to churn up other demoralizing developments. There had been no such thing as promotions, and, according to the grapevine, our European counterparts were sparkling with higher rank. One of the most frustrating things was the lack of information about length of combat tours. All were anxious to know how many missions would determine our combat stay overseas.

Ground crew personnel had their own brand of problems and mishaps, as they performed around-the-clock maintenance on the Superfortresses. They worried about the length of their tours of duty. No news was forthcoming for the flight crews. Most of them went about their work with the attitude that they were there for the duration, hoping they wouldn't have an unavoidable mishap, such as the one Sgt. Arthur Geminder, with the 504th BG, of the 313th Wing on Tinian Island, almost had: "I was put in charge of the wash rack, washing down dirty B-29s. For help, they were sending me guys who were given extra duties, or guys who had screwed up. The second lieutenant, who was my boss, told me to

Patches *flew with the 875th BS, 497th BG, and was damaged during one of Japan's early retaliation raids on Isley Field in 1944.* Marshall

be very careful with the system of cleaning, which was no more than an air compressor and a drum of kerosene.

"The mixture was sprayed on the planes with long nozzles. There was a gauge on the drum which was not to exceed 150lb. And, yes, you guessed it—I don't know which one of us was responsible, the extra-duty guys, the screw ups, or who—all of a sudden, a loud boom that sounded as if a bomb had gone off shook the area. I glanced around to see the drum flying sky high. The drum, still loaded with lots of kerosene, went up to at least 200ft before reversing its assent and began falling. It landed within a few feet of the B-29 we were washing. I have often wondered what would have happened if that half-filled drum had hit that plane, causing an explosion, which would have destroyed that big B-29. I would be paying for that plane for the rest of my life, I'm sure.

"The name of the aircraft was the *F.D.R.*"

Big Time Operator *was assigned to the Lt. W. M. Bloomfield crew, 9th BG, Tinian Island.* Larry Smith

*Chapter 11*

# First Fire Raid on Tokyo

By March 8, 1945, rumors about the upcoming B-29 maximum-effort mission were revealed as facts. Those who attended the briefing for that first all-out incendiary raid on Tokyo will never forget the almost shock-effect it had on the crews who would participate. General LeMay was calling for an unbelievable change of policy in the method B-29s would attack Japan. He was advocating such a radical change that most of his own staff thought the loss rate of B-29s and crews would reach astronomical numbers of up to 75 percent. The rumor that came out of that staff meeting was LeMay's so-called reply: "Well, if those figures happen to be correct, then we'll have to send for more B-29 combat crews, won't we?"

The first shocker at the mission briefing was: "The altitude over the target will be 5,000–8,000ft."

The next shocker caused even deeper groans: "All gunners, except one, will stand down for the Tokyo mission. That gunner will ride in the tail gunner position and act as scanner-observer only. No ammunition will be carried because the gun barrels will be removed, saving at least 3,000 extra pounds and thus increasing the bomb payload by that much."

The final shocker was the worst: "This will be an all-night flight; take off at about 6:00pm, hit the target soon after midnight, and return to base after sunup the next day. Crews will fly individually to and from and over the target, and drop their bombs in a selected urban area marked by twelve B-29 pathfinders. These planes will take off an hour ahead of the main strike forces and start fires around the area to be saturated by succeeding planes dropping inside the 'ring of fire'."

All three wings, now in the Marianas—the 73rd, the 313th, and the 314th—would participate in the mission. It would be the largest concentration of B-29s to strike Japan so far, with 325 B-29s scheduled to participate. All planes would drop their load of napalm incendiary bombs in the same general area of urban Tokyo.

Every crew had to adhere to the planned route and cruise control. This was absolutely necessary for the mission to succeed with a minimum of losses due to planes running into each other as they converged upon the target area before arriving in an area that would be illuminated by searchlights and fires. Each squadron in every group participating was assigned certain altitudes. All planes would have enough fuel to make the round trip, but no deviations could be made to or from the target. The navigator and flight engineer would be responsible for spotting any changes in the flight plan. The radar operator would assist the navigator in picking up known landmarks, such as the small islands along the flight path. He was also responsible for monitoring his set and letting the pilots know if blips other than known objects showed up on his screen, indicating that the plane might be on a collision course with another plane in the area.

The decision to use firebombs on Tokyo was made in Washington, but the low-level altitude, over the targets, was LeMay's own decision. According to some of the better known "history-watchers," that decision was one of seven of the most important decisions made by field commanders in World War II that changed the course of the war and had a great effect on bringing it to an end.

Some of the US military leaders, including Chester Nimitz, were against using incendiary bombs on urban areas. Some considered it morally wrong to kill civilians, especially women and children. Others thought that burning down wooden shacks would not win the war, that industries had to be destroyed before any war could be won.

When LeMay first revealed his plans for the fire raids on all major cities of Japan, his staff couldn't believe he was serious. His experts argued their points against his proposals, and each time, the general had a convincing answer for why his plan would work. Why would he take such

*Bulldozer operators, building North Field at Tinian Island, wave at a flight of B-29s from Saipan as they pass in salute.* Josh Curtis

an unnecessary risk, he was asked, in removing all the guns on this mission? LeMay's answer: According to intelligence reports, there were only two night fighter groups in all four of the main Japanese home islands, so the risk that they could effectively attack a steady stream of B-29s flying over the city would be minimal.

With the B-29s flying at such a low altitude, some thought, the automatic antiaircraft guns would have a field day shooting them down. LeMay's answer: According to Intelligence reports, only two B-29s had been lost to antiaircraft guns. Unlike the German antiaircraft weapons, which were manipulated by radar, the Japanese guns were fired in conjunc-

tion with searchlights and were not controlled automatically by radar, thus allowing a wide range of inaccuracy in hitting fast-moving B-29 targets. Therefore, the general said, the risk of losing large numbers of our planes to Japanese antiaircraft guns would be unlikely.

Also of some concern was the matter of spacing the planes. The B-29s would take off from the three different islands, and planners hoped to get the planes over the target in the shortest time possible. Since the newly arrived 314th BW was located about 125mi south of Saipan and Tinian Island, they would be the first to leave the ground. Calculators determined they should begin their takeoff about 45–50min ahead of the attacking forces on Saipan and Tinian Island.

A takeoff policy had long since been determined for the B-29s participating in bombing missions. It would take a heavily loaded airplane about 1min, after applying power, to begin

the takeoff roll to reach the "point of no return," or near the end of the 8,800ft runways, where there would be no chance of safely aborting the takeoff. A flagman would signal the next plane to begin rolling. During a mission, at either of the bases in the Marianas, a B-29 on each runway would leave the ground at 1min intervals. Each of the bases had two parallel runways, and takeoff rolls were staggered at 30sec intervals, which meant that two planes were leaving the ground each minute.

LeMay didn't see the bombing of urban areas in the Japanese cities as unethical or immoral. It was a known fact, he said, that much of the Japanese industries' war effort took place in the homes of the Japanese people. Therefore, if the goal was to completely destroy Japan's industrial ability to continue the war, this aspect of their production would have to be destroyed also. The American people were also, by now, familiar with the fate of our

*Destiny's Tot was assigned to Capt. William Wienert's crew of the 9th BG, Tinian Island.* Larry Smith

prisoners of war in Japanese POW camps, and sought retribution.

The maximum payload of forty M-69 incendiary bombs was cased in clusters weighing 500lb each. Each B-29, loaded with bombs and fuel, would register a gross weight of up to 140,000lb. On the Tokyo raid, each plane would average only about 6 tons of bombs, or almost 12,000lb of incendiaries.

Metal straps contained the incendiary bomb clusters, and the straps were fused to break at a pre-determined height above the ground, causing the small, individual bombs to scatter over a large area. One maximum load of clusters would cover an area up to 0.5mi wide and about 1.5mi long. The jellied substance in the bombs would ignite upon impact, and the fire was very difficult to extinguish. Water would spread the fire rather than douse it.

LeMay designated Gen. Thomas S. Power his spotter over Tokyo that night. After leading his 314th BW on the mission, he would drop his bombs and then climb to 10,000ft or above, and send reports back to Guam on how the raid was progressing.

## Sea of Flames Erupts in Tokyo

March 9, 1945, finally arrived. This would be the day of reckoning for LeMay's low-level advocates of fire-bombing urban areas in Tokyo. Late in the afternoon, crews at Saipan and Tinian Island were ready to climb aboard their B-29s. LeMay stood by at North Field, Guam, to watch General Power lead the 314th BW crews on the most daring B-29 mission ever undertaken, to Japan. He would be carrying M-47 incendiaries, as would a few of the other leaders, but the main strike force would unload the napalm M-69 incendiaries.

It was a few minutes after 6:00pm when this author and crewmates cranked up our Superfortress, newly named *Mary Ann* in honor of our

*One of the nights Toyama burned.* Chuck Spieth

*A close-up of the incendiary 500lb cluster, before the tail fin is attached. Straps around the cluster could be fused to break at varied altitudes above ground, which scattered the 37lb napalm incendiary bombs.* Hurth Thompkins

ground crew chief's daughter born since her dad left the States for Saipan, and prepared to taxi out to takeoff position. Since our hardstand was located near the eastern end of the runway and there was a prevailing easterly wind on Saipan, we had to use up lots of gas to get to the western end of the takeoff strip. There was nothing we could do about the long taxi ride to takeoff position, but on this particular afternoon the thought did cross my mind, *What if we should need this gas we're having to waste to get back to Isley Field tomorrow morning?*

We waved at the line of chaplains lined up near the point where we turned onto the runway, and they were waving at each plane and wishing us well on the mission. The takeoff was normal. Crossing the overrun above the Magicienne Bay, we leveled out just above the water and held our northeasterly course about 5min, and then when we passed Kagman Point, we began turning in a northerly direction toward Tokyo. The trip up was uneventful. Intercom conversation was

subdued, and about all conversation that took place, other than normal business from the navigator telling us to make corrections, was the excitement generated by the beautiful setting sun on our left. There were only a few clouds and they seemed to dance around the beautiful reddish glow of the sun.

Our flight route to Tokyo this night carried us very close to Iwo Jima, and the fighting taking place down below telegraphed a message to us that the struggle for the island was not yet over, and people were still dying down there.

With each mission to Japan, the same ugly feeling seemed to rear its head after passing Iwo Jima: Would our luck hold one more time? Maybe when the Marines finally capture the island, I thought, it will pass away, but on this mission, the feeling was still there. To me, the feeling moved to another level, and precautions became more important, because now we were approaching closer and closer to the front door of the enemy.

An hour or so after passing Iwo Jima, we entered the now-familiar weather front that seemed to linger somewhere along the line between Iwo Jima and Japan. We were flying at about 2,000ft altitude, but decided to get down a little lower to prevent the possibility of colliding with another B-29 on the way to Tokyo. Our powerful R-3350 engines continued their monotonous roar that let us know that all was well so far.

Finally, our navigator, Jim O'Donnel, asked for a small correction and said it was time to start our climb to our bombing altitude. This was a crucial part of the trip up to the target. We were ordered to fly with our navigational lights off when north of Iwo Jima because of the possibility of there being Japanese ships below to take shots at us. You'd have to be very close to another ship in the soup, anyway, before you could see it, so we were climbing through zero-visibility weather and having to rely on the radar operator to warn us if we were on a collision course with another B-29. Finally, at about 5,000ft, we broke out of the clouds and looked upon one of the most horrifying scenes we had ever witnessed. We were still 50mi or so from landfall, and we could see the fires in Tokyo. Scanning searchlights filled the sky, trying to pick up approaching B-29s. We saw our first B-29 as we came closer to the searchlights. It was a strange feeling to see a few of our planes caught in the lights; you could tell they were being fired on because of the tracer bullets going up to them. We knew that several hundred B-29s should be all around us. Since we were in about the middle of the bomber stream, those nearest us were merging into the same route as our drop zone. How had we missed hitting a plane while climbing in that weather front? Now as we neared what seemed a fiery holocaust, we didn't have time to dwell on what might happen. It was time now to exert all our energy in trying to survive. We donned our dark glasses to try to avoid being blinded if caught in the searchlights. We noticed two B-29s were caught in the lights. When one light would get locked on, other lights would scan over to also lock on, and then they sent up barrages of flak. A B-29 caught in four or five searchlights is a beautiful but horrifying sight. You knew that its crew could be shot out of the sky any minute, but the beautiful silver B-29 gleamed a ghostly white, and you prayed that the people inside would make it through another minute or two.

For awhile, we flew parallel between the two B-29s caught in the searchlights, and lucky for us, all lights in the area were concentrating on those two to give gunners on the ground more time to shoot them down. Finally, we were caught in a fast-moving beam which, after scanning past us, switched back and caught us. It was brighter than daylight. We finally escaped the lights, but a much tougher chore lay ahead. By this time, we were passing over some of the area where the fire was beginning to meet and become a conflagration. Looking down into the streets of Tokyo, you could see flames coming from house windows, and the smell of burning debris was bad, but as we moved on further and opened our bomb bays, we were sickened by the sweet smell of burning human flesh. It was nauseating; I missed

at least two meals before I could eat anything again.

As we dropped our bombs and started to turn to get out of the smoke and flames reaching up to more than 10,000ft by this time, we hit a wind shear. We were lucky. We flew directly into a strong updraft heat thermal that had a G-force stronger than anything I had witnessed in my flying career. We were sucked up like a feather at a tremendous speed. Commander Cox and I both were completely demobilized. We were pinned to our seats, and it was impossible to lift an arm to control the airplane. Within seconds, it turned us loose, and we had gained more than 5,000ft almost instantly. If we had not hit the thermal head-on, we would have experienced what some other crews did in this and other incendiary raids. Several crews who sur-

*T. N. Teeny II was assigned to the Capt. Wendell Hutchison crew of the 1st BS, 9th BG, Tinian Island.* Larry Smith

vived the experience simply were flipped over on their back, but were lucky enough to get their plane under control before diving into the ground, one of the wings catching in the updraft and flipped the plane over.

For more than 2hr, the B-29s dropped bombs on one of the world's largest cities, and the results of that raid were so successful that there was never another word said about the B-29s not living up to their potential in the Pacific.

General Norstad had come to the Marianas to see how things were going at LeMay's 21st BC headquarters at Guam. After he was briefed on the up-

*Daylight raid on Osaka, June 1, 1945. Note that the fires are beginning to spread.* Chuck Spieth

*A ten-plane flight of Superfortresses from the 29th BG, Guam, heads north.* Andy Doty

coming fire raid on Tokyo, scheduled to take place March 9–10, he sent word back to Washington to stand by for word from an outstanding show. When the news about the most successful mission yet performed by the B-29s was released, nobody in Washington had a broader smile than General Arnold. His deep-rooted faith in the plane was now vindicated.

The fires started by the B-29s that night in Tokyo, aided by a 75mph wind, destroyed more than 16sq-mi of the city. Totally demolished were almost 25 percent of all buildings in Tokyo, or more than 267,171 structures. To the B-29 crews that witnessed the events unfolding below them, it was as described as "a nightmare out of Dante's inferno." Tokyo officials estimated that 83,783 people were killed outright, more than would die in the Hiroshima and Nagasaki atomic blasts later. At least 50,000 more were injured in the holocaust and the homes of more than 1,000,000 Tokyo residents were destroyed.

LeMay remained at his headquarters until he received the coded messages from General Powers, who was observing the massive inferno as it developed. The messages were transmitted over 2–3hr as a continuous stream of Superfortresses added their bomb loads on the city. Powers described the raid and its obvious results to LeMay while circling over the area until the last plane departed for its home base.

Raymond ("Hap") Halloran, navigator on the Snuffy Smith crew, had been a prisoner of war since his plane was shot down over Tokyo on January 27, 1945, when the B-29 Superfortresses swooped in over the city at low altitude and dropped their payloads. Halloran, along with some other POWs, was in solitary confinement, in what he called a horse stall, about 5ft wide and 8ft long. Located at the military police compound called Kempai Tai, he was about two or three blocks from the Imperial Palace. Hap recalls some of his thoughts that night: "An antiaircraft gun emplacement was located nearby, and when it was fired, the ground shook. I had often wondered if the guns were shooting down some of my friends, or if the B-29s were really doing much damage when they came over. No bombs had, so far,

fallen near our compound, and of course I had no way of judging.

"Sometime after midnight, I guessed, I was awakened by loud shouts and screaming coming, evidently, from people in the streets outside the compound. As I lay there in my darkened cell, I finally realized an air raid was in progress. I then began hearing the roar of airplanes that seemed to be directly over us at very low altitude. I couldn't imagine what the hell was happening. At first I thought the planes were Japanese, but soon I could recognize the roar that sounded mighty familiar—that of a B-29. It seemed they were coming over, sporadically, every minute or two. Near the ceiling of my cell was a small

opening, the only one in the room, and when I stood up I could see a huge orange glow from fires nearby.

"The frightening shouts and crying continued till late in the morning before dawn as more planes continued to come over. The fires spread rapidly, I was told, aided by a hurricane-force wind, and the resulting inferno looked as if the whole universe was on fire.

"I was suddenly seized with the terrifying thought that I might be burned to death. As the night wore on, and the loud commotion outside the compound continued, I had a fear that the frightened civilians might storm the compound and kill all of us POWs. But beneath the fears for my personal safety, I had a comforting feeling that

*Nip Clipper assigned to the Capt. M. I. Ashland crew, 9th BG, Tinian Island. This aircraft was shot down August 8, 1945, during a daylight raid on Yawata, Japan. The* Clipper *was being flown by the Carl Holden crew that day, and ten of the eleven men on board were taken prisoner by the Japanese. The eleventh crew member was never recovered from sea. Larry Smith*

our B-29 boys were getting the job done, and if they could keep this up, the war would soon be over.

"A guard told me the next morning that there was talk that the prisoners may be shot because of the many civilian deaths caused by the B-29s' attacks on the city. That, of course, was not a comforting thought."

## Chapter 12

# Preparing for the Knockout Blow

Bolstered by the outstanding success of the March 10 incendiary raid on Tokyo, General LeMay's 21st BC in the Mariana Islands served notice to the military leaders, but also to the Japanese people in the streets of their cities.

In rapid-fire succession, the three wings of Superfortresses from Saipan, Tinian Island, and Guam carried out incendiary raids on Nagoya, Osaka, and Kobe, all important industrial cities and considered major contributors to the Japanese war effort. During the fourteen-day maximum-effort attacks, the six missions, including the Tokyo raid of March 10, 1,729 B-29s took part. They dropped a combined total of 10,858 tons—23,887,600lb—of incendiary clusters on urban areas of the cities. The missions, each carried out at night and flying individually en route to and over the targets, were flown at altitudes ranging from a low of 4,000ft to a maximum of 9,800ft. Twenty-six Superfortresses were lost during the six missions, fourteen of them in the March 9–10 Tokyo raid.

*A flight of B-29s from the 498th BG at Saipan practices formation flying near the coast of Saipan. The gun barrels were often removed for low-level fire raids, but guns and gunners were carried on most regular bombing missions. 73rd BW Photo/Harold Dreeze*

During this blitz, Tokyo, Osaka, and Kobe were hit only once, while three strikes were made on Nagoya, one of the most heavily saturated industrial cities. Adding up the results of the six strikes, LeMay was assured that the gamble he had taken paid off. The B-29s had fewer mechanical mishaps during the low-altitude attacks, and they had completely destroyed 32sq-mi in four of Japan's greatest cities.

After the six incendiary raids, LeMay received a message from General Arnold, requesting that he relay a message to all three wing commanders. He also instructed that the message be read to all combat crews. The message: "The series of five major strikes which you have performed in fewer than ten days constitute an impressive achievement, reflecting the spirit of your crews, but equally the determinations and the devotion to duty of your ground personnel. Every member of your command is to be commended for his vital share in this superior accomplishment. This is a significant sample of what the Jap can expect in the future. Good luck and good bombing." Arnold's message related to the five incendiary raids preceding the March 9–10 Tokyo fire raid.

That message was a real morale booster, but some of us thought that the many people working in the factories back in the States, building and testing the B-29, should also receive some of the accolades. The Superfortress had now developed into a real workhorse, manned by more confident crews that were getting results.

Nowhere was this more clear than on Iwo Jima. Two weeks after that island was invaded, the first B-29 landed for fuel and repairs, before taking off amidst fanatic fighting to return to its base in the Marianas. Lieutenant Malo and crew of the 9th BG, at Tinian Island, had trouble with fuel transfer over Japan, and because of this and other damage sustained, were faced with the choice of either trying to land on a small fighter strip near the southern tip of the island adjacent to Mount Suribachi or ditch in the ocean. Malo decided to try landing on the volcanic-ash 4,000ft runway. Like all Superfort pilots, he was used to landing on 8,000ft or longer runways, and he thought the outcome might be somewhat doubtful.

The control tower told Malo about the obstructions and fighting going on around the runway. He landed safely, made a few repairs, added enough fuel to get back to Tinian Island, and took off—becoming the first B-29 to land at Iwo Jima. This crew's luck ran out before the end of the war, however. On another mission to Japan, they were shot down and killed.

After Malo's successful stop at Iwo Jima, all crews in the Marianas were warned not to attempt a landing there

Capt. Louis J. Whitten and crew, flying Twentieth Century Sweetheart, *dropped supplies on a POW camp in Shanghai on September 7, 1945.* Josh Curtis

*Lt. Frank Carrico and his crew of the 882nd BS, 500th BG, flying* Pride of the Yankees *on a mission to Tokyo, were attacked by Japanese fighters. The no. 2 engine was riddled by gunfire and immediately caught fire. Luckily, the engines prop ran away, blowing the fire out. Four more attacks disabled the no. 1 engine, but the aircraft flew on, all the way to Saipan, a distance of 1,500mi over water. The odds of making it back such a distance with two engines out on the same side are incredibly low, but the* Pride of the Yankees *accomplished this feat twice. The second time the* Pride *lost engines no. 1 and 2 over Tokyo (May 25, 1945), the crew decided to land on Iwo Jima. When they arrived over Iwo, the whole area was fogged in, so the crew headed to Saipan, where they landed several hours later.* Hurth Thompkins

unless theirs was an extreme emergency. For the next two weeks before the island was secured, a small number did land there, including this author and his crew.

Weather forecasting continued to give mission planners major problems. Neither the Russians nor Chinese would help LeMay collect weather data from that part of the world to make reliable forecasts for upcoming weather over the Japanese home islands. Consequently, there was no way to determine weather over a given target 24hr before a scheduled mission.

Finally, a small weather-observer unit composed of eight trained observers and forecasters, called "The Fightin' 55th," was sent to the Marianas to work with the 21st BC. These men, including Jack C. Grantham and

"Ham" Howard, came up with the idea of sending combat crew-manned B-29s, with one of the weathermen aboard with his instruments and equipment, to Japan to send a report back before or while a mission was being planned. Other unit members included Ed Everts, Al Louchard, Bob Moore, Juke Nielson, and Dick Worthen. This worked out very well.

Targets were selected according to good weather advantages. Finally, "weather ships" became a major part of scheduled missions, with up to three weather plane trips to and from the selected target area to forecast weather for the upcoming strike. These planes usually flew across the main island of Honshu, if the mission was to take place anywhere in that vicinity, and from one end to the other, and even west of the island sometimes to check weather in the Sea of Japan. These weather missions culminated at command headquarters at Guam, where the weather observer made his report.

My first "weather strike" and a brush with history on Iwo Jima came during the maximum-effort fire raids in March. We were scheduled to take off before dawn on March 16, fly to Japan, cross Honshu, and generally check the weather conditions all over the island. A weather observer was with us. Altitude was to be 30,000ft over Japan, but as we neared the coastline of Honshu, we experienced a few backfires on one of the engines. Flight engineer John Huckins checked the oil and recommended we not climb any further since oil pressure was not

what it should be. The skies over Japan looked peaceful and almost clear, so rather than continue to climb above the 26,000ft we had already reached, we remained at that level. We felt it was more or less imperative to make a stab at crossing Honshu and send back weather conditions for the scheduled incendiary strike that night on Kobe, so we proceeded across the mountains just north of Mount Fuji. As we made our turn to set a heading to return home, Huckins announced that the oil pressure in the ailing engine had dropped to near zero, so Commander John Cox told him to feather the engine. Crossing over a peaceful-looking bay near the coastline on our return route, we began getting fire from a large destroyer which we had not seen down below. As this was happening, Huckins made another startling announcement: The oil pressure in another engine was beginning to falter. We'd soon be flying with only two engines.

We were flying on a wing and a prayer, and with two engines out, it was difficult to maintain altitude all the way from Japan. We had made a decision, and had set our heading for Iwo Jima. Hopefully, we could make an emergency landing there, and avoid having to ditch our plane in the ferocious Pacific Ocean. Our base at Saipan was still hundreds of miles away. The date: March 16, 1945.

As we neared the gourd-shaped 7mi-long piece of volcanic no-man's land, we could see the fighting taking place with smoke and flashes from artillery guns covering a big part of the northern sector. We called Hotrocks tower for a straight-in approach to the short fighter strip near the base of Mount Suribachi on the southern tip of the island. There was no way to land on a runway under construction on the plateau just north of the fighter strip. The scene throughout the island was one of desolation, and on our descent, the closer we got to the landing strip, the sulfuric stench, mixed with a sweet smell of death, seemed to seep into our cockpit. We landed safely after skidding all the way down the soft volcanic-ash runway. A crowd of Marines, looking as if they were fresh out of the trenches or fox holes, came over to look at our giant Superfortress and chat with us. They tried to make us feel like heroes, but we responded with, "Not us. You fellows are the heroes!" We had to stay over for engine repairs, and that is how I got a real brush with history. On Saipan, the climate is tropical, never cold, but at Iwo Jima it was a different story the night of March 16, 1945. I was not quite sure if I shivered because I was cold or if it was fright.

The Star shells kept the whole island lit up throughout the night, and when dawn finally came, we were told the Island commander had declared Iwo Jima secure. "Secure, hell!" we said, "Those bullets are still flying and people are still dying." But the morning of March 17 went down in history as the date our Marines captured Iwo Jima. Now for almost half a century since that date, like more than 20,000 other B-29 flyers who made emergency landings on Iwo Jima, I still pause periodically and utter an almost-silent prayer: "Thank God for the Marines and Iwo Jima!"

The massive six-mission firebomb blitz depleted the M-69 incendiary bomb supply, but there would be no let-up in attacks against Japan. Now that Iwo Jima had been captured, it was rapidly being turned into a major air base capable of handling large numbers of B-29s low on fuel returning from regular strategic bombing missions. Also, the P-51s were being moved up to Iwo Jima and would shortly begin escorting the Super-

*The 500th BG's Big Z Superfortress shower incendiary clusters on a target below.* 73rd BW Photo/Harold Dreeze

*Lt. Chuck Spieth and crew pose in front of their B-29 while ground crew men inspect the no. 2 engine.* Chuck Spieth

*Bugger of the 331st BG, 315th BW, has varied mission markers. The parachuting symbol indicates that the crew flew a POW supply drop after the war. The loaded donkey symbol probably indicated that the crew made a forced landing and had to use every method available to get back to base.* George Harrington/Josh Curtis

fortresses over Japan and making further attacks on airfields, shipyards, and other targets before joining up with a B-29 "mother ship" to escort them on the 700mi flight back to Iwo Jima. There would be no let up while awaiting for the incendiary bomb supply to be replenished.

The second phase of the attack on the Japanese homeland began as March wound down. The promised aerial mining of harbors and ports around the home islands was about to begin. As far back as January 1945, Admiral Nimitz tried to persuade General LeMay to start the aerial mining and keep it going continuously, but LeMay insisted and General Arnold agreed that the 20th AF had to get on with its primary responsibility of destroying selected industrial targets. LeMay said that when more B-29s joined the attack, he would begin the mining project, but not until the last of March or April.

The Navy assigned a detachment of mining warfare experts, headed by Cdr. Ellis A. Johnston, to the 21st BC, with orders to instruct the B-29 crews in aerial mining. The 313th BW was assigned the task of delivering the mines to the many harbors and straits in and around all of Japan's main islands, plus some harbors in Korea. This phase was to be known as Operation Starvation. The 58th BW had carried out some very successful mining missions at Singapore, Saigon, Johore Straits, and other targets, before winding down its CBI operation at the end of March. The 58th BWs' last mining mission was a thirty-three–plane strike against the Port of Singapore on March 28–29.

On March 27, the 313th BW sent 102 B-29s on their initial mining drop on Shimonoseki Straits. Flying at altitudes of 5,000–8,000ft, they dropped 571 tons of aerial mines, some with fuses delayed, to explode when ships passed over. On March 30–31, the 313th went back to the same target. Included this time were ninety-four B-29s carrying 513 tons of mines. The 314th BW sent one of its groups, the 19th, back to Nagoya with all-purpose bombs.

As the aerial mining project was getting underway, Nimitz made another urgent request to LeMay for more help from the B-29s. The Navy had experienced a few suicidal attacks by Japanese fighters during the Philippine operation. The invasion of Okinawa was scheduled to begin April 1, and Nimitz asked LeMay to attack the airfields on Kyushu Island, where he thought the suicide missions would be launched from ships and invasion forces just a little over 300mi south of those fields.

LeMay was again reluctant to change courses in his planned attacks, especially since he thought the Japanese were reeling from the effects of his latest major attacks. He did agree to send his Superfortresses to attack the airfields on Kyushu. On March 31, he sent the 73rd and 314th BWs to bomb airfields while the 313th BW dropped mines in Shimonoseki Straits.

The invasion of Okinawa took place on Easter morning, and the B-29 attack on Kyushu seemed to have been effective. For the next four or five days, the Japanese kamikaze planes stayed away. Then things changed drastically. On April 6, they came in force. Japanese bombers attacked the invaders on land and more than 300 kamikaze pilots began diving into the ships off shore. Admiral Nimitz called for more help with the airfields, and on April 8, General LeMay's B-29s struck six Kyushu airfields. For a short time again, the kamikazes didn't come, but for three weeks, LeMay had to divert his attacks from scheduled targets to the airfields on Kyushu.

On April 7, the 73rd BW went back to Tokyo. This time it would be different. For the first time since the beginning of the B-29 assault on Japan, we would have escort service from the now operative 7th Fighter Command's P-51s off Iwo Jima. This would be a daylight mission going in at the unusually low altitude of 11,000–15,650ft. All four groups would rendezvous just off the coast of Japan, at bombing altitudes. We had orders to circle until all planes assembled by groups, and by then, if the P-51s had not arrived to form a protective umbrella over us, we were to make three more big circles before going in without them. Shortly after starting our second circle, we saw the specks approaching, and as they came to us and positioned themselves in battle formation, I thought that was the most beautiful sight I had ever witnessed: 121 B-29s heading toward their target with about fifty P-51s hovering above them.

As we neared the coastline, I glanced down and saw a twin-engine Japanese fighter climbing up to attack us. The P-51 pilots directly above our plane saw him also, and two P-51s dove straight down across our nose and shot the plane down. Two parachutes appeared before we got out of sight. Capts. Robert T. Down and Richard H. Hintermeier, the two P-51 pilots who attacked the Japanese plane, were credited with shooting down the first Japanese plane, flying land-based American fighter planes, over the Japanese home islands.

Iwo Jima became a beehive of activity after the P-51s moved in; they and the P-61 Black Widows left temporary quarters at Saipan to help locate lost B-29s. The new occupants were trying to make the place livable, even though the many caves that had been bull-dozed shut contained dead bodies.

Soon after Iwo Jima was captured and the tally had been totaled up, word got back to Saipan that some of the statisticians in Washington wondered if the price paid for capturing such a small piece of rock was worth it. The numbers were indeed impressive: When the fighting ended in March 1945, more than 6,800 American Marines had paid the supreme sacrifice, and more than 19,000 were wounded. Only 1,000 of the estimated 21,000 Japanese soldiers defending the island were taken prisoner. The rest died.

Everyone who set foot on Iwo Jima called the volcanic ash-covered piece of no-man's land a "hell on earth."

Maj. Harry C. Crim, commander of one of the P-51 squadrons sent to escort B-29s over the targets in Japan, describes the locale best: "Iwo Jima was perhaps one of the most hostile ground environments a person could find himself in. Dante, in his visions of Hell, could have used Iwo for a model. Nature provided an active volcano, and men provided the war."

As soon as Iwo Jima was made ready to accept B-29s in trouble on a regular basis, a detachment of aircraft mechanics was sent to service the planes that needed fuel or repair. The only trouble was that most of the men sent had received no training on B-29s. As the number of landings increased, the B-29s stacked up to the extent that parking space became a premium. Somebody finally came up with a solution: One experienced me-chanic from each squadron operating from the Marianas, twenty in all, were sent to Iwo Jima to straighten out this tangled mess and to organize an efficient operation. Each mechanic was a specialist in a given field—hydraulics, electrical systems, instruments, and engines. At first, they thought their tour of duty on Iwo Jima would be a short one, but they were sadly mistaken. They all were there when the war ended six months later.

One of these specialists was Allen Hassell, an engine mechanic. He recalls how shocked he and others were when they landed on what he called a "hell on earth": "I am in total agreement with Major Crim's assessment of Iwo Jima being the most hostile ground environment a person could find himself in. The first thing we saw after debarking from the plane that brought us to such a godforsaken place was the steam escaping from the ground all around us. My first thoughts were, *Gosh! The ground is on fire!* The stench from the escaping sulfur fumes made the place smell like a rotten-egg dump. When the truck came to pick us up and carry us to our living area, I got another rude awakening about our new abode. I jumped into the cab with the driver, thinking maybe I could get some 'inside poop' from him. Our conversation went something like this:

"'Do they have any showers around here?'

"'Showers?' he replied, 'I wake up every morning with my eyelids stuck together!'

"'How's the food?'

"'Ha! Ha! Rotten!'

"That conversation served notice that we were in for many more surprises before we settled down to a workable routine. Living conditions, however, never did improve much! When I returned to Saipan, after the Japs threw in the towel, most of my old friends had long since rotated back to the States. But I had lived a part of the war that I could truthfully tell people who listened and who may express some doubts that I had truly 'served in hell on earth and came back!'"

## Chapter 13

# Build-up for Countdown

The fighting in and around Okinawa by the second week in April 1945 was not progressing very well. The kamikaze planes were still giving the Navy ships a bad time and the Japanese soldiers were putting up a strong defense against the US Army units. As expected, rumor had the B-29s scheduled for a major strike at Okinawa, in support of the fighting there.

There must have been something to the latest rumors, because this author's crew was selected to fly a weather strike to Okinawa, with a weather observer aboard to check the weather for an upcoming major strike there. This would be our second "easy" mission. Some of the crews called weather missions "milk runs," even though they were exposed to the full force of the enemy alone over his territory. We believed scuttlebutt about weather strikes being easy until we had our brush with history at Iwo Jima on March 16–17. This mission, however, would be routine, we were almost certain. We knew the Navy's 58th Task Force was off the coast of Okinawa, and what better protection could we have with all that power on our side?

The flight to our turn-around point, just off the coast of Okinawa,

Twentieth Century Fox *flew with the 501st BG, 315th BW, Guam.* Josh Curtis

was very boring. At 30,000ft, we felt secure against enemy fighter attacks, so we let our guard down. If there ever was a relaxed crew on a combat mission in enemy territory, it was our entire crew that day. On homeward-bound flights, John Sutherland, our tail gunner, would crawl through the tunnel and, after giving the front-end troops the news of what was going in the rear of the plane, would lay between commander John Cox and me and watch the auto-pilot for us. He was pretty good at keeping the indicator lights on the instrument out, which means the plane is flying straight and level when no light is bleeping.

I'm sure we need not worry about a court-martial at this late date, so now it can be told. I can swear to it that every man aboard our plane went to sleep, including the weather observer and our tail gunner, who was the only man supposedly watching the controls of the aircraft at that time.

No one knew how long we remained asleep, but we all suddenly had a rude awakening. Kendal Chance, our central fire control gunner, was the first to shout the alarm that we were being attacked by bogies. But his warnings were ineffective, since four bogies dived down across our nose, and we suddenly had a sinking feeling that we were about to get our ticket punched.

All I could say was, "What the hell!"

Cox came alive and yelled, "Check the back-end and see if the gunners have the gun sights on."

It's too bad if you go into battle with your gun sights off, because it takes a few minutes for them to warm up before becoming operative to fire the guns. No! The guns had not been turned on, so there we were like a ship dead in the water.

Our "secure" position at 30,000ft above a solid overcast didn't seem "secure" anymore. By this time, the bogies were coming in for another attack. But, by this time, also, the whole crew was alert, and the sleepiness had been wiped from our eyes—and some sharp aircraft identification expert on the crew yelled over the intercom, "Oh, heck! They're US Marine planes."

One of the pilots pulled right up under our wing and made an attempt at hand-signaling to us. I signaled to him that I was turning our radio to the frequency he was supposed to be on, and so we made contact. The first thing I heard him say was, "Texas base, we have found the 'bogie' and have identified it as a 'friendly monster'."

He went on to tell me that our IFF (Identification Friend or Foe) was inoperative, and that we were showing up on "Texas Base," his aircraft carrier below, as a bogie. "You better get out

*The* City of Memphis *screeched in amid a stream of smoke. Handwerker and crew flew with the 19th BG, 314th BW, at Guam.* Jim Handwerker

*Aircraft commander Jim Handwerker, center, standing, and crew brought the* City of Memphis *all the way from Tokyo to Guam the night of April 1, 1945, after two engines on the same side were lost over the target. Handwerker was awarded the Silver Star.* Jim Handwerker

of the area as fast as you can. We have the whole 58th Task Force around here."

"For God's sake, be sure and emphasize that we are extremely friendly. How about you fellows staying with us awhile to keep them from shooting us down?"

We had a very friendly visit with the Marine pilots, and they stayed with us about 30min to "protect" us from our own Navy ships below.

Bombing strategy took on a new look in April. Multi-wing mass raids to a single target gave way to fewer planes involved in some of the raids. The 73rd BW usually sent out all four of its groups on a strike, but the 313th and 314th scheduled their attacks in squadron and group flights to a single target. Almost daily, B-29s roamed the skies over Japan, especially after beginning the attack on airfields on Kyushu.

Two three-wing attacks took place during April 13–14 when 348 B-29s dropped 2,124 tons of incendiary bomb clusters on Tokyo arsenal from altitudes of 6,000–11,000ft. Seven Superfortresses were lost that night. The night of April 15, the 313th and the 314th BWs dropped 1,110 tons of incendiaries on the urban area of Kawasaki, a city just south of Tokyo. Twelve B-29s were lost that night.

While joining in the attacks on the airfields on Kyushu, at times the 313th continued mine-laying flights. Twice during the month, they mined the port at Hiroshima, and twice they dropped mines in Shimonoseki Straits.

On April 12, General O'Donnell's 73rd BW was scheduled to try once again to knock out the illusive target no. 357, the Musashino Engine Factory at Tokyo; 114 B-29s were scheduled to participate. Again, the P-51s off Iwo Jima would escort the B-29s on this mission. Both the 313th BW, with eighty-two planes scheduled, and the 314th BW, with eighty-five B-29s, were scheduled to hit a chemical plant at Koriyama, about 125mi north of Tokyo.

Action during the daylight raid on Koriyama would result in the first and

only Medal of Honor to a B-29 combat crew member of the 20th AF in World War II. The recipient of the award Sgt. Henry E. ("Red") Erwin, the radio operator on Capt. George A. Simeral's crew of the 52nd BS, 29th BG, 314th BW.

Captain Simeral was a flight leader, and on this particular mission, his flight would be leading the squadron, with the squadron commander, Lt. Col. Eugene Strouse, in the right seat. Simeral remembers the incident vividly: "We arrived over Aoga Shima, our rendezvous area, and began to fly the prescribed pattern to pick up the formation. I motioned for Erwin to fire some flares and then a smoke bomb to attract the attention of our other aircraft in the area and to identify us as the lead plane.

"The flares dropped through the tube without incident, but when Erwin pulled the pin on the phosphorous flare, it malfunctioned and exploded, blowing particles of phosphorous into his eyes and burning off most of his right ear, part of his nose, and most of the skin from his right arm. Patches of skin were seared from his face. Red said afterwards that he felt no pain at the time, but knew he had to get the flare out of the plane.

"The forward section of the plane filled with dense white smoke and became so thick that I could not see my instrument panel. We were at 1,000ft

*An unusual shot of Mount Fuji in Japan, looking out over the left wing and engines of a B-29 en route to its target in Tokyo.* Kelcie Teague

and fortunately on auto-pilot, except for the elevators. My biggest concern was to avoid placing too much pressure on the control column and causing us to stall, which would have been fatal at that low an altitude.

"In the meantime, Red had packed up the burning phosphorous bomb and crawled with it toward the cockpit. He went past the navigator, who was in the tunnel observing through his blister, unlatched the navigator's table from the gun turret, and lurched toward the co-pilot, shouting for him to open the window.

"With superhuman effort, he raised himself up in front of Colonel Strouse and threw the burning bomb out the window."

On April 19, 1945, at the hospital at Guam, Maj. Gen. Willis H. Hale, commanding general of the Army Air Forces, Pacific Ocean Area, presented Sergeant Erwin, with the Medal of Honor. Standing in the room by his bed were Maj. Gen. Curtis E. LeMay, and Brig. Gen. Thomas Power, Erwin's wing commander. Also present were squadron commanders of the 29th BG and the crew of his B-29. Erwin's gallantry and heroism, above and beyond the call of duty, saved the lives of his comrades.

## Balls of Fire

In his foreword to the 9th BG's *War Journal*, commanding officer Col.

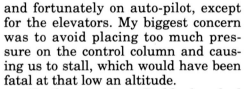

*Brig. Gen. Thomas Power, commander of the 314th BW, Guam, had his personal B-29 dressed up with all the flight and service groups painted on, showing their records.* Kelcie Teague

Henry C. Huglin said of the 2,500 men in his group: "...[They] were forged in the crucible of war into a brilliantly smooth-working team whose accomplishments will forever be indelibly inscribed in the war annals of the United States as a glowing tribute to themselves and to their country."

As one of the four groups that made up the 313th BW, the 9th BG took part in the aerial mining of the home ports of Japan, as well as many of the incendiary fire raids. The *War Journal* had this recorded account about the group's incendiary attacks: "April 13–14, 1945—With today's effort, we resumed our incendiary attacks against Japan's major cities. Our target was the Tokyo Arsenal area. We had another perfect score, with twenty-eight aircraft scheduled, twenty-eight airborne, twenty-eight striking the primary, and twenty-eight returning safely to base. Sixteen fighter attacks were made and antiaircraft fire was moderate to intense. This mission was one of our most successful and resulted in destruction of approximately 11 sq-mi of the city. April 15–16, 1945—Swiftly we followed up our sec-

ond big raid on Tokyo with a blow the next night, at the adjoining city of Kawasaki. This was our toughest, as well as our costliest, mission. Over fifty enemy aircraft were encountered. Approximately a dozen 'Balls of Fire' were sighted by our crews. With over 300 aircraft going over the target, the danger of mid-air collision was ever-present. The antiaircraft fire was both accurate and intense. We were in it longer, too. Heat thermals, one of the serious perils on these raids, were unusually severe. There were thirteen aircraft lost in the Bomber Command. Four of them were ours."

The fire raids on Japanese cities in 1945 instilled memories that will last forever. Anyone who was there witnessing the most destructive fires in the history of the world, as they developed into conflagrations, can close his eyes, even after half a century, and still "see" the devastating holocaust.

At first, combat crews who had to carry out those unbelievable orders vented their fury on General LeMay, the architect of such an unorthodox way of using the high-altitude bomber. Van R. Parker, an aircraft commander in the 28th BS, 19th BG, had a lot of misgivings about LeMay when he heard about the upcoming fire raids. He relates: "Down through the years, I have been amused with published ac-

*And the rains came. This was the scene soon after the 314th BW arrived at North Field, Guam—not a pleasant welcome. Kelcie Teague*

*Fires begin to spread as Superfortresses drop incendiaries on Tarumiza, Kyushu.*

counts of thoughts of the combat crew personnel regarding General LeMay's decision to go to low-level firebombing raids on the Japanese cities. My reaction at the time was one of outrage. I felt violated and condemned to a quick demise before I had hardly gotten started in combat. The most good I could say about LeMay was that he had taken full leave of his senses.

"After World War II, I decided to make the USAAF my career, and I got to know General LeMay pretty well, and one day I asked him what was the toughest decision he had ever made. He responded without hesitation, 'My decision to send B-29s in at low level over Japan.'

"The low-level fire raids also caused me to make a personal, unorthodox decision. Following the first Tokyo fire raid, having witnessed the inferno from a very low altitude, I vowed that I would never again wear a parachute over the Japanese homeland. I didn't."

The stress from making these low-level fire raids was not only on the crews, but also on the B-29s themselves, especially when they had to withstand heat thermals after the fires had built into a giant conflagration. Wells Johnson, a flight engineer with the 680th BS, 504th BG, on Tinian Island, describes the experiences one of his friends had after hitting a strong heat thermal: "My friend told me about his experience while his crew and mine were taking a four-day rest leave. He said the updrafts that grabbed their B-29 were so intense that their own bombs, just released, reversed direction and came back into the bomb bays, knocking off a bomb bay door and damaging the vertical stabilizer. He said water flasks and loose equipment seemed to float in mid-air. The over-the-target updrafts were so forceful, and likely very hot, that the B-29 was flipped over, and they found themselves heading back. Maj. Robert Langdale, the aircraft commander, was equal to the task, righting the big bird, making a 180deg turn, and heading back toward the exit route. After the scary maneuvers, the drag of the missing bomb bay door, and other damage, they made it all the way back to Tinian Island without a

*Capt. Paul E. Jones lines his crew up in front of the* Bataan Avenger, *before takeoff. The* Bataan Avenger *was flipped over on her back during a heat thermal updraft over Osaka on March 13, 1945. No one was seriously injured.* Thomas

*Smoke from fires at a target city reach up past bombing altitude.* Chuck Spieth

stop at Iwo. None of the crew was injured, except emotionally."

At Saipan, this author often wondered if Admiral Nimitz or any of his staff knew just how much the Navy bolstered the morale of some of the people in the 73rd BW. Some of the groups organized an "Island Whiskey Pool" and charged a membership fee of fifty dollars. The "whiskey ship" always came in about once a month, and members had the privilege of buying their quota, usually two-fifths of whiskey and one-fifth of rum or gin. Elmer Huhta, an intelligence officer in the 872nd BS, 500th Group, 73rd BW, Saipan, tells how he was invited to join the club: "Shortly after I got to Saipan, a young lieutenant from the 21st BC headquarters, then temporarily located at Saipan, came to me and demanded fifty dollars for membership in the Island Liquor Pool. I asked him if it was mandatory that I join the pool, and he replied, 'Hell, yes. All offi-

cers in the 73rd BW have to get in!' After he had explained the rules, including the provision that my money would be refunded when I departed the island, and most of all, the privilege of purchasing incoming whiskey, rum, and gin about once a month for $1.25 a bottle, I quickly handed him my money. As he turned to leave, with a smirk on his face, I could swear he muttered, 'To hell with the ammo, pass the booze!'

"It was almost as if the Marines up in the hills and the Seabees could smell the ships that arrived with our booze, because they all turned up in the 73rd BW area as soon as the ships began unloading. They would happily pay up to $100 a fifth to those of us who were willing to part with some of our spirits. The Marines were no dummies. For a captured Jap sword, the going rate was $150."

As April droned on, all wings continued their support of the Navy and Army at Okinawa by continually bombing airfields on Kyushu. The missions averaged twenty-five or thirty planes on any given target, but they were continuously going back to the airfield to keep them inoperable. There were two exceptions during the latter part of the month. On April 24,

General LeMay sent three wings to bomb an aircraft engine factory at Tachikawa. One-hundred thirty-one B-29s participated, carrying 474 tons of high-explosive bombs. Bombing altitude was 10,000–14,500ft. Five B-29s failed to return. One-hundred six planes loaded with 378 tons of bombs went back to Tachikawa to bomb the air depot from an altitude of 1,700–2,150ft. No B-29s were lost in this raid. A total of forty-seven planes were lost and 120 B-29s made emergency landings at Iwo Jima en route to home bases after missions to Japan during April.

Iwo Jima was fast becoming a way station for B-29s or a mid-way point to stop and get needed repairs or fuel en route to their home bases after bombing raids on Japan. The weather was always causing problems in that part of the Pacific Ocean, and sometimes prevented badly damaged B-29s from landing; those crews were forced to bail out over the island and let their planes continue flying on auto-pilot with hopes that the aircraft would fly out of the area before running out of gas and plunging into the ocean. An abandoned B-29 flying itself near a busy landing strip in the middle of the ocean could present a dangerous situation with other aircraft in the area. To prevent such a tragic mishap from happening, the P-61 squadron at Iwo

*B-29 mechanics in the Marianas were never done. Another engine change is underway.* Chuck Spieth

Jima was given the assignment of shooting down abandoned B-29s.

Robert D. Thum, a Black Widow pilot in the 549th Night Fighter Squadron, says he shot down two B-29s during his stay at Iwo Jima: "It was kind of a strange feeling to attack one of those beautiful Superfortresses. There was a bit of danger in pulling up to an airplane flying on its own, because you would never know when it would 'turn on you'. I would fly in very close to get a clear view to see if anyone was still in the cockpit. After making the decision that it was clear of personnel, it became a fighter pilot's most exciting challenge in shooting down the B-29."

During a twenty-five–day period beginning April 17 and lasting through May 11, when the airfield bombings ceased, 2,104 sorties were flown by the B-29s from the 73rd, 313th, and 314th BWs. All these missions were daylight strikes on seventeen airfields, and there was seldom a

day that B-29s were not over Japan's two southernmost islands. The pattern for scheduled attacks during the last half of the attacks would send planes from each wing to several different airfields the same day. For instance, on May 3, the 314th BW attacked six airfields with eleven planes. The 313th Wing's policy was essentially the same.

The 313th did, however, revert from the airfield attacks back to mining missions. On May 5–6, all four groups sent ninety-seven B-29s carrying 577 tons of mines back to Shimonoseki Straits.

## 58th Wing Moves to Tinian Island

During April, the 58th BW completed its move to the newly constructed West Field, located south of the four-runway North Field on Tinian Island, and General Ramey was ready to launch his first attack on the Japanese homeland by May 5. On that date, the 58th BW joined the 73rd BW in a 170-plane attack on Hiro, Japan. Two B-29s were lost on this mission, and sixty-eight planes had to use Iwo Jima's hospitality for repairs and refueling.

Also at this time, the 20th BC was merged into the 21st BC, with General LeMay remaining in command. With the full strength of the 20th AF's B-29s now concentrated in the Mariana Islands, General LeMay, as well as General Arnold in Washington, was anxious to get back to the task of completing what the B-29s were supposed to do: knock Japan out of the war.

With the obligation to assist the Navy at Okinawa now behind him, and with a new supply of the highly successful napalm M-69 incendiary bombs on hand, LeMay was ready. While the 313th Wing was winding down the airfield attacks, on May 10, the 314th Wing sent 132 B-29s to Otake to drop 549 tons of explosives on industrial and oil refinery facilities. One plane was lost during this strike, and twelve planes landed at Iwo Jima.

On May 10, the 58th BW, making their second strike against Japan from the Marianas, sent eighty-eight B-29s carrying 383 tons of explosives to hit industrial and oil storage facilities at O'Shima. On that same date, the 73rd BW sent a 260-plus–plane strike to Tokuyama, one to hit a fuel station facility and the other to hit a coal facility.

On May 14, General LeMay was able to schedule, for the first time, a 500-plus–plane mission. Using all four wings for the first maximum-effort incendiary raid since the April 13–14 fire raid on the Tokyo Arsenal, he launched 524 B-29s carrying 2,515 tons of M-69s on a daylight, 16,000–20,000ft altitude attack on Nagoya. A second fire raid, on May 16–17, with 516 planes participating, hit Nagoya's urban area again. This time, they went in at a lower altitude of 600–1,858ft, carrying a heavier load of 3,609 tons of M-69 clusters. Eleven planes were lost on the first raid, and three were lost on the second. Sixteen planes were forced to land at Iwo Jima on the second raid flown after the island was captured. Tachikawa was attacked next by 309 B-29s attacking from 13,000–26,600ft. And one group from the 313th BW was keeping up their constant attack, dropping mines mostly in Shimonoseki Straits.

On May 23–24, a record-breaking 558 planes hit the Tokyo urban area with firebombs again. This was the largest single-mission attack to date

for the B-29s, the planes carried a record 3,646 tons of bombs and dropped them from 7,000–15,100ft. Seventeen Superfortresses were lost on this mission, and forty-nine had to land at Iwo Jima. The Japanese antiaircraft gunners were improving, as were attacks from a few night fighters and what some observed as pilotless Baka Bombs.

On May 25–26, the B-29s saturated the Tokyo urban area with firebombs once again, using 498 bombers. But again, the Japanese defenders were ready and waiting. A record twenty-six B-29s were shot down or were unable to make it back that night. This turned out to be the biggest loss of B-29s over Japan on a single mission during the war. These two Tokyo raids destroyed an addi-

tional 18sq-mi in the heart of the city near the Imperial Palace.

Every B-29 combat crew had been warned not to drop bombs on the Imperial Palace compound, but during this second mission, parts of the Palace grounds buildings and the Palace itself received fire damage from flying debris. It was learned after the war the Emperor and Empress were in their air raid shelter during the raid and were not injured.

Time and time again, the B-29 Superfortress proved its metal in bringing its crew back after being heavily damaged. There are numerous cases where the pilots brought their planes back after losing two engines or fuselage or suffering tremendous wing damage.

Aircraft commander Claude E.

Goin' Jessie, *the "goingest" B-29 in the 20th AF. Larry Smith*

Hensinger, of the 679th BS, 444th BG, 58th BW, made it back to Iwo Jima from the May 23 incendiary raid on Tokyo in *Jo* after being rammed by another B-29 over the target area. The fantastic story of this plane's combat exploits probably would not have been known Stateside had it not been for the sheet metal workers at the Martin Superfortress plant in Omaha, Nebraska. After working on the plane during its production, they left a note hidden in the cockpit, asking the crew that would be assigned to *Jo* to please keep them informed about their combat experiences. Viva P. Turnbull, one

*The flight crew of* Goin' Jessie. *The crew included John Fleming, aircraft commander; Charles Chauncey, pilot; Jack Cremer, navigator; Julius Chilipka, bombardier. Kneeling: Prushko, Rice, Scribner, Coldman, Waldron and Roncace.* Charles Chauncey

of the workers, was named correspondent with the yet-to-be-assigned combat crew members. Hensinger kept the metal workers informed of his crew's experiences on Tinian Island and of their combat missions, including the May 23 mission to Tokyo.

The following is a play-by-play account of *Jo's* last hours, as related by Hensinger: "We took off from Tinian Island on the night of May 23 to firebomb Tokyo. Everything went fine until after 'bombs-away,' when the Superfort flew into a large smoke cloud. In the next instant, there was a terrific jar and crash of metal. Whether we had suffered a direct flak hit or had collided with another B-29 was not of any importance at the time, for things began to happen to *Jo*. The pilot's control column went limp and the no. 1 engine quit. The co-pilot and pilot rudder controls went out, all instruments were knocked out on no. 1 and 2 engines, and we soon found ourselves

headed back over Tokyo as a result of the blow.

"The only thing working in the cockpit, it seemed, was the auto-pilot, and that was what got us back to Iwo Jima. We were able to manipulate the ailerons and rudder with the auto-pilot controls, and were able to keep the plane on a straight and level flight. I decided on a wheels-down landing attempt at Iwo, but with no brakes, I knew that would present a real problem. We decided to tie parachutes in the tail gun position and open them just before touchdown to help stop the plane. After a hectic ride down the runway and off the end overrun, a stretch of very rough ground, *Jo* came to a final stop. *Jo* was so beat-up she was never to fly again! But the whole crew debarked from the plane uninjured."

After the two all-out efforts against Tokyo in May, the damage caused to date was over 50 percent total destruction in the entire city. In his assessment of the damage done, General LeMay said he thought the heavy loss of B-29s over Tokyo in May was worth it. Forty-three Superforts were lost in those two missions.

To wind up missions in May, LeMay sent 510 B-29s carrying 2,570

tons of firebombs dropped their loads in the urban area of Yokohama. Seven B-29s were lost on this mission and thirty-nine had to make emergency stop-overs at Iwo Jima. This was a daylight mission with the Mustangs off Iwo Jima escorting the B-29s.

With the success of the May fire raids and the 21st BC's increased strength—with the addition of the veteran 58th BW and new 315th BW—General LeMay was convinced more than ever that the B-29s could knock Japan out of the war without a land invasion. He had already informed General Norstad that his command was now capable of launching 500 or more planes on any given target in Japan, and proposed that his more powerful force be used to further intensify the strikes against Japan. The USAAF had an opportunity to prove the "power of the strategic air arm," destroying Japan's ability and will to wage war "if its maximum capacity is exerted unstintingly during the next six months." Those were strong words, shared by many USAAF people in high places, even as the policy makers were putting in place the works for a ground invasion of Japan to be executed no later than November 1, 1945.

With the Superfortress build-up in the Marianas, it was almost a miracle that there were very few major accidents during takeoffs and landings. One of the worst accidents, with several fatalities, occurred during May 1945. It happened during the mass launching of 313th BW B-29s at North Field on Tinian Island during the early evening of May 23, and the resulting conflagration that suddenly burst into the sky above North Field could be seen from Saipan.

Larry Smith, central fire control gunner on Captain Hutchison's crew, 1st BS, 9th BG, remembers seeing the disaster that destroyed four B-29s and killed ten of the eleven-man crew of *Thunderin' Loretta*, plus two ground crewmen. All planes in the 9th BG were loaded with six 2,000lb mines scheduled to be dropped in Shimonoseki Straits that night: Smith's plane was next in line for takeoff after Lt. William Caldwell, aircraft commander of *Thunderin' Loretta*, released his brakes and added full power for takeoff. Sixty seconds after Caldwell began his roll, Captain Hutchison began his takeoff roll. "About a quarter of the distance down the runway, during our takeoff run, I heard our radio operator, Frank Cappozzo, yell out, 'We're getting the red light from the tower, Captain!' Frank's sentence was hardly finished before the engines had been cut and the brakes applied hard, as Hutch and Pounteny, the aircraft commander and pilot, observed the tragedy unfolding in front of them.

"Before I could scramble back into my top gunner's position, from my takeoff position, to see what was happening, we heard a loud explosion. Caldwell's plane had veered off the runway to the right and collided head-on with a parked B-29. Fifty-caliber ammunition was going off in all directions. The six mines in Caldwell's plane exploded individually. With every explosion, the wings of our plane lifted a little from the concussion, even though it must have been three-quarters of a mile away.

"The runway ahead of us was littered with debris. I could see the entire tail section of Caldwell's aircraft lying some distance behind the conflagration, apparently having been blown off when the first mine exploded.

"We were directed to make a 180deg turn and taxi to another runway to take off for the mission. We continued on to Japan that night in half shock, not knowing the results of the tragedy we had witnessed, until our return.

"The entire Caldwell crew, with the exception of the tail gunner, who jumped from the plane before the explosion, died instantly. And it was a miracle that only two ground crewmen near the parked B-29s were killed."

While the tragedy was unfolding across the channel on North Field, Tinian Island, the 73rd BW on Saipan was taking off for another incendiary raid on Tokyo. This author was among those witnessing the explosion on Tinian Island. We wondered how many people were losing their lives at that moment. It was the worst accident that happened to the B-29 crews in the Marianas.

And it was about as tragic as the accident that took place in the 44th BS, 40th BG, 58th BW while stationed in India. In this accident, nine people

were killed outright and twenty-one were wounded, some seriously. All were crew chiefs and ground crewmen attempting to download one of the planes carrying fragmentation clusters, to be replaced with demolition bombs. One of the clusters accidentally fell and exploded, setting off a fire that spread rapidly, engulfing the B-29. Fragments spread to another plane nearby, which caught fire and was destroyed. Six other B-29s were heavily damaged.

As the strength of the 21st BC increased, so did the popularity of the B-29 Superfortress in the Marianas. A mass launching of a full wing of B-29s was spectacular, and people not associated with the plane would come to the bases to watch the takeoffs. On Saipan, a field hospital on the bluffs to the north and overlooking Magicienne Bay afforded an outstanding view of the 73rd BW takeoffs. We were told that patients would ask to be wheeled out on the porch to watch. Nurses were glad to oblige because then they could watch also. Rumor had it that doctors even pushed operation schedules up so that they, too, could watch the spectacle.

The Marines, Seabees, and Navy personnel were always trying to hitch a ride on a B-29 during an "engineering hop." After an engine change, the plane had to be "slow timed" and the compass had to be aligned. This chore usually fell to the crew that the B-29 was assigned to. During my stay on Saipan, we had to make several hops, which lasted an hour or two. Each time we went to the line to take our plane up, there was always a small group from the Navy asking if they could go with us. On our first hop, we took four chief petty officers from a Seabee battalion stationed on the northern end of the island. We stayed out about 2hr that day, buzzing all the non-captured islands in the area, such as Pagan Island and Rota. The chiefs thought the ride was great, and we told them they'd have to come back and do it again sometime. We were trying to set them up for a return favor.

Before they left us after the ride, we asked them if they could direct us to somebody who could give us some plywood. Since each Quonset hut in the officer's quarters had men from two crews, we needed a back porch so that the crew returning from a mission could sleep while the other men could play cards without disturbing them. We needed enough plywood to build a covered patio-type addition to our hut and, if possible, individual clothes closets and shelves beside each bed.

The next day, a huge 6x6 truck stopped in front of our hut and some men unloaded the whole truckload. From then on, we acted as a kind of travel agent for those chiefs. We'd call them up when we had friends who were going to take their plane up for an engineering hop and make arrangements for the chiefs to be included on the flight.

B-29 crews became staunch friends of the Navy permanent-duty personnel located down near the harbor—including officers who could get you in The World's Longest Bar. The bar was several big Butler huts joined together, and the overall length was separated into three sections, one for junior-grade officers, one for field-grade, and one for senior-grade officers. They served double-size bourbon with Coke, including ice, all for twenty-five cents a drink.

The crews also tried to develop friendships with the Navy cooks. We made friends with a group of them one day when we carried them up on one of our test hops. They invited us down to their enlisted mess hall for a midnight snack. They said not to come until after midnight because by that time most of the officers in charge would have gone to bed, and they could cook us up what we wanted. Now that sounded like the best deal on the island, especially compared to the K-rations: the powdered eggs, the Spam if we were lucky or something that resembled steak, which we called "Argentina horse flesh."

Our first trip to the Navy mess hall revealed that we weren't the only B-29 guys who had made deals with the cooks. We sweated out a line while the cooks kept frying real eggs and ham or ham-and-egg omelets. No question about it, anytime those cooks wanted a ride in a B-29, we saw they got it. And we told them that the next war we fought, we were going Navy!

There was much ado about "nowhere to go, and nothing to do, and no women, even to look at" at the B-29 bases in the Marianas. You had to make your own entertainment, whether it was playing cards or borrowing a jeep or weapons carrier to look over the island. Some, however, got three-day passes to visit some of the other islands.

Clyde A. Emswiler, crew chief on B-29 T-Square-29, the *Tanaka Termite*, with the 874th BS, 498th BG, 73rd BW on Saipan, found a way to get a pass and visit a friend on Tinian Island. He is still amused at what happened to him after his return from that visit: "Wartime duty on a god-forsaken Pacific island was a far cry from being stationed near cities like London in the European theater of war, or in other civilized areas where there were girls.

"When we left the States for overseas destinations, we knew it was farewell to sex life until we got back to civilization. Granted, on Saipan, there were a few nurses at the hospitals and later a few Red Cross girls who passed out doughnuts and coffee to the flight crews. But these girls I saw were all rank-conscious. Even my master-sergeant stripes were not enough rank to get their attention.

"One day I asked for, and was granted, a three-day pass to go over to Tinian Island, which was just 3mi across the channel from Saipan. I got word from home that one of my hometown buddies was stationed on Tinian Island. I asked my buddy at Saipan to get a pass and go over to Tinian Island with me. We knew in advance that the woman situation at Tinian Island was the same as on Saipan, so we had no thought of womanizing during the visit. We had no problem catching a hop over to Tinian Island, found my old friend, had a good visit, and when our three days were up, we caught a plane back over to Saipan. So much for our visit to Tinian Island, and you'd think this would be the end of the trip.

"Lo and behold, on checking the bulletin board in our Orderly Room, we found a notice ordering the two of us, because of our visit to Tinian Island, to report to the dispensary for a 'short-arm inspection!'"

## The Fighter Escort Fiasco

Continuing the four-wing missions, with a renewed supply of M-69 napalm clusters on hand, General LeMay sent a strike force of 509 B-29s on a daylight mission to drop on the urban area of Osaka. Bombing altitude ranged from 18,000–28,000ft, and scheduled to escort the Superfortresses over the target area were P-51s from three fighter groups from Iwo Jima. Three modified B-29s, called Navigation B-29s, would lead the fighters, one for each group, to the Japanese coastline. The navigation planes would then circle in the same area until the P-51s completed the escort duty over the target and return to their designated spot to be led back to Iwo Jima. B-29 weather aircraft were also on hand to try to forecast weather before any flights the P-51s made from Iwo Jima.

On June 1, 1945, the stage was set for the big raid on Osaka, but the P-51s, because of foul weather, suffered the worst disaster since the December 7, 1941, Japanese attacks on Wheeler and Bellows Fields on Oahu. The 15th, 21st, and newly arrived 506th Fighter Groups participated in the mission.

Maj. Robert W. Moore, commander of the 45th Fighter Squadron (FS), 15th Fighter Group (FG), who was leading the escort mission, explains how the tragedy happened: "I had an elevated ringside seat and saw the whole thing as it happened. I was leading the 45th FS of the 15th FG, and Col. John Mitchell was the leader of Blue Flight in my squadron. Earlier in the war, Mitchell had led the P-38 strike from Guadalcanal that intercepted and shot down Japanese Admiral Yamamoto over Kihili Airfield on Bouganville.

"About 250mi north of Iwo Jima, we began to encounter varied cloud layers. A weather B-29 ahead of us had radioed back that he had penetrated a small frontal area without any problem, and thought we would be able to do the same. Instead of getting better, the weather got worse, and the three navigator B-29s flew into a solid cloud front. The 506th FG tried to keep them in sight and dove down through the 21st FG in the process. Some pilots—flying close formation one second and totally blind the next—suffered disorientation and subsequently fatal vertigo, while others were victims of mid-air collisions. Many of the pilots radioed their distressed situations, and a bedlam of 'Mayday! Mayday! I'm bailing out!' ensued. This cacophony of distress calls made me aware that a major tragedy was in the making.

"Because of the weather, our entire command had to abort the mission and, luckily, we made it back to Iwo. Final tabulation revealed we lost twenty-seven planes that day and twenty-four pilots. Two pilots from the 506th FG were picked up very soon after the fiasco. The third, 2nd Lt. Arthur A. Burry, a member of my 45th FS, was flying with the 47th FS that day, and he was picked up on June 7 by a submarine.

"What really hurt was that we had lost so many close comrades—not to the enemy, but to the weather. And without a shot having been fired!"

Many things seemed to have gone wrong on the June 1 mission. Eighty-one B-29s in the strike force had to make emergency landings at Iwo Jima, and ten were lost over the target or en route home that day.

Capt. Arthur Behrens of the 458th BS, 330th BG, 314th Wing, had not reached the drop zone and still had his bomb load aboard when he received a direct hit from an antiaircraft gun. The plane suffered serious damage to the control cables on Behrens' side of the cockpit. Co-pilot Lt. Robert M. Woliver was trying to help Behrens when another shell exploded in the cockpit, killing Behrens and seriously wounding Woliver. They were flying as the high group that day at 20,000ft, and when they were hit the second time, the plane went out of control. Woliver finally got the plane under control, but was down to about 200ft above the water at that time. Years later, he wrote his friend, Cleve R. Anno, an aircraft commander in the 29th BG, that, "If the hand of God wasn't involved that

day, I'll eat my hat! In getting the plane under control from our fast descent, we wandered around so much, the navigator couldn't get any kind of fix on our location. The IFF switches up front were destroyed by the explosion, but our radar operator, Wallace Mussallm, had an emergency switch in his compartment and, luckily, it worked. He turned it on and prayed that someone would hear it.

"About this time, another 'miracle' happened. Art Shepherd and his radar operator were flying along, not too far away, in their P-61 Black Widow. They were about to return to their Iwo Jima base because their primary radar set had malfunctioned. However, they did have an operational IFF scope, which, through a stroke of luck, picked up the IFF signal from our plane, permitting them to find the B-29, way off course."

The story doesn't end here. Even though Shepherd was able to guide Woliver's plane to Iwo Jima, with so many B-29s milling around, all trying to land on the one runway, it was another matter to get the crew safely on

*Coming home, on the downwind leg in a landing pattern at Isley Field, Saipan.* Chuck Spieth

the ground. Woliver began circling the island and the crew members started bailing out of the plane, hoping to come down on the island. After several circles, all the crew got out of the airplane and landed safely. Unable to leave the plane on his own, Woliver would have gone down with Captain Behren's body, which was still strapped in its seat. But Lt. John Logerot, the bombardier, noticed his friend's predicament and threw him from the doomed plane before jumping himself, thus saving Woliver's life.

After everyone was out of the B-29, Shepherd shot down the Superfortress, the *City of Osceola*. Captain Behren's body went down with the plane.

June 1 was indeed a rough day for the 21st BC. It had lost seven B-29s and twenty-seven P-51s of its 567th Fighter Command.

*Who notices the name on this 3rd PRS Superfortress?* John Mitchell

*Chapter 14*

# Last Two Months before the A-Bomb

When General Ramey brought his veteran 58th BW out of India and China to join with the three B-29 wings then operating from the Mariana Islands against the Japanese homeland, little did he, or anyone else for that matter, know what happened to at least three of his B-29s that made emergency landings on Russian soil.

The fate of the interned B-29 crews was not known until January 1945, when they, with Soviet approval, "escaped" over the Iranian border to freedom. It was much later before the general public knew what happened to the three B-29s.

The urban area of Kobe was next to receive another maximum-effort fire raid. This time, 530 B-29s dropped 3,079 tons of M-69 napalm clusters from 13,000–18,000ft. It was a daylight mission and Kobe was covered with a solid overcast. The bombs were dropped by radar.

The days of missing targets by a wide margin were behind the B-29 crews. Most of the navigators and radar operators with better training were fairly accurate. This is why General LeMay told General Arnold during his visit to the Marianas in June that the days of loading the planes for a mission, then having to postpone the mission because of weather over the target, were long gone. "The crews," he told his commander, "now have more confidence in their radar units, so we

are now hitting the targets regardless of bad weather over the targets."

The June 5 Kobe strike was the last mission where B-29 losses were numbered in double digits. Eleven Superfortresses were lost on that mission, and forty-three had to make emergency landings at Iwo Jima.

For the rest of June, with a few exceptions, the strategy was to bomb multiple targets each day. As many as seven cities were hit in any given day. In addition to continuing the mining of Shimonoseki Straits and other ports at such places as Fukuoka, the 313th BW also joined the 58th, 73rd, and 314th BWs in another daylight incendiary raid on the urban area of Osaka on June 15. Five hundred eleven B-29s took part in the mission, and all planes returned to their bases. On June 20, the 73rd and 313th BWs sent 237 B-29s to drop 1,525 tons of incendiaries on Fukuoka; two B-29s were lost.

## The 315th Wing Arrives

The new 315th BW settled in at the not-yet-completed Northwest Field on Guam, amid rains and flooded living areas.

But before the 315th Wing could get a single combat mission tucked away, they had to stand by for a top brass dedication ceremony concerning one of their own B-29s. It so happened that General Arnold was making his

first visit to the B-29 outfits in the Marianas in June. Somebody had the idea of naming one of the Superfortresses in honor of Admiral Nimitz, who had done such a good job of seeing that the B-29s got what was needed, so a brand-new Superfortress from the 501st BG was selected, and the name *Fleet Admiral Nimitz* with a five-star flag was printed on the nose of the airplane. A painting of the plane now hangs in the Admiral Nimitz Center. Colonel Boyd, 501st BG commander, took part in the ceremony before a crowd of 315th BW spectators and the crew of the *Fleet Admiral Nimitz*, standing at attention. Speeches were given by General Arnold, Admiral Nimitz, and 315th BW commander Gen. Frank Armstrong.

Col. George E. Harrington, the 315th BW's supply chief, said the 315th was supposed to have been located at West Field on Tinian Island and was packed for overseas shipment when orders were received from 21st BC on Guam that plans had been changed.

The uniqueness of the 315th is recalled by Stephen M. Bandorsky, radar navigator, 502nd BG: "All four groups of the 315th BW—the 16th, 331st, 501st, and the 502nd—trained [with a focus on night missions] in aircraft built by the Bell Aircraft Corp. at its Marietta, Georgia, plant, between January and September 1945. These planes were the only true variant of the B-29 ever manufactured. It was called the B-29B, and was a stripped-down version of the standard B-29. The General Electric remote-controlled aiming system was not installed since the only armament on the plane was its tail guns, twin .50cal machine guns, and a 20mm cannon. A variety of other components were also omitted in order to save overall weight and thereby increase the aircraft's bomb-carrying capacity. The resulting reduced, unladened weight of the plane of 69,000lb lessened the strain on the engines and airframe and permitted the bomb load to be increased from 6 tons to 9 tons."

They came ready to show off their new Eagle radar units, capable of identifying a single building in a selected target area by using a wing-shaped radar vane beneath the fuselage. The Eagle radar system was developed by MIT's Radiation Lab, and was designed specifically for bombardment. It was so secret that no B-29 equipped with this system was ever permitted to be photographed, even for official purposes.

"All missions were planned and briefing materials provided that were specifically oriented to radar bombing," Bandorsky remembered. "Premission briefings were so thorough, that the RDOBs had to spend hours

---

### Russian Superfortresses

Several years ago, Mauno A. Salo, then a member of the board of directors of the American Aviation Historical Society, sent me an article pertaining to the "lost" B-29s in Russia, with a note that it contained a part of the B-29 history that is not well known. The article, which Salo said was written by an unknown British author, is a documentation of a detailed account of what happened to the crew of the three B-29s confiscated after landing at Vladivostok, Russia, and another crew that had to bail out of their damaged B-29 over Russian soil.

The three B-29s "captured" by the Russians were Superfortresses nicknamed *Ramp Tramp*, serial number (s/n) 42-6256, flown by Capt. Howard R. Jarrell from the 770th BS, 462nd BG; *Ding How*, s/n 42-6358, flown by Lt. William Micklish of the 79th BS, 468th BG; and the *General H. H. Arnold Special*, s/n 42-6365, flown by Capt. Weston H. Price from the 794th BS, 468th BG. The fourth B-29 retained by Russian authorities was s/n 42-93829, from the 395th BS, 40th BG. It crashed in Russia.

The B-29 crews that landed at Vladivostok were treated as an enemy—fired upon by antiaircraft guns and escorted to a landing field by fighters. The crewmen were stunned at their receptions, since the Soviet Union was supposed to be an ally of the United States in World War II.

At the urgency of the American consul, O. Edmund Chubb, the crewmen were allowed to "escape," but the Soviets would not release the aircraft. They used the Soviet-Japanese Alliance as a cover to impound the airplanes and to intern the crews.

With the three flyable B-29s in their hands, Soviet authorities began a project to build their own Superfortress. They quickly put into action a program of the highest priority: to manufacture exact copies of the American B-29 bomber. Overall responsibility was given to Soviet bomber designer A. N. Tupolev, with A. B. Shvetsoz supervising the production of a direct copy of the R-3350 engine. A wide section of Soviet manufacturing industry and research expertise was brought into the program. Two of the B-29s were stripped down into components and sub-assemblies for technical evaluation. The third B-29 was kept in flying condition for flight-test evaluation.

Many industrial, scientific, and technological problems had to be overcome. A factory on the Volga River was given the task of producing twenty pre-production aircraft for testing various systems. Two factories behind the Ural Mountains were given instructions to tool up for serious production in the summer of 1946. The last of the twenty pre-production aircraft, designated as the Tu-4, were delivered to the flight-test center during the late autumn of 1947. As with the B-29, the Tu-4 was beset by numerous technical and mechanical problems, such as failures in the propeller-feathering mechanisms and the electrically operated landing gear systems, engine fires, and airlocks in the fuel and oil pressure systems of the Shvetsov ASh-73TK engines.

The Soviets must have encountered more problems with the brakes and tires than they bargained for because third parties, acting for the Soviet government, tried to purchase tires, wheels, and brake assemblies in America in 1946. This was brought out during testimony of Gen. Carl Spaatz, USAF chief of staff, before President Truman's Air Policy Committee.

The Soviet copy of the B-29 made its first public appearance at the Soviet Aviation Day Parade on August 3, 1947, when three of the twenty pre-production Tu-4s flew across Tushino Aerodrome in Moscow. They were accompanied by a transport version that used the same wings, engines, and tail assembly on a redesigned fuselage, designated as the Tu-70.

More than 1,400 exact duplications of the B-29 Superfortress were built by the Soviet Union and were the principal component of their long-range aviation arm until the early I950s. With one stroke, the Soviets had revolutionized their thinking on manned bomber design and tactical deployment.

Rudy L. Thompson, a flight engineer in the 770th BS, 462nd BG, adds a bit of flavor to the story of the Soviets copying the *Ramp Tramp*: "There were many real heroes in the 20th AF who carried out the air assault against the Japanese homeland, and in the end dropped the bombs that forced Japan to capitulate. There were those who say they weren't even 'assistant heroes.' But some of us experienced a part of history being made and deserve a bit of the glory. My claim to fame is that I was the flight engineer on the first B-29 the Russians 'captured' and later copied.

"Our plane was named the *Ramp Tramp* because she was a real dog. That name fit her perfectly—always on the ramp undergoing repairs. The reason our crew was not flying the *Tramp* the day the Russians took control of her was that the 771st BS was short of B-29s and they borrowed our plane for Captain Jarrell and crew to fly to Anshan, Manchuria, to attack the Showa Steel Works. We eventually got a new B-29, which we immediately named *Ramp Tramp II*. We took her to Tinian Island, where we later lost her during takeoff on a mission to Tokyo."

studying radar-targeting materials and were required to draw the details from memory."

General LeMay decided that the 315th would be charged with destroying the oil refineries all over Japan. Even though several missions had already been sent to bomb such targets as the Army Fuel Depot at Iwakuni, he knew that some of the fuel and oil refineries were still operating.

For the 315th's first mission over Japan, thirty-five B-29Bs were sent to bomb the oil refinery and industrial section of Yokkaichi on June 26–27. They dropped 143 tons of bombs from 14,000–17,400ft. Thirty-six Superfortresses went to Kadamatsu on June 29–30 and with 209 tons of bombs hit the oil refinery there. Both missions produced excellent results, and the 315th got off to a good start.

## With Fame Came Celebrities and Journalists

During the spring and summer of 1945, several Hollywood celebrities came to the Marianas to entertain the troops that flew and serviced the B-29s. One night, this author and three or four buddies were at the bar of the 499th BG's Officers' Club on Saipan, when somebody opened the front door and let out one of the loudest yells we'd ever heard. In walked the very popular movie comedian, Joe E. Brown. That was one of his trademarks: opening his big mouth and yelling as loudly as he could. Well, he came in and shot the bull with us for a while. He told us that he got word a month or so before, from the War Department, that his son, a B-17 pilot in Europe, had been killed when his plane was shot down.

Not long before Okinawa was captured, Ernie Pyle, America's most popular war correspondent, came to Saipan. He had a nephew on the island and he wanted to check up on the B-29. He stayed for a few days in the Quonset hut of Gerald Robinson, commander of the 875th BS, 498th BG.

Robinson remembers Pyle's excitement in getting to ride in a B-29: "I was privileged to take Ernie up on his only flight of a B-29. Less than two weeks later, while riding in the front seat of a jeep in Ie Shima Island, near Okinawa, a Japanese sniper shot him through

the head, killing him instantly.

"These are some of the things he wrote about his B-29 ride with us: 'I sat on a box between the pilots, both on takeoff and landing, and as much as I've flown, that was still a thrill. These islands are all relatively small, and you're no sooner off the ground, than you're out over water, and that feels funny. If the air is a little rough, it gives you a very odd sensation sitting way up there in the nose. For the B-29 is so big that instead of bumping or dropping, the nose has a willowy motion, sort of like sitting out on the end of a green limb when it's swaying around.'"

Ralph Marr, tail gunner with the 15th BS, 16th BG, is proud of the fact that his was the only B-29 crew that lived in the pages of a major magazine. The *Saturday Evening Post* assigned one of its top war correspondents, Richard Tregaskis, to "live and fly with us on the Road to Tokyo, and to report the action first-hand in a weekly series of stories." Capt. Bob ("Pappy") Hain, who flew fifty missions over Europe, was the crew's aircraft commander.

## The *Lucky Irish* and *Bataan Avenger*

One of the greatest "sweat jobs" a B-29 combat crew had to endure while

*A picture taken by author on June 1, 1945, just prior to entering boiling smoke clouds over Osaka, Japan. Note the B-29 below left wing. Flak from Japanese navy ships hit the nose of Captain Wilkerson's plane and it spun down. All perished. Marshall*

flying a bombing mission to and from the Japanese homeland from the Marianas was the countdown to rotation home. Thirty missions had been set for a combat tour, but the closer a crew came to that magic number, the tougher it became to sweat out the next trip to Japan.

By June 1945, opposition, especially fighter attacks, had diminished to the point that sometimes there was not a single enemy fighter in the air. But they were still able to put up flak barrages that could knock a Superfortress down, there were those terrible weather fronts to fly through on the 3,000mi round trip to and from the target, and there was always that fickle finger of fate, always lingering around the corner—as recorded about the crew of the *Lucky Irish*: As the bombing raids increased with the strong build-up of B-29s coming from the islands, the magic number thirty rolled around for some of the crews. My number thirty came up after the June 7 maximum-effort fire raid on Kobe. My crew and I were dished a

A B-29 Superfortress at Dalhart, Texas, Air Base, shows the Eagle radar antenna beneath fuselage. This is a rare picture of this secret weapon used by 315th BW. The Eagle system, known officially as the AN/APQ-7 radar set, was a great improvement over the older AN/APQ-13 radar units in the B-29As. The Eagle was capable of identifying a single building in a selected target area, allowing the radar operator and bombardier to coordinate their efforts to aim the bombs more accurately. W. H. Keathley

double lucky deal. We had not only survived the thirty-mission tour, but also survived the thirty-mission cut off, by one day. The day after completing our tour of combat duty, we were placed on a holding list, awaiting transportation back to the States for reassignment.

Lt. William A. Kelley, aircraft commander of *Lucky Irish*, remarked after the thirtieth and final mission, "The unusual thing about our crew is that nothing unusual has ever happened to us."

The combat tour of the crew had been unbelievably routine. Assigned to the 870th BS, 497th BG, on Saipan, they began their combat tour on the first B-29 raid on Tokyo, November 24, 1944. None of the men had received the slightest injury, the aircraft had hardly been scratched, and they had flown every mission as scheduled and never aborted. The central fire control gunner, Glenn W. Jomes, complained, "Our good luck seems to charm away the opposition and keeps me from getting any gunnery practice."

Actually, this was the third *Lucky Irish* flown by Kelley's crew. The first was destroyed on the runway at

Saipan by Japanese aircraft from Iwo Jima. The second *Lucky Irish* was lost somewhere north of Iwo Jima on a mission to Japan, having been assigned to another crew for this mission. Yet, flight after flight, the original crew of A-Square-28 wallowed in Irish luck.

The *Irish* were an extremely close crew. They had trained together for more than a year and flown in combat over the vastness of the western Pacific and the Japanese homeland for another six months. Now they were going home: the first Superfortress crew to complete its combat tour of duty, thirty missions. The plane they were to fly back to the United States was the *Dauntless Dotty*, the lead plane for the first B-29 raid on Tokyo on November 24, 1944.

As Kelley and crew boarded the plane for home, he didn't know that his first child, a daughter, had been born a few hours earlier. Compared to the 3,000mi nonstop flights to and from Japan, the return flight would be simple: Saipan to Kwajalein in the Marshalls, Hawaii, and then to California. With an outstanding record of fifty-three missions over Japan and 176,000 combat miles, *Dotty* had just been overhauled. They departed Saipan in the twilight hours of June 6, 1945, and reached Kwajalein just before midnight. They had a snack in the mess hall, and the crew voted on whether to remain overnight and get a little sleep or refuel and proceed to Hawaii. To a man, they decided to push on. At 3am, they were airborne, and 40sec later, the *Dauntless Dotty* plunged into the Pacific Ocean, never to be seen again. Ten of the thirteen men on board perished instantly.

Lt. John F. Neveille, the co-pilot, was thrown through the nose of the aircraft and survived, as did Glenn Gregory, the tail gunner, and Charles McMurry, the left gunner.

News of that crew's disaster wasn't known for some time later, but had this author and his crew known, our mode of transportation back to the States may have been changed. The *Lucky Irish* crew left Saipan on their fatal flight one day before we completed our tour and were eligible for rotation back to the States. We were asked how we wanted to return home: by a Navy transport ship, by Air Transport Command, or wait for a war-weary B-29 to become available and fly it back to the States. We settled on waiting for a "war weary." We had a boring three-week wait before our B-29 was brought from the 6th BG on Tinian Island. We were to return the plane to the States for a complete overhaul, including repair of structural damage suffered during an incendiary raid on Osaka. The name of the aircraft was the *Bataan Avenger*. A newspaper clipping pasted on the pilots' instrument panel told part of the story of the *Avenger*: Before building the plane, workers at the Boeing Aircraft Co. plant in Wichita, Kansas, raised the money to purchase it, and they prophesied that some day the airplane would return to Kansas, victoriously. The flight back to the States was uneventful, if you can overlook the anxiousness that accompanies a person returning from a combat tour of duty. We had to leave the plane in California, after authorities turned deaf ears to our pleas to let us fly the *Avenger* on to Wichita, Kansas. What a gala event that would have been!

## B-29s Roam Japanese Skies

By June 1945, the B-29s, now with five wings roaming the skies over Japan, had greatly weakened the opposition. B-29 losses were decreasing at a rapid rate. This meant that the Superfortresses had, at last, overcome the deficiencies that had caused so much early trouble.

As the war continued, strategies changed to suit the situations. With the 313th and 315th BWs tightening their stranglehold on the Japanese population, it was becoming increasingly difficult to get food or oil and gas from outside sources. They tried dropping barrels of much-needed food into the Inland Sea from Asian shores, hoping the easterly currents would deposit it on Japanese western shores. The Japanese air force was curtailed due to the depletion of their oil and fuel supplies, destroyed by B-29s of the 315th BW. Japanese planes didn't have enough fuel to attack Superfortresses now roaming their skies.

The 58th, 73rd, and 314th BWs attacked sixty-six cities in Japan, sometimes with assistance from the 313th BW. The 315th never participated in a combined mission with other units, but instead, with their Eagle radar system, put their full effort into destroying the oil and fuel industry and storage facilities.

Regular attacks were made on cities with as few people as 40,004 (Isezaki) to the larger cities with populations of 6,778,804 or more (Tokyo). LeMay finally had printed notices dropped from B-29s over a city, warning the population to vacate the premises or suffer the consequences, prior to a mission.

William C. Leiby, bombardier with the 28th BS, 19th BG, relates a June 26, 1945, mission his crew, flying the *City of Austin*, made: "Our mission was to the Kawasaki Aircraft Factory at Kagamigahara, Japan. As we were rendezvousing just off the coast of Osaka, Japanese fighters rose to attack our formation. They shot down one of our B-29s and our squadron leader ordered us to leave the formation and drop down to see if we could assist the ditching plane's crew.

"We circled the downed flyers, dropping food, water, emergency radio equipment, and life rafts. Our radio

*The ground crew of the 3rd PRS's* Double Exposure *know how to clean their airplane.*
John Mitchell

*An unusual shot of the V-Square-25, which flew with the 878th BS, 499th BG, Saipan.*
Ray Brashear

*Two officers chat beside a Superfortress that honors the 4th Marines.* Dick Field

operator finally contacted a nearby submarine, who came to the rescue of the downed flyers immediately. After our submarine surfaced near the crew in the water, we headed for a couple of two-masted Japanese schooners that had set out from shore toward the downed crewmen. We tried dropping two bombs on the boats, but missed. Our aircraft commander, Lt. Ed Gammel, then made a higher pass at the boats, bringing the nose down as we got in range so that we could fire all six of our .50cal guns at the same time. As we passed over, the tail gunner got in some good shots. The first boat immediately caught fire and began burning, and we noticed that the second boat was badly damaged. The submarine picked up the downed crewmen and we set our course to our return route to Guam."

## Balls of Fire Myth Resolved

As the B-29s increased their missions over Japan into the summer of 1945, so did the crew reports of seeing "balls of fire" following them during their return to base. Some of the gunners fired on the elusive bright light that followed them for miles, and some of the pilots even used sharp, often violent, evasive maneuvers in an effort to shake off what they considered an enemy aircraft with powerful lights to direct Japanese fighter planes to them. But, the pilots said, it was useless, for the lights would stay with them, regardless of the action taken.

In all reports, there was one consistent point: The balls of fire, the airborne-searchlights, or whatever they appeared to be, would always appear off the right wing when going into the Japanese homeland and off the left wing as they returned to their Mariana bases.

By early July, the fireball myth was resolved. All B-29 bomber crews were summarily briefed as follows: "Fly all over the sky, fire all you want, you're not going to shoot this one down. Those 'balls of fire' you've seen out there is the planet Venus, which is extremely brilliant in this region of the world at this time of the year."

Fresh from a record-setting performance in June of amassing a total of more than 6,200 combat hours, Lt. Col. Charles M. Eisenhart's 505th BG was assigned the task of flying all the mining missions. With an average of thirty B-29s on each flight, the 505th scheduled missions every other night to lay mines in areas covering most of the harbors, especially the Shimonoseki Straits, to tighten the stranglehold around Japan's home islands. The group's action was instrumental in virtually halting the 1.5 million tons of merchant shipping Japan needed for her survival. The 505th's effort was the continuation of Operation Starvation, which had been assigned to the 313th BW by General LeMay.

## First Capitulation Feelers Appear

Following the B-29s' most destructive raids on Japan's major cities, some Japanese civilian leaders read the handwriting on the wall and argued for discussions to begin in an effort to find ways to end the war. By this time, Tokyo, Nagoya, Kobe, Osaka, Yokohama, and Kawasaki lay in ruin. The combined total urban area of these cities had a total of 257.2sq-mi, of which the B-29s had totally destroyed 105.6sq-mi of the built-up areas. Many of the factories had been burned or put out of operation. Millions of Japanese families had lost their homes during the massive fire raids, and the blockade of all Japanese ports had rendered shipping impossible. It was time now to try and stop the war.

A new Premier, Adm. Kantaro Suzuki, had taken over the Japanese cabinet in April, and the civilian leadership thought Suzuki could be persuaded to at least discuss ways to end the war. Suzuki, who had taken over the top job from Hideki Tojo in April, finally realized that his country was in desperate straits and something had to be done.

Suzuki agreed to seek Moscow's intercession at the right time, but it was not until July that he persuaded his foreign minister, Shigenori Togo, to formally direct the Japanese ambassador in Moscow, Naotake Sato, to seek help from the Soviet leaders. He hoped that their influence with the Allies could help in trying to stop the war.

The Japanese government, still influenced by military leaders as late as July 1945, looked upon themselves as the ones to establish and maintain a lasting peace.

Togo's instructions to Sato seemed to counteract any proposal for stopping the war. Knowing that the United States and England weren't about to lay down any weapons and would

*Ray Brashear checks engines during start-up. Note the sixteen missions emblems and three victories over Japanese fighters displayed on his plane.* Ray Brashear

*Superfortresses from the 878 BS, 499th BG, Saipan, on the way to a target.* Ray Brashear

press the attack unless the Japanese would agree to an unconditional surrender, Togo nevertheless instructed Sato to inform the Soviets that this condition would not be accepted by Japan and that if the United States and England persisted in this demand, Japan had no alternative but to see the war through in an all-out effort, for the sake of survival and honor of the homeland.

In Sato's opinion, the Soviets would not go along with any Japanese proposals, and he thought Tokyo's view of the world situation was unrealistic. He told the Foreign Minister this and that, in his opinion, England and America were planning to "take the right of maintaining peace away from Japan." He voiced doubts that Japan was in a position or had the reserve strength to resist the war further, and questioned whether it was necessary to further sacrifice the lives of hundreds of thousands of soldiers and millions of other innocent residents of cities and metropolitan areas.

This would certainly be the outcome if the Imperial General Headquarters continued to gird for such a war of resistance, he predicted.

The fact that the B-29s were able to bomb cities and towns across Japan almost unchallenged was somewhat of a mystery among General LeMay and other Allied leaders. The reasons were not fully known until after the war: Expecting an invasion of their homeland, Japanese military leaders had hoarded at least 8,000 aircraft and hid them in undetected areas, built one-way runways scattered throughout the country, and waited. Most of the airplanes would be flown by kamikaze pilots. The Japanese thought that by delaying an invasion, they could hold out indefinitely and thus demand better surrender terms.

With little or no air opposition, General LeMay continued the leaflet propaganda drops on cities that would be hit the next day. The civilian desire to continue the war correspondingly declined.

## The Manhattan Project and the 509th Composite Group

In the best-kept secret the US Government ever involved itself with, a mysterious special project code-named the Manhattan Engineer District, with Brig. Gen. Leslie Groves directing, began work on producing the atomic bomb in 1942. By 1943, it was time to think about how the B-29 would have to be modified to deliver the bomb to a target. General Arnold

instructed his chief assistant for air material, now Maj. Gen. Oliver P. Echols, to have a B-29 modified to meet specifications for carrying the bomb. Echols selected his assistant, Col. Roscoe Wilson, as the special project officer to get the job done. Wilson called on now Col. Donald Putt at Wright Field, who happened to have been the first USAAF officer to fly a B-29, to help carry out the highly secret project.

A B-29 was borrowed from the 58th BW, and its bomb bay was modified to accommodate two bombs of different sizes: one, nicknamed Little Boy, which would be 28in in diameter and 120in long and weigh 9,000lb; and another, nicknamed Fat Man, which would be 60in in diameter and 128in long and weigh about 10,000lb. The bombs would be used separately, not loaded at the same time.

After modifications were done and tested with simulated bombs of the size and weight of the two atomic bombs, a contract was awarded to a firm in Omaha, Nebraska, to modify at least fourteen B-29Bs immediately. The A-bomb modification order eventually was increased to fifty-four, but only forty-six B-29s were modified before war's end.

General Arnold selected Lt. Col. Paul W. Tibbets, Jr., to command a

*As the missions against Japan accelerated, so did the scrap pile on Tinian of wrecked Superfortresses and other aircraft.* Bill Rooney

new, self-sustaining combat unit, called the 509th Composite Group (CG), in the summer of 1944. Tibbets had been flight-testing the B-29s since shortly after production of the Superfortress began. Before joining the B-29 testing program, Tibbets had completed twenty-five combat missions in B-17s over Europe and North Africa, and he was considered an outstanding pilot.

When Tibbets assumed command of the new combat unit, he alone was informed of the nature of his mission. His initial duties were to find an isolated spot in the United States where the unusual training program could be carried out with the least chances for leaks of what the ultra-secret unit was training for. He was also responsible for selecting personnel for the unit. Wendover, Utah, was selected as the training site. For the nucleus of his combat unit, he chose the 393rd BS, which was then in training with the 6th BG, a unit of the 313th BW, in Nebraska. Maj. Charles W. Sweeney, commander of the 393rd BS, moved

his unit to Wendover in September 1944. The 320th Troop Carrier Squadron with its C-54s was attached to the group to move the group's personnel anywhere in the world. The 320th would be called the Green Hornet Airline. The 509th CG also was provided with its own engineer squadron, an air material squadron, and a military police company. By the time the 509th deployed to Tinian Island in 1945, its total strength came to 225 officers and 1,542 enlisted men.

By July, the entire 509th CG was in place on Tinian Island, and located in a special section near North Field, the entire operation was somewhat of a mystery to personnel from the nearby 313th BW.

To emphasize how secretive the 509th CG was, even General LeMay, commander of the 21st BC, was not aware of the atomic bomb program until March 1945. It was then that Col. Elmer E. Kirkpatrick, an engineering officer associated with the project, came to the Marianas to supervise the special construction at Tinian Island in preparation for the arrival of the 509th CG and to inform LeMay of its true nature and how it would fit in with the 21st BC. Soon after, General Arnold informed LeMay about the 509th's mission also, and told him that although the 509th CG would be un-

der the 21st BC's control, since the unit would be operating under an experimental nature, it would be controlled initially from his Washington headquarters. General LeMay had nothing to do but go along with his boss. Admiral Nimitz was informed of the secret operation also in February by Cdr. Frederick L. Ashworth, who had been assigned to the 509th and made a special trip to Guam to inform the admiral.

### Goin' Jessie

The Superfortresses continued to saturate cities across Japan during July and early August. The efficiency of these airplanes and their ground crews was reaching new heights.

Charles G. Chauncey, pilot on the John D. Fleming crew of the 5th BS, 9th BG, on Tinian Island, tells how proud his crew was about the accomplishments of their *Goin' Jessie*: "When we picked up our brand-new Boeing-Wichita–built B-29, s/n 42-24856, at the Herrington, Kansas, staging base and headed west for our combat destination home on Tinian Island, little did we realize that *Goin' Jessie* would be such a prophetic name.

"In combat, *Goin' Jessie* racked up all kinds of records. On July 10, 1945, at 0118 o'clock over Wakayama, Japan, *Jessie* was credited with dropping the 2,000,000th ton of bombs dropped by the USAAF on the Axis since World War II began. Colonel Luschen, squadron commander, who was riding with us that day, verified the bomb drop and claimed the record for the aircraft. But that accomplishment was minor compared to record-setters that followed.

"We were certain we had a good flight crew, thought we had a good airplane, and we had what we considered an excellent ground crew headed by M/Sgt. Einar S. ('Curley') Klabo. Our thoughts were all justified indeed. We never had to abort a combat mission. *Goin Jessie* lived up to our expectation all the way.

"When we left for the States, after completing our thirty-five–mission combat tour, Lt. William Reynolds and crew took over *Goin Jessie*, and kept the no-abort record intact, up to and including the final large-scale bombing raid on Japan on August 14, 1945. It was *Goin' Jessie*'s fiftieth mission without a single abort. That record means that not once did a crew have to return to base without completing the assigned mission because of mechanical troubles, an outstanding accomplishment indeed.

"When the war ended, *Jessie* had flown 808 combat hours, or 135,000mi, or five-and-one-half times around the world, and had dropped 645,000lb of explosives on targets in Japan.

"Accomplishing this amazing combat record, Jessie had used twelve engines, three sets of tires, 295,000gal of gas, and more than 5,000gal of oil.

"For such an outstanding performance of keeping *Goin' Jessie* going, Sergeant Klabo, who had remained crew chief for the entire record-setting performance of *Goin' Jessie*, was awarded the Legion of Merit medal."

Colonel Huglin, commander of the 9th BG, remembers the circumstances surrounding the awarding of the medal to Sergeant Klabo the day Gen. Carl Spaatz, newly named commander of the US Strategic Air Forces in the Pacific, came to Tinian Island: "General Davis, the 313th BW commander, sent word to us group commanders of the Wing to come to his headquarters to be present at the briefing for General Spaatz and to have lunch with him.

"While driving my jeep to Wing Headquarters, I was speculating on what I would tell the General if he should say to me, 'Well, Colonel, what problems do you have that I can help with?'

"Well, wonder of wonders, I was placed next to General Spaatz at lunch, and he said just that to me! I told him that most everything was going very well in our operations and maintenance, but I was having trouble getting awards for our deserving men in a reasonable length of time. I cited, in particular, Master Sergeant Klabo, the crew chief of a B-29 nicknamed *Goin' Jessie*, which had completed almost fifty combat missions with a perfect maintenance record. I thought Sergeant Klabo deserved a prompt award of the Legion of Merit. General Spaatz said, 'I agree. And furthermore, I will present it to him this afternoon.' And he did. Now, that is command action!"

*A bit of flak harassed a flight of B-29s over Tokyo.* 73rd BW Photo/Chuck Spieth

*The harbor at Guam.* Bill Rooney

117

## Chapter 15

# Final Blow of World War II

The final days of World War II were ticking down to the final onslaught by the middle of July 1945. Colonel Tibbets, with his 509th CG's full complement of men and machines in place at their Tinian Island home base—even before the first test explosion of the nuclear bomb—was anxiously awaiting the word "Go." Confidence displayed by the scientists and engineers of the Manhattan Engineer District project over-shadowed uncertainty. The ultimate climax was near.

Early on the morning of July 16, two B-29 Superfortresses at Kirkland Field in Albuquerque, New Mexico, took off after a short delay because of weather conditions over their target. The Superfortresses were equipped with a variety of instruments, electronic devices, cameras, and other equipment to record the fireball's intensity and other phenomena that was expected to occur during the explosion of an atomic bomb. The "bomb" was attached to a 100ft-tall steel tower located at a site called Trinity, in the white-sands desert west of Alamogordo, New Mexico. The two B-29s were still several miles from the test sight when a tremendous explosion occurred. The time was a few seconds past 5:20am, and the pilots gasped in amazement at the brightness of the explosion, described by Gen. Leslie Groves as equal to several suns at midday. The explosion, rattled windows in houses over 100mi away in Albuquerque, New Mexico.

At exactly the same time of the explosion, Jim Teague, a B-29 flight engineer in transition training at the Alamogordo Air Base, was pre-flighting his B-29 in preparation for a training flight, when all of a sudden it seemed, he said, "the entire universe lit up and we could see as plain as day." He had just asked his helper to bring the crew chief lights around so he could see to inspect an engine. His helper said, "You don't need a light, the sun is coming up." Teague's reply was, "The sun, hell! That light is coming from the west—a plane must have exploded. At about that time, a major sped down the flight line in his jeep, waving to the crews about ready to crank their planes and take off. 'All planes, cut your engines. We've got orders to delay your takeoff.' It was not until after August 6, 1945, the day Hiroshima was bombed, that we found out why all our planes were grounded for a short time that morning on July 16."

Word of a successful atomic bomb test was flashed to President Truman, who was attending an Allied conference at Potsdam. The president informed Winston Churchill and Chiang Kai-shek about the successful test, and a declaration was issued, calling upon the Japanese government to surrender immediately. The declaration warned that the alternative would be Japan's prompt and complete destruction. Japan's Premier Suzuki dismissed the declaration with a strong determination to fight on to a successful conclusion.

The stage was set. President Truman had approved the dropping of the A-bomb on Japan, so the time set to drop the first atomic bomb was as soon as weather would permit after August 3. Gen. George Marshall and Secretary of State Henry Stimson approved the mission sent to them at Potsdam by acting chief of staff, Gen. Thomas T. Handy, on July 24, and the clock began to tick. The mission directive was dispatched to Gen. Carl Spaatz, who was directed to send a copy of the document to Admiral Nimitz and General MacArthur.

The target for the first drop would be one of a list of four cities: Hiroshima, Kokura, Niigata, or Nagasaki.

As Tibbets' 509th CG stood by awaiting favorable weather, the 21st BC went about sending Superfortresses loaded with mines and firebombs across Japan. B-29s from all five wings were on the prowl over Japan during the night of August 1–2. A

*Pilots, man your planes! P-51s of the 21st FG on Iwo Jima ready for takeoff, as seen beneath the three-story tail of a Superfortress "Mother Ship." Josh Curtis*

*P-51s of the 567th Fighter Command arrived at Iwo Jima soon after the island was captured on March 16, 1945: The Mustangs* *were a beautiful sight on the ground but were much prettier when escorting B-29s over Japan.* Marshall

*Adm. Chester Nimitz addresses an assembly during the ceremony dedicating a B-29 named in his honor, while the crew of the* *plane and Colonel Hubbard and General Armstrong look on.* John Mitchell

record-breaking 836 Superfortresses took part in the mission.

As if waiting for the weather to dictate the exact time when Colonel Tibbets would load up and head for the as-yet-unknown target in Japan with his "secret weapon," General LeMay waited until the night of August 5 to send another force of 635 Superforts to Japan, loaded with fire-bombs, mines, and explosives. The B-29s were back at their bases before an early-morning departure of another B-29, this one with the name *Enola Gay* freshly painted on its nose. Piloted by Tibbets, that B-29 took off from North Field on Tinian Island on a mission that would send shock waves around the world. It was 2:45am, the morning of August 6, 1945.

## Hiroshima's Fate Sealed

Three B-29s loaded with weather-observing instruments, proceeded Tibbets' departure by about 1hr. Their mission was to fly to the area of the selected targets in Japan and check and report weather conditions back to the *Enola Gay* as the flight to Japan developed. The city of Hiroshima, with a population of 245,000 residents, had already been selected as the primary target, if the weather was favorable for a visual drop. If not, one of the other three cities would have been the target.

Maj. Claude Eatherly, flying *Straight Flush*, led the weather planes off the runway at North Field, followed by *Jabbitt III* and *Full House*. The latter two planes were to check weather conditions at Kokura and Nagasaki, respectively. At Iwo Jima, Lt. Charles McKnight and his crew stood by in another Superfortress, to take the place of *Enola Gay* if mechanical trouble developed before they reached Iwo Jima. Their stand-by services were not needed.

Two B-29s following the *Enola Gay* off the runway at North Field would play a vital role in the mission. The second plane off was the camera plane, flown by Maj. George Marquardt, followed by Maj. Charles W. Sweeney's plane, loaded with blast gauges and other instruments.

*Straight Flush* reached Hiroshima shortly after 7am. After crossing over the city twice, Major Eatherly flashed

the word to Tinian Island and to the en route *Enola Gay* that Hiroshima was clear for a visual bomb drop. Hiroshima would be the target.

After passing Iwo Jima, Tibbets and the accompanying planes began their climb to a bombing altitude of 31,500ft. Navy Capt. William ("Deke") Parson, the weaponeer, armed the bomb as the three planes headed for Hiroshima. At 9:15am, the bombardier pushed the button that released the bomb, and 2min later, the explosion took place, timed to go off 2,000ft above the ground. The blast killed more than 78,000 people in Hiroshima and injured another 51,000. More than 48,000 buildings in the city were completely destroyed and an additional 22,178 were badly damaged. More than 176,000 people were made homeless.

During the training for the atomic bombing missions, Colonel Tibbets never clarified the special weapon they were training to drop. He always called it "the Gimmick," never mentioning the term "atomic bomb."

The day before the strike, Colonel Tibbets ordered the name *Enola Gay* be painted on the nose of the plane. The Superfortress actually was assigned to Capt. Robert Lewis, one of Tibbets' hand-picked pilots. Lewis first saw the new name just prior to take-off. According to some who were there, he asked, "Who the hell did that?" He was told that the name *Enola Gay* was painted there by order of Tibbets, and that it was Tibbets' mother's name.

There was no let-up with the dropping of the atomic bomb on Hiroshima. The Superfortresses from the 58th, 73rd, and 313th BWs struck the Toyokawa Arsenal in a 151-plane daylight raid, dropping 124 tons of explosives from 19,000–23,600ft. Again on the night of August 7, the 505th BG of

*Diamond Y-3 flew with the 501st BG, 315th BW, Guam. The 315th came to Guam a few months before the Japanese surrendered. Most of their planes were painted black underneath and up the sides to hide them from the Japanese searchlights.* Bill Rooney

the 313th BW sent thirty-two B-29s loaded with 189 tons of mines to drop on seven different targets.

The Japanese government, determined to continue the war at all costs, attempted to downplay the atomic attack on Hiroshima. This brought out a 245 B-29 force, on August 8, from the 58th, 73rd, and 313th BWs, again to drop incendiary bombs on the urban area of Yawata in the southern island of Kyushu. At the same time, the 314th BW struck an industrial area of Tokyo with a sixty-plane force. The Japanese fighters and antiaircraft still

*The* Enola Gay *is parked in its hardstand after dropping the first atomic bomb. Lt. Col. Paul Tibbets, commander of the 509th CG was at the controls of this aircraft when the world was introduced to the power of atomic energy as the bomb demolished the city of Hiroshima, Japan.* Warren Thompson

had a little fight, knocking down four B-29s during the Yawata raid and three at Tokyo.

## Second Atomic Bomb

The Japanese showed no indications of being ready to end the war under Allied terms, so a second atomic mission was scheduled for August 9.

After the destruction of Hiroshima, Foreign Minister Togo, along with other Japanese leaders, realized that if their government didn't surrender immediately, their cities were in jeopardy of being totally destroyed and their people killed. On August 8, while the second atomic mission was being readied, Togo met with Emperor Hirohito and advised him to accept the Potsdam Declaration quickly. The Emperor agreed, and said it was time to try to prevent another tragedy like Hiroshima. Togo dispatched the Emperor's message to Premier Suzuki, who, regrettably, was unable to convene the foot-dragging Supreme War Council until the next day.

The plutonium bomb called Fat Man, weighing about 12,000lb, was already loaded on the B-29 called *Bock's Car*, and was ready to leave for the second atomic strike against Japan. Major Sweeney was the aircraft commander, and Fred Olivi was co-pilot that day. The strike plane on the second mission was supposed to have been the *Great Artiste*, but since it had been used as one of the two observation planes on the Hiroshima strike, the wired instruments had not been removed in time to load the bomb for the second mission. Capt. Fred Bock flew one of the observation planes on the second strike.

As in the first mission, alternate targets were selected for the second atomic strike. Kokura was selected as the primary target, with Nagasaki named as alternate. If weather prevented a visual drop at the primary target, they were to proceed to the alternate target immediately.

Jake Beser, the radar countermeasure operator for both missions, said the "Hollywood premier" atmosphere was non-existent for the second mission. It was almost as if they were about to leave on a routine B-29 mission to Japan, similar to the mass raids in the past. Beser was the only person to fly on both strike aircraft, and was considered the most experienced man available to monitor the sensitive equipment. He recalls that the second mission got off to a bad start from the very beginning and got worse as time passed: "I was beginning to feel the effects of the lack of sleep when we got to *Bock's Car* and sat down on the Colonel's jeep until it was time to go. The appointed time came and went, and we still were sitting there. Something was causing a delay in our departure.

"Major Sweeney came over to Colonel Tibbets' jeep several times, and they removed themselves from our presence and had several animated discussions. At one point, Fred Asworth, the assigned weaponeer for this mission, was made privy to the discussions, but obviously neither Bill Laurence, the *New York Times* correspondent who was assigned to cover the mission, nor I could contribute to it, so we weren't told what the trouble was. I learned from one of my enlisted men that there were two concerns: one, the weather over Japan was not clearing as expected; and two, there was some kind of problem with the bomb bay fuel transfer."

The anxious moments before take-off were only a prelude of what was to come. Major Sweeney proceeded to Kokuro to find the entire area covered with a thick layer of smoke, caused by the mass incendiary raid on Yawata the night before. Yawata and Kokuro were located near each other, and the dense smoke still covered both cities. There was nothing to do but to proceed to Nagasaki, the alternate target. There was a nine-tenths cloud coverage over that city also. Sweeney made the decision to fly a second and possibly a third run over the city while Capt. Kermit Beahan searched for a hole in the overcast. By this time, the flight engineer told Sweeney that something would have to be done soon, or they would run out of fuel and not make it back to Iwo Jima. Sweeney tried one more fly-over and this time, Captain Beahan yelled that he could see a slight opening in the clouds. He immediately lowered the bomb bays and prepared to drop the bomb. He flipped the switch, and Fat Man was on its way. A few seconds later, Nagasaki disappeared under the familiar fireball and mushroom clouds that raced toward the sky. An estimated 35,000 people died.

Troubles for the crew were a long way from over. The troublesome fuel transfer pump, discussed back at Tinian Island before takeoff, refused to transfer fuel from one of the storage tanks. A quick check indicated that there was not enough fuel left to make it back to Iwo Jima, so Major Sweeney decided to try the shorter distance to Okinawa, which was not given as an alternate landing site, even though preparations were being made to accommodate General Doolittle's 8th Air Force.

The crew of *Bock's Car* finally found a field, but it was a fighter strip. Sweeney decided to try to land there anyway, because it was doubtful that they could make it any farther. The last foul-up came when the men in the tower refused to believe that *Bock's Car* had been over Japan and dropped the atomic bomb. Finally, Sweeney turned and started the final approach for the short fighter strip, ignoring the tower personnel trying to wave him off. He just barely made it, borrowed some gas, took off, and returned to Tinian Island.

The atomic bomb dropped on Nagasaki was the last one dropped in anger. It served its purpose despite the anxiety it caused that day among the *Bock's Car* crew. Fred Olivi, co-pilot on the plane had this observation of the part he played in the last atomic bomb dropped: "As a participant in the bombing of Nagasaki, I hope that it marked the final chapter in the history of atomic warfare. I will never forget the sight of that ugly mushroom cloud arising from the ruins of Nagasaki.

"The night following the bombing, we huddled around our radios on Tinian Island and heard Japan sue for peace. For the first time, I began to realize the significance of our mission and the importance of our group. Two B-29s altered the course of history."

It would be five days before the Japanese government finally threw in the towel. During this time, hundreds of Japanese citizens became victims of the B-29 onslaught. It was not before the Emperor himself met with the War Cabinet, and in an unprecedented address to the military leaders, which

Sleepy Time Gal *was assigned to the 498th BG, 73rd BW, Saipan.* Dickson

was broadcast to the citizens of Japan, he insisted that Japan should surrender. Capitulation was expected momentarily.

On the night of August 14, no effort had been made by the Japanese government to make contact or formally seek an end of hostilities with the Allies. Hundreds of Superfortresses were scheduled for another strike at targets throughout Japan, and the crews were all told to carefully listen to their radios on the way up to their targets. They were instructed to abort their mission, drop their bombs in the ocean, and return to their bases, if word that the war had ended was received. The message never came that

night, and the Superfortresses completed their last combat mission of World War II.

It would be during the morning of August 15, 1945, that word of Japan's surrender finally came.

## Air-Sea Rescue

By the end of World War II, it was appropriate to note and give thanks that the air-sea rescue operation had come of age. With an outstanding record, statistics prove it was highly successful in saving many men who

軍閥の日本を鞭て亡び行く一国家を救ふ事は諸君

軍閥が国家に倒れたる時更に悪に逃げる報告所

軍閥が国難す倒れたる時中に逃げ報告所

国家を救ひ空襲が居るか亡ぶ説明し土就か部に居て

日本は様に不倒れ明し土就敢然し不居て居る所

*A copy of one of several leaflets dropped over Japanese cities. During the last few months of the war, many tons of propaganda leaflets were dropped on populated areas of Japan in an attempt to bring the truth of the war's progress. Japanese citizens had not been told that Japan was losing the war. The leaflets were designed to inform the civilians of Japan's military losses and reverses and to warn them of the impending bombing and burning of their cities.* Andy Doty

were forced to ditch during the air assault against Japan.

At the peak of the air-sea rescue operation in the Pacific, there were fourteen submarines, twenty-one Navy seaplanes, nine B-29 Super Dumbos, and five surface vessels patrolling the waters between Japan and the Mariana Islands. A total of 2,400 men were assigned to air-sea rescue duty. Of the 1,310 B-29 crew members known to have gone down or ditched at sea, 654, or about 50 percent, were rescued.

## Missions of Mercy

When the shooting stopped, the 20th AF set up a project called "Missions of Mercy," to search out and drop medical supplies, food, and clothing to Allied prisoners of war held by the Japanese.

Prisoner of war camps were eventually found in Japan, China, Manchuria, and Korea. The last supply drop by the Superfortresses was on September 20, 1945. By that time, 1,066 B-29s had participated in 900 effective missions to 154 camps. An estimated 63,500 Allied prisoners were provided 4,470 tons of supplies.

During the 'Missions of Mercy," eight B-29s were lost with seventy-seven crew members aboard.

When the prisoners of war were finally liberated, many stories of outrageous atrocities were told. Many prisoners died during captivity. Some had endured the hardships and abuse

*Major Track, 411 BS, 502nd BG, 315th BW, flying* The Uninvited, *claims the distinction of being the last crew to bomb Japan in World War II. They were the last plane over target at Akita the night of August 14, 1945.* George Harrington

since the fall of the Philippines during the early days of the war, as was the plight of Earl Barton, a crew chief with the 30th BS, 19th BG, stationed at Clark Field in the Philippines when their base was overrun. He eventually ended up at a prisoner of war camp called Shinagawa, located in the Tokyo area. Barton will never forget the inhumane treatment he and others received: "I wound up in a camp near Tokyo, where I witnessed the B-29 bombings and fire raids on Tokyo. What a spectacular show! It was tremendous! After three-and-one-half years of imprisonment, I felt the Japanese deserved every bomb showered on them.

"The B-29 raids literally blew and burned us out of Tokyo. Personally, I never got enough. I wanted the whole island destroyed! The Japanese treated us like caged animals. We were spat on, kicked, forced to eat crap, jeered at, stabbed, poked, slapped, beaten, humiliated, and tortured both physically and mentally. What a relief it was to see and hear the American planes coming over and knowing that the war would have to end soon.

"When people ask me what the fire raids on Tokyo were like, I sum it by quoting an old Army saying, 'The wind blew, the shit flew, and visibility was obscured for days.'"

## The Show of Force Mission

The surrender date was set for September 2, 1945. All the main characters who were instrumental in bringing Japan to the surrender table were there on the main deck of the battleship *Missouri*, docked in Tokyo Bay and surrounded by hundreds of US Navy ships. At the head table sat General of the Army Douglas MacArthur presiding over the historic event. Directly behind him stood General LeMay, Admiral Nimitz, and others most responsible for the day's event. Also standing tall was Lt. Gen. Jonathan Wainwright. He looked frail, skinny, and clearly visible in his eyes were the years of abuse he had endured since it came his lot, back on May 5, 1941, to surrender the last stronghold of the American army at Corregidor to the conquering Japanese army.

While the ceremony was taking place aboard the *Missouri*, the big stars of the show roared in from the south, displaying what was billed as "The Show of Force." In battle formation, more than 500 B-29 Superfortresses, representing every unit of the 20th AF, roared across Tokyo Bay, in what was a spine-tingling display of power. Certainly nobody attending the surrender ceremony, including the Japanese official who signed the docu-ments in the name of the Emperor, would doubt that had it not been for the Superfortresses, the ceremony would not be taking place on that date.

## Tallying the Score

The 20th AF operated for fifteen months, had suffered 3,015 casualties—dead, wounded, and missing, and had lost 414 bombers. Only 147 of the bombers lost were attributed to flak or fighter attacks. They had dropped almost 170,000 tons of bombs on enemy targets, and had flown 34,790 sorties during the war.

A couple of significant quotes came to light sometime later. Prince Konoye of the Japanese Royal Family said, "Fundamentally, the thing that brought about the determination to make peace was the prolonged bombing by the B-29s."

Premier Suzuki, who evidently had trouble convincing the War Plans Committee that the war was lost, said, "I, myself, on the basis of the B-29 raids, felt that the cause was hopeless."

A lot of water had gone under the bridges, and the oceans' tides had risen and fallen many times since President Roosevelt pronounced December 7, 1941, the "Day of Infamy."

*Chapter 16*

# Between the Wars

With the war ended, all thoughts turned to going home. For some, beginning the long trip eastward wasn't long coming. A point system was used to determine who went home first.

To get some people home fast, the Superfortresses were turned into transports and loaded with human cargo, rather than supplies or bombs. They called it Operation Sunset.

Since there was no more use for so many Superfortresses in the Marianas bases, a rotation system was set up for men and planes. Operation Sunset originated at Saipan, since the 73rd BW crewmen had been in the Pacific longer than those in other wings, with the exception of the 58th BW, which had transferred from the CBI theater. If a full combat crew were eligible for rotation, they would bring a B-29 back to the States, including additional men. Personal effects were loaded on the aircraft. The Air Transport Command, plus Navy cargo or transport

*And then there was one! Long gone are the thousands of B-29 Superfortresses that played a major role in winning World War II, with the exception of fewer than twenty-five on static display in the United States and some foreign countries. Only one is still flying: Fifi, reclaimed and owned by the Confederate Air Force of Texas, participates around the country in Air Shows, much to the delight of those of us who flew them in combat. Glenn Chaney*

*B-29s line up at Isley Field, Saipan, awaiting orders to load supplies in planes to be dropped at POW camps. Josh Curtis*

ships, also brought some of the Sun-setters home.

Some of the last wings to arrive in the Marianas, such as the 315th, and the 314th at Guam, were ordered to remain on station to maintain a stable force until other decisions were made.

## B-29 Boneyards

Arrangements were made to deliver the returning B-29s to what some called "boneyards" or open storage areas. Many of the Superfortresses were stored in western states, where the dry humidity would not deteriorate or rust the aircraft as much as if they were stored in more humid areas. Many of the B-29s were mothballed, with exposed parts enclosed in a cocoon to prevent deterioration. These aircraft could be recalled in a very

*A prisoner of war camp where Americans were held in Japan. Note the initials "P.O.W." painted on the tops of buildings to aid supply aircraft to find them.* John D. Kremer

short time and put back in service if needed. Large numbers of B-29s were stored at Davis-Monthan Air Force Base (AFB) at Tucson, and at China Lake, California, Pyote, Texas, and Tinker Field, Oklahoma.

Many of the Superfortresses fell prey to the chopping block. Consumers were starved for aluminum pots and pans, and since the B-29 was now living out its usefulness as a bomber, entrepreneurs decided they could produce a lot of cookware with all that aluminum.

Norman Lent, who served as a flight engineer in the 3rd PRS during the war and was then working for Lockheed, watched salvage people at Pyote, Texas, convert Superfortresses to aluminum ingots: "The Texas Railroad Co. set up shop at Pyote to scrap out B-29s by the hundreds. They had blast furnaces going day and night to melt down the big bombers. For me, it was a heart-breaking, gruesome sight.

"The salvagers would tow the planes to an area where they removed the engines and some of the internal needs. After this, they would flip the plane over on its back and chop holes in the leading edges of the wings so that they could remove the fuel valves. After the landing gear and wheels were removed, a large knife, which was dropped from a high boom, would cut the fuselage and wings into pieces. A crane would then pick up the pieces and drop them into a furnace, where the once-proud warbirds were converted into almost-pure aluminum ingots. All of the B-29s that remained at Pyote after we had selected the ones to de-moth were scrapped out in this manner."

### B-29s Fulfill Post-War Tasks

Not all B-29s were destined for scrapping after the war, however. They remained the Strategic Air

*Food and medical supplies were dropped over the POW camps.* 73rd BW Photo/ Hurth Thompkins

Force's top bomber until 1948, when they were replaced with the revised Superfortress version, then called the B-50. Soon after that, a brand-new bomber, the B-36, appeared. The B-29s were then designated medium bombers. It was something of a demotion for the most advanced bomber of World War II.

## Bikini Atomic Tests

One of the major undertakings after World War II was a project involving further testing with atomic bomb explosions. Operation Crossroads would involve 242 ships, including aircraft carriers, battleships, and cruisers from US, Japanese, and German fleets; 10,000 instruments; and more than 42,000 people. The exercise took place at Bikini Atoll, located 200mi west of Kwajalein.

Two atomic bombs were exploded in separate events, one dropped from a B-29 Superfortress and one at an underwater position near the center of the dispersed ships. The 509th CG was, again, selected to drop the bomb. Col. Paul Tibbets was assigned the duty of dropping the Fat Man-type bomb, and he would again be flying the *Enola Gay*.

The USAAF's element, known as Task Force 1.5, consisted of about 2,000 personnel, drawn mostly from the Strategic Air Forces and under the command of Gen. Roger Ramey. Five B-29s code-named Silverplates and modified to drop an atomic bomb, took part in the exercise. Also participating were one standard B-29 and eight F-13As from the 3rd PRS, responsible for taking pictures after the drop. The Air Weather Service sent three RB-29s to check weather over the test site before the drop.

July 1, 1946, was designated the drop date, which was code-named Able Day. Because of mechanical troubles on drop day, the *Enola Gay* was grounded and *Dave's Dream* was substituted, with another pilot flying it.

Five ships were sunk by the atomic explosion and nine were heavily damaged.

The Superfortresses were also involved in the second phase of "Operation Crossroads." The underwater explosion took place several weeks after Able Day, and the B-29s were used for

support functions, such as photographic and data collection.

## The Tanker's Role

With the advent of jet fighters, the Air Force had to activate an entirely new type of a support unit for the short-range aircraft. The new designa-

*Barrels of supplies were dropped in this photograph. Note POWs outside the buildings anxiously awaiting the landing of the containers.* Hurth Thompkins

A 500th BG ground crewman stands by with a fire extinguisher while an engine is started. The 500th BG aircraft were last to leave Saipan in Operation Sunset Project at the end of the war. During this operation, the mighty bombers were used as transports to carry the group's personnel home. USAAF Photo

tion for the unit was air refueling squadrons, and the B-29s were ideal for this task of in-flight refueling.

The Air Force borrowed a British-developed system of trailing hoses and grapnel hooks. Another modification had to convert B-29s to tankers with the aircraft coming from the Strategic Air Forces. In 1948, the Boeing plant at Wichita was re-opened for the express purpose of modifying the B-29s as tankers. These aircraft were designated KB-29Ms. Seventy four B-29s were converted to tankers at the Wichita plant.

## The Air Weather Service

World War II experiences with the weather, especially in the Pacific, convinced the USAAF of the need for better weather observation and monitoring, and led to the development of a tracking system to locate and report bad weather, such as typhoons and hurricanes.

The Air Weather Service was organized in 1946 and, using RB-29s, soon became global weather watchers. The first flight over the top of a hurricane was made by an Air Weather Service B-29 on October 7, 1946, and on March 17, 1947, the first RB-29 flight over the North Pole was made.

In 1950, after a complete overhaul, the RB-29s were redesignated again, this time to WB-29.

Col. Ray Brashear was operations officer for the 514th Weather Reconnaissance Squadron, later changed to the 54th Strategic Reconnaissance Squadron at North Guam Air Base, and then again to Anderson AFB. He relates some of the tactics used to

Gen. Jonathan Wainwright, left, whose lot it was to surrender the Philippines to the Japanese early in World War II, paid a visit to Boeing-Wichita after his release and recuperation from the long confinement in prisoner of war camps, to see the Bataan Avenger. Boeing Archives

track weather in that part of the world: "The area south and west of Guam is where most typhoons developed. The path of individual typhoons is very erratic, but generally makes a sweeping curve northwest, then north, and finally northeast if they do not dissipate sooner. Some developed and died without ever touching land. Others, at different times, roared across the Philippines, Formosa, Okinawa, the China coast, and even Japan. Needless to say, everyone in that part of the world was vitally interested in the location, strength, and general movement of the storm. Ships at sea had a most urgent need to know where the typhoon was and its general direction and speed of movement.

"When a tropical storm or typhoon developed, the 514th made a morning and afternoon fix on its location. This required flying into the eye to determine the intensity of each quadrant. Depending on its proximity to a suitable refueling base, one airplane might make the morning fix and then linger in the storm area for the late afternoon fix before heading for Iwo Jima, Clark USAAF Base in the Philippines, Okinawa, or back to Guam."

Jim O'Donnell remained in service a while after the war because, he said, "the USAAF suddenly found themselves short of good experienced overwater navigators." He was assigned to a weather squadron in Guam and he recalls one of the flights he made to the Philippines checking on a typhoon; it was the most violent storm he had ever encountered: "Our B-29 was thrown around like a straw, about like [by] the heat thermals over Japan during fire raids. When we landed at Clark AFB, we noticed that the rivets were torn from the fuselage in places. We had to leave the plane at Clark Field, and we learned later it was scrapped."

## B-29s Loaned to RAF

Eighty B-29s were "loaned" to the British RAF in 1950. The RAF gave the ex-Superfortresses a new name, Washington, and used them for long-

range observations and to experiment with some very heavy bombs.

All of the B-29s were eventually returned to the USAF.

## The B-50

As World War II was heading for the last round-up, Boeing Aircraft Co. was still determined to eliminate the remaining deficiencies in its B-29 Superfortress. Designers came up with a much-improved version of the Superfortress at about the time that the Japanese threw in the towel. The new version was called the B-29D. It had many changes but still resembled the original B-29. The most notable difference was the tail, which was 5ft taller than that of the B-29, bringing the overall height over 33ft.

The 2,200hp Wright R-3350 engines were replaced by 3,500hp Pratt & Whitney R-4350 engines. The B-29D's 141ft wingspan was about the same as that of the original B-29s, as was its 99ft length. Gross weight was increased to 173,000lb, and top speed was 380mph at 25,000ft altitude. Service ceiling was rated at 36,000ft, load was 20,000lb maximum, and range was 4,900mi.

*Robert Robbins, left, holds the distinction of having served as experimental test pilot at Boeing, and accumulated more than 470hr on the no. 1 XB-29. During the last few years, he has flown Fifi, becoming the only living person known to have flown the first and the last B-29. Robbins poses at an air show in Florida with Glenn Chaney. Glenn Chaney*

In December 1945, the B-29D was redesignated the B-50. It served as an interim bomber, along with some not-yet-retired B-29s, until the jet-powered B-47 came on line.

Boeing built 370 B-50s during the period of 1945 to 1953. There were three bomber conversions—the RB-50 for reconnaissance, the WB-50 for weather, and the KB-50 for tanker service—as well as a version for training (the TB-50) and for testing (the DB-50). Some of the KB-50Js were fitted with two General Electric J-47 turbojet engines of 5,000lb thrust to increase speed for refueling jet aircraft.

The B-50s did not see combat in Korea, but did serve as tankers during the Vietnam War. They were retired from service in 1965.

## Chapter 17

# B-29s in Korea

They called it the Korean Conflict, the Limited War, or a Political War, but whatever the nomenclature, it was a plain war to the foot soldiers and the air crewmen who risked their lives in the air above the 38th parallel in Korea. The shrapnel from flak barrages and bullets from Soviet-built MiG fighters were just as deadly as the hits that snuffed out the lives of young airmen over Europe and Japan in World War II.

Historians kept dispatching their fading-glory stories about the swan song of the B-29 Superfortress, but on June 25, 1950, just a few months short of her seventh birthday, the gallant old B-29 was called on, once again, to go to war. For two-and-one-half years, she again showed her mettle, despite limitations and restrictions dictated by politicians.

It was on that date, again a Sunday morning, that a horde of Communist North Koreans crossed the 38th parallel and attacked the Republic of Korea to the south. For the southern Korean soldiers guarding the border, it was no contest. The invading North Koreans swept through their ranks and headed south, bent on capturing South Korea.

Beat Up Bastard *bombed the North Koreans from Kadena Air Base on Okinawa.* R. Mann

The nearest US Air Force (USAF) outfit to the trouble spot was the veteran 19th BG, the only combat unit now assigned to the once-proud and potent 20th AF. The 19th BG was located at Anderson AFB on Guam, known during World War II as North Field, where it served with distinction as one of the four B-29 BGs of the 314th BW.

General MacArthur, serving as United Nations Supreme Commander, headquartered in Tokyo, was instructed to support the South Koreans. He immediately ordered the 19th BG, with its twenty-two B-29 strike force, to answer the call and move to Kadena Air Base on Okinawa, from where it would launch an attack on North Korea.

It took the 19th BG only 19hr after receiving MacArthur's orders to strike their opening blow in the Korean War. An element of four B-29s flew to the Munsan area to search out and drop their bombs on targets of opportunity. The planes all returned safely to their base.

As the war heated up, the USAF sent two more of its B-29 groups to make up the Far East Air Force (FEAF), commanded by Maj. Gen. "Rosey" O'Donnell. Joining the FEAF to begin attacks on Korea were the 22nd and 92nd BGs. Col. Jim Edmundson, who served as commander of the 468th BG, 58th BW in India,

China, and Tinian Island in World War II, commanded the 22nd BG. O'Donnell's FEAF was headquartered in Yokota, Japan. In July, two more B-29 groups, the 98th and the 307th, were sent to Japan to join the FEAF.

President Truman let it be known that he was against indiscriminate bombing of North Korea, and bombers were not to fly beyond the borders of North Korea.

By mid-September, General O'Donnell was satisfied that all major strategic targets in North Korea had been neutralized, and he ordered the 22nd and 92nd BGs to return to the United States. With the air war well in hand, he told the other two groups they probably could spend Christmas back in the United States.

But by November, things began to take on a different hew along the Yalu River. The Chinese began a build-up of soldiers and equipment just across the river, poised to join the fray and engulf the American and South Korean troops. General O'Donnell sent his bombers to the bridges across the Yalu, but the river had begun freezing over, making it possible for the Chinese to cross on the ice. By July, the North Koreans had acquired enough MiG fighters that they could mount major air strikes. General MacArthur ordered General O'Donnell to send B-29s to the airfield in North Korea to attempt to neutralize them, but they

*Tail gunner Albert E. Conder and crew of 92nd BG, 325th BS, shown taking off from RAF Station Southorp, England, prior to Korean War.* Albert Conder

had to pull back to try and stop the invaders from the north. It was touch and go, but B-29s from the 19th BG had some success dropping "Raisin" bombs, which were directed to the target by radio beams. These bombs were the forerunners of the "smart" bombs used against Iraq in Operation Desert Storm.

Negotiations for a peace settlement had been started in 1950, but progress was almost nonexistent.

*B-29 of the 580th Air Resupply Squadron on a search and rescue mission assigned at Burtonwood, England, 1953.* Robert Tharratt

*Albert Conder remembers the cold weather during the winter of 1953 at Lowrey Field, Colorado, where he received gunnery training.* Albert Conder

Albert E. Conder, a central fire control gunner with the 92nd BG, tells of how fate stepped in and saved his life as he watched his good friends being shot down near Sinanju in North Korea: "In December 1948, I was assigned to a crew in the 92nd BG, 325th BS, commanded by 1st Lt. James T. Patrick. This crew had a permanently assigned aircraft, a B-29, no. 2084.

"No. 2084, held a very special place in my heart. It was the first B-29

*Typhoon Goon II, a fully modified WB-29 of the 54th Strategic Reconnaissance Squadron (Weather), formerly the 514th Weather Reconnaissance Squadron. The Unit was located at Guam, 1949–1951.* Ray Brashear

B-29 pilots practice formation flying near their base at Lowrey Field, Colorado, before shipping out to join the FEAF command. Albert Conder

that I ever flew on. It was assigned to our crew for more than eighteen months and during that time, we had flown it to Bermuda, England, Africa, Germany, the Azores, Alaska, and all over the United States.

"I saw it come to an untimely end on September 10, 1950, along with

Band leader Phil Harris had a popular novelty song he called "The Thing." Every time he described "the thing" or its contents, a loud drum beat drowned out his words. No one ever found out what "the thing" was. However, crew chief Sergeant Leighty knew The Thing was his WB-29. The plane flew with the 514th Weather Reconnaissance Squadron, later the 54th Squadron during the Korean War. Ray Brashear some of my very good friends and former crewmates.

"My crew was flying on no. 7326, the lead ship of a three-aircraft formation. The target was far into North Korea, near Sinanju. No. 2084 was flying the right-wing position. As we headed for the target, three shots were fired by antiaircraft guns at our formation. The first was just behind us, the second came between us and no. 2084, actually between the left wing and the horizontal stabilizer of the tail section. The next shot hit engine no. 2 of 2084. I was monitoring the command radio and heard Maj. Zane M. Hoit call a 'Mayday'.

"Major Hoit stated also, that he was going to attempt to make it to the Yellow Sea for a possible ditching. Luck was not with him or his crew, for just few minutes later, the left wing folded and no. 2084 began its death dive.

"I was able to observe everything very clearly from my position as the CFC, top gunner. I counted five 'chutes as the crew exited the falling plane, watching in horror as one of the five landed in the burning wreckage on the ground. Patrick, followed by our left wingman, took our ship down to a very low altitude, in an attempt to help our stranded crewmates. We dropped our survival kits, along with guns and ammo we had on board. We also made several strafing runs, in an attempt to give air-sea rescue time to arrive. As we circled the crash site, we could see what appeared to be thousands of either soldiers or people heading for no. 2084. It looked like an army of ants.

"It was apparent very soon that the air-sea rescue would be of no help, and it was with sad hearts and lumps in our throats that we finally had to leave those brave men to their fate and return to our home base, Yokota AFB, Japan.

"Shortly before we had been ordered to the Far East to participate in the Korean War, Lieutenant Patrick and the flight engineer, T/Sgt. Joseph C. Goslin had been transferred from our crew to another crew. Patrick became the commander of the crew flying no. 7326. I was extremely upset with this turn of events, because I wanted to continue on as the CFC

*A nice inflight of a brand new, sleek WB-29. It arrived in Guam in early 1951 ready for assignment with 514th Weather Reconnaissance Squadron based at North Guam AFB, later named Andersen AFB. The weather squadron tracked weather in support of the Korean War from Guam over Japan to a point near Russia. Ray Brashear*

*A close view of a WB-29. Symbols on the nose indicate nine typhoon penetrations. The crackerbox on the aft fuselage contained weather monitoring equipment and seen below the no. 2 is weather monitoring radar. This plane also flew with the 514th Weather Squadron. Ray Brashear*

*First Lieutenant Carlyle G. Townswick commanded B-29 number 066 during the Korean War. The aircraft known as* Townswick Terrors. *The crew flew missions against North Korea from Yokota AFB in Japan with the 325th BS, 92nd BG.* Conders

*The Lt. James T. Patrick crew pose in front of* United Notions *at their base at Yokota AFB, Japan. Ten days after this picture was taken,* United Notions *was shot down over North Korea, with another crew flying the plane. Standing left to right: 1st Lt. James T. Patrick, 1st Lt. James S. Murphy, 1st Lt. John B. Wood, Jr. Capt. James R. Cole, and Maj. Homer E. Chatfield. Kneeling, left to right , M/Sgt. Edward D. Hodsdon, S/Sgt. William T. Ayres, and S/Sgt. Paul A. Lenart.* Condor

gunner on his crew. He felt the same way, and with some persuasion, he was successful in effecting my transfer also. I honestly feel that Lieutenant Patrick saved my life, because without his help and the grace of God, I would have been on board no. 2084 that fateful September day in 1950.

"After the armistice, and prisoners were returned, we were told that four of the survivors from no. 2084 had been seen in POW camps in Manchuria. None ever returned."

The 580th Air Resupply and Communications Wing was a little-known unit that saw distinguished service in the Korean War. Robert C. Tharratt

tells about the unit's assignments during the Korean War: "The 580th Air Resupply and Communications Wing was the first of three special B-29 units that flew during the Korean War. Two squadrons [580th and 581st], equipped with modified B-29s with only the tail turret for armament, were reactivated from storage at Warner-Robins Field, Georgia, and began training at Mountain Home AFB, Idaho, early in 1951. The lower-aft turret hole was padded and used to parachute Army Special Forces at night during escape and invasion exercises in the German Alps. Bomb bays were modified to handle cargo, fuel tanks, parachute containers, or leaflet delivery equipment."

The first wing commander was Col. John Kane, a Congressional Medal of Honor recipient in World War II. Colonel Kane participated in the ill-fated first low-level B-24 raid on the Ploesti oil fields in 1943.

The 580th was deployed to Wheelus AFB in Tripoli, Libya, in October 1952 and the 581st went to Clark AFB in the Philippines shortly thereafter. Coincidentally, it was from a North African airbase that Colonel

Kane flew his B-24 on the Ploesti raid just nine years earlier. The final air resupply and communications squadron, the 582nd, trained at Mountain Home and deployed to Molesworth, England, in 1953.

Dubbed "psychological warfare" units, these squadrons were ideally suited for a variety of assignments. Many B-29 flights were long-range night missions to deliver leaflets and supplies, equipment, and personnel to "friendly, isolated forces" in remote areas. The Alps of Southern Europe, North African and Asian deserts in the distant Arabian Gulf, and the battlefield of North Korea, adjacent to Iron Curtain countries, served as an ideal training ground to develop the skill and precision necessary to carry out successful clandestine operations.

Many of the missions were hazardous low-level night flights to avoid radar detection. During one moonless-night transition mission in 1953, B-29 no. 44-61681 literally flew into the ground in the desert near Wheelus Field. Miraculously, six of the ten crew members survived. This aircraft, nicknamed *The Incendiary Blonde*, had flown sixteen missions with the 20th

*Circle-W-084 of the 325 BS, 92nd BG is shown dropping demolition bombs on targets in North Korea. The plane was based at Yokota AFB, Japan, and was part of the FEAF, commanded by Maj. Gen. Emmett O'Donnell, who commanded the 73rd BW at Saipan during World War II.* Conder

South Sea Sinner *was assigned to the 19th BG and bombed targets in North Korea from Kadena Air Base in Okinawa. The 19th BG was the last group of the old 20th Air Force of World War II fame. When* North Korea crossed the 38th parallel to start the Korean War, the 19th BG B-29s were the first to drop bombs on the North Korean invaders. R. Mann

AF during World War II. Three other aircraft from the 580th were lost during the six years of operations. The 581st and 582nd suffered similar operational losses.

The B-29s of the 581st were assigned to duty on Okinawa and flew on leaflet missions over North Korea in 1952–1953. In January 1953, a 581st B-29 was shot down over Manchuria, and the USAF crew reportedly were imprisoned as spies until 1955. The 580th remained in Libya after the Korean War to carry out special assignments during the Cold War build-up. The 580th returned to the United States in 1957 for deactivation, and the 581st and 582nd in 1958, closing another interesting but little-known chapter in the history of the B-29 Superfortress.

America's F-86 Sabre Jets were sent to Korea to try and protect the B-29s from the superior MiG Jets, but the early-model Sabres were no match for the Soviet-built MiG-15, so the B-29s tried night raids and were more successful, until the MiGs learned

Never Hoppen *also flew with the 19th BG from their base on Okinawa.* R. Mann

Nose artists never missed a stroke between wars as the 19th BG B-29s prove with sophisticated works like this on Top of the Mark. *The black belly indicated the plane did a lot of low-altitude, night flying.* R. Mann

some night fighter tricks and were successful in shooting down several B-29s.

FEAF planners were successful with their strategic campaign of sustained attacks on North Korea's hydroelectricity facilities. They selected four complexes for destruction: Sui-Ho, Chosin, Fusen, and Kyosen. The Navy contributed with carrier-born aircraft from Task Force 77 off the coast of Korea. The raids began on June 24 with the B-29s going in for the first time that night against Chosin. By June 27, it was estimated that nine-tenths of North Korea's electrical-generating capacity had been destroyed.

On July 27, 1953, negotiations for a cease fire were agreed to by all parties, and the Korea Conflict had ended after three years, one month, and two days. It was obvious the B-29 Superfortress had fought its last battle.

The old, tired B-29s had done a respectable job. They had dropped a total of 167,000 tons of bombs on the enemy, and in so doing, lost sixteen B-29s to enemy fighters, four to antiaircraft guns, and fourteen to other causes.

A job well done!

Bug's Buster *bombed North Korea as one of the 19th BG's fleet of B-29s flying missions from Kadena.* R. Mann

140

# Appendices

## B-29 Production Summary

| Type | No. Built | Plant |
|---|:---:|---:|
| XB-29-BO | 3 | Boeing-Seattle |
| YB-29-BW | 14 | Boeing-Wichita |
| B-29-BW | 1,630 | Boeing-Wichita |
| B-29-BA | 357 | Bell-Atlanta |
| B-29-MO | 531 | Martin-Omaha |
| B-29A-BN | 1,119 | Boeing-Renton |
| B-29B-BA | 311 | Bell-Atlanta |
| | 3965 Total | |

### Performance Characteristics and Technical Data

| Manufacturer/ Type | No. Built (All Models) | Span | Length | Height | Empty Wt. (Pounds) | Gross Wt. (Pounds) | Service Ceiling | Cruise/Top Speed (MPH) | Engines | H.P. | Range | Bomb Load |
|---|---|---|---|---|---|---|---|---|---|---|---|---|
| Boeing B-29 | 3,654* | 141'3" | 99' | 27'9" | 70,140 | 110,000 | 31,850' | 220/365 | Wright R-3350-23 | 2,200 | 5,830 | 20,000 |
| Boeing/Bell B-29B | 311 | 141'3" | 99' | 27'8" | 68,821 | 135,744 | 38,100' | 344/354 | Wright R-3350-57 R-3350-57A | 2,200 | 6,023 | 10,000 |

* Includes B-29s other than B-29Bs.

# Dimensions

| DIMENSION | AIRCRAFT | | | | |
|---|---|---|---|---|---|
| | **XB-29** | **YB-29** | **B-29** | **B-29A** | **B-29B** |
| Wing Span (ft. in.) | 141' 2.76" | 141' 2.76" | 141' 2.76" | 141' 2.76" | 141' 2.76" |
| Wing Root Chord (ft. in.) | 17' 0.00" | 17' 0.00" | 17' 0.00" | 17' 0.00" | 17' 0.00" |
| Wing Tip Chord (ft. in.) | 7' 5.00" | 7' 5.00" | 7' 5.00" | 7' 5.00" | 7' 5.00" |
| Wing Area (sq. ft.) | 1,736.0 | 1,736.0 | 1,736.0 | 1,739.0 | 1,736.0 |
| Aileron Span (ft. in.) | 25' 10.00" | 25' 10.00" | 25' 10.00" | 25' 10.00" | 25' 10.00" |
| Flap Span (ft. in.) | 37' 8.43" | 37' 8.43" | 37' 8.43" | 37' 8.43" | 37' 8.43" |
| Length (ft. in.) | 98' 1.92" | 99' 0.00" | 99' 0.00" | 99' 0.00" | 99' 0.00" |
| Height (ft. in.) | 27' 9.00" | 27' 9.00" | 27' 9.00" | 27' 9.00" | 27' 9.00" |
| Rudder Height (ft. in.) | 14' 7.25" | 12' 0.18" | 12' 0.18" | 12' 0.18" | 12' 0.18" |
| Horizontal Stabilizer Span (ft. in.) | 43' 0.00" | 43' 0.00" | 43' 0.00" | 43' 0.00" | 43' 0.00" |
| Horizontal Stabilizer Root Chord (ft. in.) | 11' 2.40" | 11' 2.40" | 11' 2.40" | 11' 2.40" | 11' 2.40" |
| Vertical Fin Area (sq. ft.) | 237.8 | 237.8 | 237.8 | 238.8 | 237.8 |
| Horizontal Tail Area (sq. ft.) | 330.0 | 330.0 | 330.0 | 330.0 | 330.0 |
| MLG Track (ft. in.) | 28' 5.60" | 28' 5.60" | 28' 5.60" | 28' 5.60" | 28' 5.60" |
| MLG Tire Diameter (in.) | 56.00" | 56.00" | 56.00" | 56.00" | 56.00" |
| NLG Tire Diameter (in.) | 36.00" | 36.00" | 36.00" | 36.00" | 36.00" |
| Propeller Diameter (ft. in.) | 17' 0.00" | 17' 0.00" | 16' 7.00" | 16' 7.00" | 16' 7.00" |

# Bibliography

**Books**

Anderton, David A. *B-29 Superfortress at War*. New York: Charles Scribner's Sons. 1978.

Berger, Carl. *B-29, The Superfortress*. New York: Ballantine Books, Inc. 1973.

Beser, Jacob. *Hiroshima & Nagasaki Revisited*. Memphis: Global Press. 1988.

Birdsall, Steve. *Saga of the Superfortress*. New York: Doubleday & Co., Inc. 1980.

Birdsall, Steve. *B-29 Superfortress in Action*. Carrollton, Texas: Squadron/Signal Publications, Inc. 1977.

Birdsall, Steve. *Superfortress*. Carrollton, Texas: Squadron/Signal Publications, Inc. 1980.

Gurney, Gene. *B-29 Story*. Greenwich, Connecticut: Fawcett Books. 1961.

Coffey, Thomas M. *Iron Eagle, the Turbulent Life of General Curtis LeMay*. New York: Crown Publishers. 1986.

Hudson, Lionel. *The Rats of Rangoon*. London: Leo Cooper. 1987.

Marshall, Chester. *Sky Giants over Japan*. Winona, Minnesota: Appolo Books. 1984.

Marshall, Chester. *The Global Twentieth, An Anthology, Volume 1*. Winona, Minnesota: Appolo Books. 1985.

Marshall, Chester. *The Global Twentieth, An Anthology, Volume 2*. Memphis, Tennessee: Global Press. 1987.

Marshall, Chester. *The Global Twentieth, An Anthology, Volume 3*. Memphis, Tennessee: Global Press. 1988.

Marshall, Chester. *The Global Twentieth, An Anthology, Volume 4*. Memphis, Tennessee: Global Press. 1992.

Morrison, Wilbur H. *Point of No Return*. New York: Time Books. 1979.

Pimlott, John. *B-29 Superfortress*. Secautus, New Jersey: Chartwell Books, Inc. 1980.

Prange, Gordon W. *At Dawn We Slept*. New York: McGraw-Hill Book Co. 1981.

Sargent, Mary Thomas. *Runway Towards Orion*. Grand Rapids, Michigan: Trimph Press, Inc. 1984.

Thomas, Gordon and Morgan Witts. *Enola Gay*. New York: Pocket Books. 1977.


**Albums, Histories, Documents**

"The 20th AF Album," by Dick Keenan. Published by 20th AF Association. 1982.

"Strategic Air War Against Japan," by Maj. Gen. Haywood S. Hansell, Jr. Published in 1980, under the auspices of the Airpower Research Institute, Air War College, Maxwell AFB, Alabama.

"Impact, Volume 8," sponsored by the Army Air Forces' Historical Society. Published by *Historical Times*

"The Story of the 73rd BW, the Unofficial History of the 73rd BW at Saipan." First printing 1946 by 73rd Wing headquarters. Reprinted by the Battery Press, Inc., Nashville, Tennessee. 1980.

"The Air Intelligence Report of the 21st BC." Published by 21st Bomber Command, April 1945.

"Saipan, Then and Now" (1972); "Tinian Island, Then and Now" (1977); and "Guam, Then and Now" (1979) by Glenn McClure. Published by Emerson's, Universal City, Texas.

"The Pirate's Log, a Historical Record of the Sixth BG." Published by Engineer Reproductions, Philippines. 1946.

"Story of the 505th BG, 313th BW, Tinian Island." Published by Betty Macintyre, Ogden, Utah. 1946.

"War Journal—Story of the 9th BG, Tinian Island." Published by the 9th Bomb Group. 1946.

"The Unofficial History of the 499th BG, Saipan." Published by Historical Aviation, Temple City, California. 1981

"The Story of the 315th Wing, Guam." Published by the 315th Wing Association, Cocoa Beach, Florida. 1981.

"The B-29 Bibliography," by Denny Pidhayny. Published by the 58th BW Association Recording and Historical Secretary. Updated April 1992.

# Index